Praise for *Think Like a Co*

The Commons is among the most important and hopeful concepts of our time, and once you've read this book you'll understand why!

—Bill McKibben, author *Deep Economy*

Think Like a Commoner is a brilliant, accessible, practical, path-breaking intellectual tour de force. A defining contribution to the New Economy movement and an essential read for everyone who cares about the human future. I expect to return to it as a basic reference for years to come.

—David Korten, author, *Agenda for a New Economy*, board chair YES! Magazine, and co-chair, New Economy Working Group

The commons is truly the new paradigm, the missing third link for the reform of civilization. But the commons is not a thing, but above all the expression of a cultural revolution and of subjective changes. David Bollier has done a great job of explaining the importance of this great cultural shift.

—Michel Bauwens, Founder, Foundation for Peer-to-Peer Alternatives

Our world is in need of reviving an ancient wisdom if it is to survive. David Bollier has a beautiful, bold but practical vision for our commons future and lights the path forward. I love this book!

—Maude Barlow, National Chairperson of the Council of Canadians; international water activist

It probably surprises you to know that the wealth we own together as a commons is far more valuable than the wealth that we and corporations own separately. Corporations know this and have commercialized or taken control of what we the people own – such as the public airwaves, the public lands, our genes and trillions of dollars of knowledge (eg. research and development) paid for by taxpayers – for starters. For this and more you must read Bollier's brilliant distillation of the huge variety of commons and how we can take control of what we own in order to transform our economy for us, our posterity and the planet. Once you pick it up, you'll tremble with the excitement of what we all own in the form of the commons that somehow escaped our notice in our years of formal education.

—Ralph Nader, Consumer advocate and author, *Unstoppable: The Emerging Left-Right Alliance to Dismantle the Corporate State*

THINK
LIKE A
COMMONER

THINK
LIKE A
COMMONER

A Short Introduction to the Life of the Commons

DAVID BOLLIER

new society
PUBLISHERS

For more information, including citations and recommended readings
for each chapter, go to thinklikeacommoner.com

Cover design by Diane McIntosh. Illustration © iStock (ARTQC).

Printed in Canada. First printing January 2014.

New Society Publishers acknowledges the financial support of the Government of Canada through the Canada Book Fund (CBF)for our publishing activities.

should be addressed to New Society Publishers at the address below.

To order directly from the publishers, please call toll-free
(North America) 1-800-567-6772, or order online at www.newsociety.com

Any other inquiries can be directed by mail to:

New Society Publishers
P.O. Box 189, Gabriola Island, BC V0R 1X0, Canada
(250) 247-9737

LIBRARY AND ARCHIVES CANADA CATALOGUING IN PUBLICATION

Bollier, David, author
Think like a commoner : a short introduction to the life of
the commons / David Bollier.

Includes index.
Issued in print and electronic formats.
ISBN 978-0-86571-768-8 (pbk.).—ISBN 978-1-55092-559-3 (ebook)

1. Public goods. 2. Commons. 3. Capitalism. I. Title.

HB846.5.B64 2014   306.3   C2013-907692-1
                                         C2013-907693-X

New Society Publishers' mission is to publish books that contribute in fundamental ways to building an ecologically sustainable and just society, and to do so with the least possible impact on the environment, in a manner that models this vision. We are committed to doing this not just through education, but through action. The interior pages of our bound books are printed on Forest Stewardship Council®-registered acid-free paper that is **100% post-consumer recycled** (100% old growth forest-free), processed chlorine-free, and printed with vegetable-based, low-VOC inks, with covers produced using FSC®-registered stock. New Society also works to reduce its carbon footprint, and purchases carbon offsets based on an annual audit to ensure a carbon neutral footprint. For further information, or to browse our full list of books and purchase securely, visit our website at: www.newsociety.com

MIX
Paper from
responsible sources
FSC® C016245

For Jonathan Rowe (1946–2011),
whose beautifully insightful writings about
the mysteries of the commons
remain an inspiration.

~

CONTENTS

INTRODUCTION

WHEN MY SEATMATE on the airplane turned to me and abruptly asked, "So what do you do?" I replied that I study the commons and work as an activist to try to protect it.

Polite bewilderment. "Say what?" It was not the first time. So I cited the familiar references—the Boston Common and medieval pastures—and moved on to the so-called tragedy of the commons, the meme that brainwashed a generation of undergraduates.

Sensing a quiver of interest, I ventured further, mentioning open source software, Wikipedia and Creative Commons licenses. At the risk of overwhelming my captive seatmate, I ticked off a list of commons that are rarely seen as commons: the vast public lands containing minerals and forests, the broadcast airwaves that TV stations use for free, urban spaces, the human genome. I mentioned the wonderful community festivals in my hometown, the "gift economies" of blood donation systems and the commons of language itself—a resource that is free to anyone to use, but whose letters and words are fast becoming proprietary trademarks. Then there are the fisheries, farmland and water that an estimated two billion people around the world manage as commons to meet their everyday needs.

I half expected my new friend to turn back to her book or gaze out the window at the fleecy clouds over the Great Plains. Instead she brightened. "Oh, I get it! The commons are things that no one owns and are shared by everyone."

Well put.

She mused that the park where she walks her dog and mingles with strangers is a commons—and so is the online list-serv about parenting that she belongs to. She cited a lake near her home, and the downtown plaza where all sorts of public events are held.

In the modern industrialized countries of the world, the commons tends to be a baffling, alien idea. The word may be invoked to make faux-genteel allusions to Merrie Old England ("Coxswain Commons Apartments"), but otherwise it has scant currency. We don't really have a language for naming commons—*real* commons—and so they tend to be invisible and taken for granted. The commons is not a familiar cultural category. Anything of value is usually associated with the "free market" or government. The idea that people could actually self-organize durable arrangements for managing their own resources, and that this paradigm of social governance could generate immense value—well, it seems either utopian or communistic, or at the very least, impractical. The idea that the commons could be a vehicle for social and political emancipation and societal trans-formation, as some commons advocates argue, seems just plain ridiculous.

The point of this book is to gently dispel such prejudices and provide a short introduction to the commons. After encounter-ing so much confusion about the commons over the years—and seeing how rich bodies of commons-oriented scholarship are inaccessible to the lay reader, and commons-based activism and projects are scattered, ignored or misunderstood—I decided it was time to write a short, accessible synthesis of the topic. (Confusingly, "commons" is both the singular and plural of the term, and some people make things even more confusing by using the word "common" instead of "commons.")

I want you, my reader, to imagine that you are my quizzical seatmate as we begin a short flight. You have intuitions about the commons and the need for social cooperation. You surely know about the dismal performance of corporate capitalism and government. You may even be concerned about the alarming privatization of countless public resources, the proliferation of ads in every nook of everyday life and the growing list of stubborn environmental problems.

For my part, I have many stories to tell about the power of commons to address such problems in innovative, socially minded ways. After researching and writing about countless "enclosures" of commons—in which corporate interests appropriate our shared wealth and turn it into expensive private commodities—I have learned how dangerous our ignorance of the commons is. It simply enables the private plunder of our common wealth, as the subtitle of my first book on the commons, *Silent Theft*, put it.

We have so few words to *name* the pathologies of markets and the feasible commons-based alternatives. I like to think that by naming the commons, we can learn how to reclaim it. We can begin to gain a healthy perspective on the limits of markets and learn how to participate in acts of *commoning* with others. And we can reap many benefits—economic, social, political, civic, physical, aesthetic, even spiritual—that simply can't be bought at a store.

The many misconceptions that surround the commons bother me. So I want to explain why the history of the commons and the political vision it sets forth are a cause for optimism. I want to explain how the commons can ameliorate our economic troubles by advancing a richer theory of *value* than conventional economics. This is not just an idle academic concern but an urgent practical one—because too much of the world's economic and political life revolves around voracious markets and the ecological damage and warped human relationships they engender.

Countless real-life commons—for natural resources, online information and civic life—provide a vital counterpoint. These commons integrate economic production, social cooperation, personal participation and ethical idealism into a single package. They represent a practical paradigm of self-help and collective gain. The commons is essentially a parallel economy and social order that quietly but confidently affirms that another world is possible. And more: we can build it ourselves, now.

As we will see in the pages below, the commons holds great promise for reinventing dysfunctional governments and reforming predatory markets. It can help us rein in our overly commercialized consumer culture. It can usher in new forms of "green governance" to protect the environment. At a time when our representative democracy has become a gaudy charade driven by big money and remote bureaucracies, the commons offers new forms of on-the-ground participation and responsibility that can make a real difference in people's lives.

I should stress that the commons is neither a "messaging strategy" of the sort favored by campaign publicists, nor an ideology or dogma. It is not just a new name for the "public interest." It amounts to a kind of political philosophy with specific policy approaches, but it goes much deeper because it engages us as fully human and complex creatures.

As a paradigm, the commons consists of working, evolving models of self-provisioning and stewardship that combine the economic and the social, the collective and the personal. It is humanistic at its core but also richly political in implication, because to honor the commons can risk unpleasant encounters with the power of the Market/State duopoly.

The Market and State, once very separate realms of morality and politics, are now joined at the hip: a tight alliance with a shared vision of technological progress, corporate dominance and ever-expanding economic growth and consumption. Commoners realize that this is not just a morally deficient, spiritually unsatisfying vision for humanity; it is a mad utopian fantasy. It is also ecologically unsustainable, a crumbling idol that can no longer command the respect it once took for granted.

In response, the commons sets forth a very different vision of human fulfillment and ethics, and invites people to achieve their own bottom-up, do-it-yourself styles of emancipation. It has little interest in hidebound party politics, rigid ideologies or remote centralized institutions. It seeks to build anew, or, as R. Buckminster Fuller memorably put it, "to change something, build a new model that makes the existing model obsolete."

That's what a robust commons movement around the world is doing. It is pioneering new forms of production, more open and accountable forms of governance, innovative technologies and cultures and healthy, appealing ways to live. It is a quiet revolution—self-organized, diversified and socially minded. It is pragmatic yet idealistic and, for now, only occasionally engaged in mainstream politics or public policy. Yet it has been steadily growing, in most instances outside the gaze of the mainstream media or the political establishment. It seems poised to "go wide," as they say in the movie business, because the various tribes of transnational commoners are starting to find each other. They are coordinating their work and thinking and developing ways to make common cause in the face of the growing dysfunctionalities and anti-democratic paranoia of the Market/State.

I hope that in the coming flight I can explain the refreshingly different logic and social dynamics of the commons as it is now unfolding in numerous contexts. I promise to keep things short, accessible and interesting—while pointing as much as possible to the rich complexities and unresolved questions that demand further attention. We will traverse some of the eclipsed history of the commons, revisit the smear known as the "tragedy of the commons" and see how social scientists and activists have rediscovered the commons over the past generation.

We will also explore the ways in which the commons raises profound questions about the standard market narrative about property rights, markets and value—and how it proposes very different foundational premises for a new political economy. In its deepest reaches, the commons goes way beyond the plane of economics, public policy or politics. As we will see in Chapter 10, it points us toward a very different mode of human existence (ontology) and human knowledge (epistemology) than the ones to which we have become accustomed. The commons suggests new models of human morality, behavior and aspiration that go beyond the benighted models taught in Economics 101.

No survey of the commons would be complete without an overview of the varieties of *enclosure* now dispossessing communities and degrading the environment and culture. Diverse realms of our common wealth—water, land, forests, fisheries, biodiversity, creative works, information, public spaces, indigenous cultures—are all under siege. The encouraging news is that, despite rampant market enclosures, commoners are responding with a remarkable range of hardy, innovative models. In the pages ahead, we will encounter some of the more impressive and replicable responses: the "copyleft" licenses for free software and free culture; collaborative websites and other forms of peer production; subsistence commons that share seeds, land, water and other natural resources; stakeholder trusts for managing large-scale common assets; relocalized food systems that blend community engagement with market provisioning; among many others.

Pull back to a wide-angle perspective and one can see diverse stands of history, politics and commoning crystallizing into a coherent new paradigm. Some of us dare to imagine a commons renaissance. A recent book that I co-edited with Silke Helfrich, *The Wealth of the Commons: A World Beyond Market and State,* documents the staggering international breadth and vitality of commons activities and advocacy. The commons can now be seen in German ecovillages and Chilean fisher commons; in thousands of open-access scientific journals; in an explosion of alternative currencies used by local communities; and in urban gardens that grow food and social connections.

These developments bear witness to the reality, made abundantly clear by the 2008 financial crises, that the prevailing dogmas of market individualism, private property rights and neoliberal economics cannot, and will not, deliver the kind of change we need. And yet the traditional advocates of reform, liberals and social democrats, while generally concerned with market abuses and government malfeasance, are themselves too exhausted to imagine new paths forward. They are too indentured to the Market/State mindset and cultural outlook, and too naive or spineless in the face of finance capital, to entertain new forms of governance and institutional innovation. Contemporary liberals and social democrats may pretend to want ambitious social and political transformation ("Change We Can Believe In," etc.), but the harsh political truth is that they are content to muddle through and cling to the sinecures of power.

I hope our flight together goes briskly. Before we descend, I want to contemplate the future of the commons paradigm as it confronts the aging dogmas of neoliberal ideology. How can we unseat a "free market" theology that cannot deliver on its promises and yet will not allow serious consideration of alternatives? Our archaic system of nation-states and international bodies cannot mobilize itself to deal intelligently with a gravely imperiled planetary ecosystem. It resists serious measures to improve social justice and fair distribution.

In the face of the colossal troubling dysfunction of neoliberal governance, a growing movement of commoners from India and Italy, Germany and Brazil, the US and the UK and many other regions of the world—furiously coordinating through the global Internet culture—are cobbling together a new shared imaginary for change. This is no ideological pipe dream or utopian fantasy. It is a piecemeal revolution of savvy, pragmatic dreamers determined to build living, functional alternatives in the face of many looming catastrophes.

There just might be some turbulence ahead...but for now, sit back, relax and enjoy the flight. Let's talk about the commons.

1

THE REDISCOVERY OF THE COMMONS

THE WOMEN OF ERAKULAPALLY—a small village two hours west of Hyderabad, India—spread a blanket onto the dusty ground and carefully poured sacks of brightly colored, pungent-smelling seeds into thirty piles: their treasure. For these women—all of them *dalit*, members of the poorest and lowest social caste in India—seeds are not just seeds. They are symbols of their emancipation and the recovery of their local ecosystem. The homegrown seeds have enabled thousands of women in small villages in the Andhra Pradesh region of India to escape their fate as low-paid, bonded laborers, and to remake themselves as self-reliant, proud farmers.

In 2010, when I visited Erakulapally under the auspices of the Deccan Development Society, Indian food prices were soaring by 18 percent a year, bringing social unrest and hunger to many parts of the country. But five thousand women and their families in seventy-five Andhra Pradesh villages not only had enough food for their needs—two meals a day instead of one, as previously—they had achieved food security without having to rely upon genetically modified seeds, monoculture crops, pesticides, outside experts, government subsidies or fickle markets.

Their achievement of food sovereignty, as it is called, has been remarkable because they are outcasts many times over: they are women, socially shunned "untouchables," poor, rural villagers.

During the Green Revolution of the 1960s and 1970s, governments and foundations in the West made a big push to introduce large-scale commercial rice and wheat production in so-called developing countries. This helped mitigate hunger in the short term, but it also introduced crops that are alien to many Indian ecosystems and that require harmful and expensive pesticides. The new crops are also more vulnerable to drought and volatile market prices. Tragically, the Green Revolution displaced the traditional millet-based grains that generations of villages had once grown. The expense and unpredictability of market-based monoculture crops—and the agricultural and financial failures that often resulted—are widely blamed for an epidemic of two hundred thousand farmer suicides over the past decade.

The women of Erakulapally discovered that traditional crops are far more ecologically suited to the semi-arid landscape of Andhra Pradesh and its rain patterns and soil types than proprietary seeds from the West. But to recover the old biodiverse ways of farming, the women had to ask their mothers and grandmothers to search for dozens of old nearly forgotten seeds. Eventually, in attics and family safe boxes, they found enough seeds to do a planting, and finally, after many additional rounds of cultivation, revived their traditional "mixed crop" agriculture. The practice consists of planting six or seven different seeds in the same field, which acts as a kind of "eco-insurance." No matter if there is too much or too little rain, or if the rain comes too early or too late—*some* of the seeds will grow. Families will have enough to eat no matter the weather—and there will be no need to buy expensive genetically modified seeds or synthetic pesticides and fertilizers.

The recovery of traditional agriculture did not come through "technology transfer" or government-sponsored agricultural research. It came through a do-it-yourself process of recovering the "people's knowledge" and deliberately encouraging social collaboration and seed sharing. In seed-sharing villages, every farmer now has a complete knowledge of all the seeds used, and every household has its own "gene bank," or collection of seeds, at home.

"Our seeds, our knowledge" is how the women put it: every seed is a capsule of their knowledge. No one is allowed to buy or sell seeds; they can only be shared, borrowed or traded. The seeds are not regarded as an "economic input." Villagers have a "social," almost mystical relationship with the seeds, which is a subtle but important reason that the women were able to emancipate themselves. "Every crop has a meaning in a women's life," said P. V. Satheesh of the Deccan Development Society. "The seeds are a source of dignity."

THE SEED-SHARING COMMONS of Andhra Pradesh illustrate an important feature of commons: they can arise almost anywhere and be highly generative in unlikely circumstances. There is no master inventory of commons. They can arise whenever a community decides it wishes to manage a resource in a collective manner, with a special regard for equitable access, use and sustainability.

The title of this chapter, "The Rediscovery of the Commons," has a certain ironic edge because for hundreds of millions of people around the world, the commons has never gone away. It has been a part of their daily lives for centuries. It nourishes them every day with food, firewood, irrigation water, fish, wild fruits and berries, wild game and much else. But these commons, like those of Native Americans and other indigenous peoples, have often been regarded, even today, as invisible or trivial. As most economists will tell you, only markets have the power to meet our essential needs. The recent "rediscovery" of the commons suggests otherwise. Market-obsessed industrialized societies are coming to realize that the Market and the State are not the only ways to organize society or manage resources.

But the path to understanding the commons requires a willingness to think in particulars, see the creative potential of social relationships and surrender the search for abstract universals and predictable certainties. The commons works because people come to know and experience the management of a resource in its unique aspects. They come to depend on each other and love *this* forest or *that* lake or *that* patch of farmland. The relationships between people and their resources *matter*.

History matters, too. The particular historical circumstances, leaders, cultural norms and other factors at a given moment in time can be critical to the success of a commons. Commons persist and grow because a defined group of people develop their own distinctive social practices and bodies of knowledge for managing a resource. Each commons is special because each has evolved in relationship to a specific resource, landscape, local history and set of traditions.

Consider the improbable circumstances that gave rise to one of the most successful, widely used software programs in history, the commons known as GNU/Linux.

LINUS TORVALDS was a 21-year-old undergraduate in Finland in 1991 when he decided to write his own computer operating system. It was a ridiculously ambitious project because operating systems are horrendously sprawling and complicated—things that only large corporations can afford to create and distribute. But Torvalds was fed up with the cost and complexity of Unix, a leading mainframe program, so he set out to build a Unix-like operating system that would work on his personal computer. As luck had it, the Internet was just coming into vogue as a popular medium for email and file transfers (the World Wide Web had not yet been invented).

Torvalds released an early version of his program to an online group, and within a few months, hundreds of people had volunteered useful suggestions and bits of code. Within a few years, a collaborative community of several hundred hackers had come together to work on the new program. He called it *Linux*—a wordplay that combined "Unix" with his first name, "Linus." Several years later, when the so-called Linux kernel was combined with a suite of programs known as GNU developed by Richard Stallman, founder of the Free Software Foundation, a complete operating system that could work on personal computers was born: GNU/Linux, often known simply as "Linux."

This was an astonishing and unexpected achievement. It not only demonstrated that amateurs could create a highly complex software program; it also showed that the Internet is a highly productive hosting infrastructure for social collaboration. A virtual community of self-selected hackers, with no payroll or corporate structure, had organized themselves into a fiercely creative, innovative, merit-driven commons. Remarkably, *it worked*!

The Linux experiment proved to be a foundational model for what is often known as "commons-based peer production," a type of online collaboration that invites huge numbers of people to join forces via open network platforms. The GNU/Linux model of commoning was the social pattern that later inspired collaborative projects like Wikipedia (and hundreds of less renowned wikis) and open-access scholarly journals, in which academic disciplines reclaim control over their work from commercial publishers and make it free and shareable. Linux has also made possible such recent innovations as social networking; crowdsourcing of information and fundraising; and open design and manufacturing projects such as the Global Village

Construction Set, a collection of fifty types of affordable farm equipment produced using open source principles.

As we will see in Chapter 8, the Linux experiment defied some seemingly inviolate principles of economics. It showed that the interplay of rational, self-interested individuals bargaining in the marketplace is not the only way to create wealth. Indeed, it showed that "wealth" itself is much more than fabulous sums of stocks, bonds and cash. Serious wealth can also be a community asset and the rich set of social relationships that make community possible. The Linux story is a stunning proof that the commons can be highly generative and contemporary as well as being entirely practical and effective.

THERE IS NO STANDARD FORMULA or blueprint for creating a commons; that's what examining any particular commons reveals. Nor is the commons some panacea or utopia. Commoners often disagree among themselves. There are personality clashes as well as internal debates about what works best and what's fair. There can be structural governance problems and external political interference. But commoners are intent on addressing difficult practical questions such as, What's the best way to irrigate these forty acres when water is scarce? and What's a fair way to allocate access to a dwindling fishery in this coastal bay? Commoners are also not afraid to tackle the problem of shirkers, vandals and free riders: individuals who want benefits without corresponding responsibilities.

The point is that the commons is a practical paradigm for self-governance, resource management and "living well." Commoners can often negotiate satisfactory resolutions to meet their common purposes without getting markets or government bureaucracies involved. They struggle to figure out the best structures for managing a collective resource, the procedures for making rules and operational norms that work. They understand the need to establish effective practices to prevent over-exploitation of their forest or lake or farmland. They can negotiate fair allocations of duties and entitlements. They like to ritualize and internalize their collective habits and stewardship ethic, which over time ripen into a beautiful culture.

A constant challenge is the tendency of some people to "defect" from a common agreement and undermine potential schemes that would otherwise benefit everyone. This can lead to private profiteering from a collective resource or, worse, a chaotic free-for-all that destroys the resource. This is known as a "collective action problem." Social scientists spend a lot of time studying why collective action problems can be so intractable and how they may be overcome. We will explore this issue further in Chapter 2.

It helps to understand that commons are not just *things* or *resources*. Outsiders to commons scholarship are prone to this mistake, either because they are economists who tend to objectify everything or because they are commoners declaring that a certain resource *ought to be governed* as a commons (what I call an "aspirational commons"). Commons certainly include physical and intangible resources of all sorts, but they are more accurately defined as paradigms that combine a distinct community with a set of social practices, values and norms that are used to manage a resource. Put another way, a commons is *a resource + a community + a set of social protocols*. The three are an integrated, interdependent whole.

Seen from this perspective, the question is not whether Pink Lake in Senegal or genomic databases on the Internet are commons, but rather whether a particular community is motivated to manage such a resource as a commons; and can it come up with the rules, norms and enforceable sanctions to make the system work? When put this way, it is interesting to consider the improbable types of common-pool sources that can be governed as commons.

A CLAN OF MUSCLE-BOUND SURFERS on the North Shore of Oahu, Hawaii, share a passion for catching big waves at Banzai Pipeline Beach. The Pipeline has been likened to the Mount Everest of surfing—a place where the best go to prove their mettle and talent. Not surprisingly, there is enormous competition over who is entitled to ride which waves—and resentment against outsiders who don't respect the surfing protocols that the local crowd has developed. "It's a dangerous environment, and without a self-governing control pattern, it would just be chaos out there," Randy Rarick, executive director of the Vans Triple Crown of Surfing competition, told a reporter for the *New York Times*. Another surfer pointed out that "there are serious consequences if you drop in on somebody and they got hurt, or if you wipe out and hurt yourself."

To deal with these issues, a self-organized social collective known as the Wolfpak came together to manage how people may use a beloved but scarce local resource: the massive waves. Wolfpak members have evolved their own rules for the orderly, safe and fair use of the waves, and for maintaining their own community. They decide who can catch which waves, and they punish those who violate their social code of surfing etiquette. Isaiah Helekunihi Walker, a history professor who has written about the surfing culture on North Shore, noted, "For the Hawaiians, respect is an important concept, particularly when it comes to being in the ocean." When surfers from Australia and South Africa arrived at the beach, boasting of their prowess, the locals at the Pipeline didn't take it very well.

There have sometimes been conflicts among surfers, especially between locals and outsiders. Which raises an interesting question: Who is the more legitimate steward of the Pipeline, the local surfing fans or the state authorities, who have the legal authority to manage the beach? Should the concerns of local surfers be allowed to trump those of outsiders? Whose commons is it, anyway? And what are the fairest, most effective means for protecting it?

The Wolfpak commons resembles certain Boston neighborhoods that have come up with their own rules of managing street parking during the snowy winter months. When Boston is hit with a big snow, it immediately becomes harder to find a place to park your car on the street. This can impose hardships on people who don't live in a detached single-family home with a garage. So in some neighborhoods, residents have developed a shared understanding that if you take the trouble to shovel out several feet of snow to create a parking space for your car, you are entitled to park there until the snow melts. People indicate their right to park in a given space by putting a rusty old folding chair or other battered household item in the empty parking spot.

It is not uncommon for outsiders to the neighborhood to try to remove the folding chairs and try to park there. Or sometimes a neighborhood resident will try to sneak into someone else's spot. This is the classic free rider problem, and it has been known to trigger scuffles and conflicts. Neighborhood residents wish to enforce their informal non-statutory rules.

Professor Elinor Ostrom once told me that *this* was a commons. I was perplexed. How? Why? She explained that the neighborhood's self-organized rules for parking during a snow represent "a shared understanding about the allocation of scarce use rights"; in this sense, it is a commons. Like the Wolfpak's allocation of access to big waves, the Boston neighborhoods' "parking commons" are a case of successful self-governance.

But from the perspective of government, neighborhood parking commons are a case of "taking matters into your own hands."

Governments tend to be jealous of their authority and hostile to even small incursions on their ability to make and enforce official policy. On the other hand, the lesson from the Wolfpak and the parking commons is that local commons can provide types of management and order that government bureaucracies and formal law cannot. Boston snowplows may not reliably clear the streets of snow, and the city government's enforcement of parking rules may be unreliable or expensive. Hawaiian authorities may not wish to hire a police officer or lifeguard to patrol Banzai Pipeline Beach (leaving a void of governance?), or such tasks may be seen as too impractical or "small" for a large bureaucracy to address.

But the commoners? They often have their own deep stores of knowledge, imagination, resourcefulness and commitment. Their informal *governance* may in fact outperform official forms of *government*.

In fact, as explicit negotiations among commoners become so engrained that they settle into habit, *custom* becomes a kind of invisible "vernacular law." Vernacular law originates in the informal social zones of society—coffeehouses, schools, the beach, "the street"—and becomes a source of effective order and moral legitimacy in its own right. Social norms such as queuing up in a line (and punishing those who cut in line) and meal etiquette (never take the last helping) are a kind of passive commoning that most of us have internalized as "the way things are done." They constitute an implicit mode of commoning for managing access to limited resources.

EACH OF THE COMMONS described above arose spontaneously, without the direction or oversight of centralized institutions or government. Each is committed to a larger collective purpose while also providing personal benefits for individuals. None is driven by a quest for money or personal fortune, at least not directly. In most commons, in fact, the market is a rather peripheral presence. Yet even without the direct involvement of markets or the state, serious production and governance occur.

The beauty of the commons as a "rediscovered" paradigm is both its generality and its particularity. It embodies certain broad principles—such as democratic participation, transparency, fairness and access for personal use—but it also manifests itself in highly idiosyncratic ways. For these reasons, I like to compare the commons to DNA. Scientists will tell you that DNA is ingeniously *under-specified* precisely so that the code of life can adapt to local circumstances. DNA is not fixed and deterministic. It is partial and adaptable. It grows and changes. A commons is like a living organism in that it co-evolves with its environment and context. It adapts to local contingencies. A forest commons in Vermont is likely to be quite different from one in Nepal or Germany, because the local ecosystems, tree types, economies, cultural histories and much else vary. And yet commons in each of these places are nonetheless commons: stable regimes for managing shared resources in fair ways for the benefit of participating commoners. The "diversity within unity" principle that commons embody is what makes the commons paradigm so versatile and powerful—and so confusing to conventional economists and policymakers.

What's critical in creating any commons, as mentioned earlier, is that a community decides that it wants to engage in the social practices of managing a resource for everyone's benefit. This is sometimes known as *commoning*. The great historian of the commons Peter Linebaugh has noted that "there is no commons without commoning." It's an important point to remember because it underscores that the commons is not only about shared resources; it's mostly about the social practices and values that we devise to manage them.

Commoning acts as a kind of moral, social and political gyroscope. It provides stability and focus. When people come together, share the same experiences and practices and accumulate a body of practical knowledge and traditions, a set of productive social circuits emerges. They create enduring patterns of social energy that can accomplish serious work. They provide ongoing benefit to the community. In this sense, a commons resembles a magnetic field of social and moral energy. The force field may be invisible to the untrained eye, and its effects may even seem a little bit magical. But it's time to face the facts: the commons constitutes a versatile system for organizing reliable flows of productive, creative social energy.

2

The Tyranny of the "Tragedy" Myth

"Picture a pasture open to all."

For at least a generation, the very idea of the commons has been marginalized and dismissed as a misguided way to manage resources: the so-called tragedy of the commons. In a short but influential essay published in *Science* in 1968, ecologist Garrett Hardin gave the story a fresh formulation and a memorable tagline.

"The tragedy of the commons develops in this way," wrote Hardin, proposing to his readers that they envision an open pasture:

> It is to be expected that each herdsman will try to keep as many cattle as possible in the commons. Such an arrangement may work reasonably satisfactorily for centuries because tribal wars, poaching and disease keep the numbers of both man and beast well below the carrying capacity of the land. Finally, however, comes the day of reckoning, that is, the day when the long-desired goal of social

stability becomes a reality. At this point, the inherent logic of the commons remorselessly generates tragedy. As a rational being, each herdsman seeks to maximize his gain. Explicitly or implicitly, more or less consciously, he asks, "What is the utility to me of adding one more animal to my herd?"

The rational herdsman concludes that the only sensible course for him to pursue is to add another animal to his herd. And another.... But this is the conclusion reached by each and every rational herdsman sharing a commons. Therein is the tragedy. Each man is locked into a system that compels him to increase his herd without limit—in a world that is limited. Ruin is the destination toward which all men rush, each pursuing his own best interest in a society that believes in the freedom of the commons. Freedom in a commons brings ruin to all.

The tragedy of the commons is one of those basic concepts that is drilled into the minds of every undergraduate, at least in economics courses. The idea is considered a basic principle of economics—a cautionary lesson about the impossibility of collective action. Once the class has been escorted through a ritual shudder, the professor whisks them along to the main attraction, the virtues of private property and free markets. Here, finally, economists reveal, we may surmount the dismal tragedy of a commons. The catechism is hammered home: individual freedom to own and trade private property in open markets is the only way to produce enduring personal satisfaction and social prosperity.

Hardin explains the logic this way: we can overcome the tragedy of the commons through a system of "mutual coercion, mutually agreed upon by the majority of the people affected." For him, the best approach is "the institution of private property coupled with legal inheritance." He concedes that this is not a perfectly just alternative, but he asserts that Darwinian natural selection is ultimately the best available option, saying, "those who are biologically more fit to be the custodians of property and power should legally inherit more." We put up with this imperfect legal order, he adds, "because we are not convinced, at the moment, that anyone has invented a better system. The alternative of the commons is too horrifying to contemplate. Injustice is preferable to total ruin."

Such musings by a libertarian-minded scientist have been catnip to conservative ideologues and economists (who are so often one and the same). They see Hardin's essay as a gospel parable that affirms some core principles of neoliberal economic ideology. It affirms the importance of "free markets" and justifies the property rights of the wealthy. It bolsters a commitment to individual rights and private property as the cornerstone of economic thought and policy. People will supposedly have the motivation to take responsibility for resources if they are guaranteed private ownership and access to free markets. Tragic outcomes—"total ruin"—can thereby be avoided. The failure of the commons, in this telling, is conflated with government itself, if only to suggest that one of the few recognized vehicles for advancing collective interests, government, will also succumb to the "tragedy" paradigm. (That is the gist of Public Choice theory, which applies standard economic logic to problems in political science.)

Over the past several decades, the tragedy of the commons has taken root as an economic truism. The Hardin essay has become a staple of undergraduate education in the US, taught not just in economics courses but in political science, sociology and other fields. It is no wonder that so many people consider the commons with such glib condescension. The commons = chaos, ruin and failure.

There is just one significant flaw in the tragedy parable. It does not accurately describe a commons. Hardin's fictional scenario sets forth a system that has no boundaries around the pasture, no rules for managing it, no punishments for over-use and no distinct community of users. *But that is not a commons.* It is an open-access regime, or a free-for-all. A commons has boundaries, rules, social norms and sanctions against free riders. A commons requires that there be a community willing to act as a conscientious steward of a resource. Hardin was confusing a commons with "no-man's-land" — and in the process, he smeared the commons as a failed paradigm for managing resources.

To be fair, Hardin was following a long line of polemicists who projected their unexamined commitments to market individualism onto the world. As we will see later, the theories of philosopher John Locke have been widely used to justify treating the New World as *terra nullius* — open, unowned land — even though it was populated by millions of Native Americans who managed their natural resources as beloved commons with unwritten but highly sophisticated rules.

Hardin's essay was inspired by his reading of an 1832 talk by William Forster Lloyd, an English lecturer who, like Hardin, was worried about overpopulation in a period of intense enclosures of land. Lloyd's talk is notable because it rehearses the same line of argument and makes the same fanciful error — that people are incapable of negotiating a solution to the "tragedy." Instead of a shared pasture, Lloyd's metaphor was a joint pool of money that could be accessed by every contributor. Lloyd asserted that each individual would quickly deplete more than his share of the pool while a private purse of money would be frugally managed.

I mention Lloyd's essay to illustrate how ridiculous yet persistent the misconceptions about the "tragedy" dynamic truly are. Commons scholar Lewis Hyde dryly notes, "Just as Hardin proposes a herdsman whose reason is unable to encompass the common good, so Lloyd supposes persons who have no way to speak with each other or make joint decisions. Both writers inject laissez-faire individualism into an old agrarian village and then gravely announce that the commons is dead. From the point of view of such a village, Lloyd's assumptions are as crazy as asking us to 'suppose a man to have a purse to which his left and right hand may freely resort, each unaware of the other.'"

This absurdity, unfortunately, is the basis for a large literature of "prisoner's dilemma" experiments that purport to show how "rational individuals" behave when confronted with "social dilemmas," such as how to allocate a limited resource. Should the "prisoner" cooperate with other potential claimants and share the limited rewards? Or should he or she defect by grabbing as much for himself as possible?

Needless to say, the complications are endless. But the basic premise of such social science experiments is rigged at the outset. Certain assumptions about the selfishness, rational calculation of individuals and lack of context (test subjects have no shared social history or culture) are embedded into the very design of the "game." Test subjects are not allowed to communicate with each other, or develop bonds of trust and shared knowledge. They are given only limited time and opportunity to learn to cooperate. They are isolated in a lab setting for a single experiment, and have no shared history or future together. Aghast at the pretzel logic of economic researchers, Lewis Hyde puckishly suggested that the "tragedy" thesis be called, instead, "The Tragedy of Unmanaged, Laissez-Faire, Common-Pool Resources with Easy Access for Noncommunicating, Self-Interested Individuals."

The dirty little secret of many prisoner's dilemma experiments is that they subtly *presuppose* a market culture of "rational" individuals. Most give little consideration to the real-life ways in which people come to cooperate and share in managing resources. That is changing now that more game theory experiments are incorporating the ideas of behavioral economics, complexity theory and evolutionary sciences into their design.

Yet the fact remains that a great deal of economic theory and policy presume a rather crude, archaic model of human being. Despite its obvious unreality, *Homo economicus*, the fictional abstract individual who actively maximizes his personal "utility function" through rational calculation, continues to hold sway as the idealized model of human agency in the cultural entity we call "the economy." Two introductory economics textbooks widely used in the US, by Samuelson and Nordhaus (2004) and Stiglitz and Walsh (2006), consider cooperative behaviors to be so inconsequential that they do not even mention the commons. If economists show any inclination to discuss the commons, you can be sure that the word "tragedy" will be lurking very nearby.

Paradoxically enough, the heedless quest for selfish gain— "rationally" pursued, of course, yet indifferent toward the collective good—is a better description of the conventional market economy than a commons. In the run-up to the 2008 financial crisis, such a mindset propelled the wizards of Wall Street to maximize private gains without regard for the systemic risks or local impacts. The real tragedy precipitated by "rational" individualism is not the tragedy of the commons, but the tragedy of the *market*.

Happily, contemporary scholarship has done much to rescue the commons from the memory hole to which it has been consigned by mainstream economics. The late American political scientist Elinor ("Lin") Ostrom of Indiana University deserves special credit for her role in expanding the frame of analysis of economic activity. In the 1970s, the economics profession plunged into a kind of religious fundamentalism. It celebrated highly abstract, quantitative models of the economy based on rational individualism, private property rights and free markets. A child of the Depression, Ostrom had always been interested in cooperative institutions working outside of markets. As a young political scientist in the 1960s, she began to question some of the core assumptions of economics, especially the idea that people are unable to cooperate in stable, sustainable ways. Sometimes working with political scientist Vincent Ostrom, her husband, she initiated a new kind of cross-disciplinary study of institutional systems that manage "common-pool resources," or CPRs.

CPRs are collective resources over which no one has private property rights or exclusive control, such as fisheries, grazing lands and groundwater. All of these resources are highly vulnerable to over-exploitation because it is difficult to stop people from using them. We might call it the "tragedy of open access." (Hardin himself later acknowledged that he should have entitled his essay "The Tragedy of an Unmanaged Commons" — an oxymoron, but never mind.)

What distinguished Ostrom's scholarship from that of so many academic economists was her painstaking empirical field-work. She visited communal landholders in Ethiopia, rubber tappers in the Amazon and fishers in the Philippines. She investigated how they negotiated cooperative schemes, and how they blended their social systems with local ecosystems. As economist Nancy Folbre of the University of Massachusetts, Amherst, explained, "She would go and actually talk to Indonesian fishermen or Maine lobstermen, and ask, 'How did you come to establish this limit on the fish catch? How did you deal with the fact that people might try to get around it?'"

From such empirical findings, Ostrom tried to figure out what makes for a successful commons. How does a community overcome its collective-action problem? The recurring challenge facing a group of principals in an interdependent situation, she wrote, is figuring out how to "organize and govern themselves to obtain continuing joint benefits when all face temptations to free-ride, shirk, or otherwise act opportunistically. Parallel questions have to do with the combinations of variables that will (1) increase the initial likelihood of self-organization, (2) enhance the capabilities of individuals to continue self-organized efforts over time, or (3) exceed the capacity of self-organization to solve CPR [common-pool resource] problems without eternal assistance of some form."

Ostrom's answer was *Governing the Commons*, a landmark 1990 book that set forth some of the basic "design principles" of effective, durable commons. These principles have been adapted and elaborated by later scholars, but her analysis remains the default framework for evaluating natural resource commons. The focus of Ostrom's work, and of the legions of academics who now study commons, has been how communities of resource users develop social norms—and sometimes formal legal rules—that enable them to use finite resources sustainably over the long term. Standard economics, after all, declares that we are selfish individuals whose wants are unlimited. The idea that we can depend on people's altruism and cooperation, economists object, is naive and unrealistic. The idea that commons can set and enforce limits on usage also seems improbable because it rejects the idea of humans having unbounded appetites.

Ostrom nonetheless showed how, in hundreds of instances, commoners do in fact meet their needs and interests in collective, cooperative ways. The villagers of Törbel, Switzerland, have managed their high alpine forests, meadows and irrigation waters since 1224. Spaniards have shared irrigation waters through *huerta* social institutions for centuries while, more recently, diverse water authorities in Los Angeles learned how to coordinate their management of scarce groundwater supplies. Many commons have flourished for hundreds of years, even in periods of drought or crisis. Their success can be traced to a community's ability to develop its own flexible, evolving rules for stewardship, oversight of access and usage, and effective punishments for rule-breakers.

Ostrom found that commons must have clearly defined boundaries so that commoners can know who has authorized rights to use a resource. Outsiders who do not contribute to the commons obviously have no rights to access or use the common-pool resource. She discovered that the rules for appropriating a resource must take account of local conditions and must include limits on what can be taken and how. For example, wild berries can only be harvested during a given period of time, or wood from the forest can only be taken from the ground and must be used for household use only, not sold at markets.

Commoners must be able to create or influence the rules that govern a commons, Ostrom noted. "If external governmental officials presume that only they have the authority to set the rules," she discovered, "then it will be very difficult for local appropriators to sustain a rule-governed CPR over the long run." Commoners must be willing to monitor how their resources are used (or abused) and must devise a system of sanctions to punish anyone who violates the rules, preferably through a gradation of increasingly serious sanctions. When disputes arise, commoners must have easy access to conflict-resolution mechanisms.

Finally, Ostrom declared that commons that are part of a larger system of governance must be "organized in multiple layers of nested enterprises." She called this "polycentric governance," meaning that the authority to appropriate a resource, monitor and enforce its use, resolve conflicts and perform other governance activities must be shared across different levels—from local to regional to national to international.

It must be emphasized that Ostrom did not regard her eight design principles as a strict blueprint for successful commons, but rather as general guidelines. It is also important to note that she focused primarily on *small-scale natural resource commons*. She did, in the latter stages of her career, explore the problems of large-scale regional or global commons and digital commons (which can scale to large sizes with great ease). But these were secondary concerns during most of her working life.

Here is another way of looking at factors that affect how a commons should be structured and managed:

+ *The character of the resource* affects how it must be managed. Finite, depletable resources such as mines have a different character than self-replenishing resources such as fisheries or forests. Commons that are "limitless" such as knowledge traditions and Internet resources (which are reproducible at virtually no cost) don't have to worry about free riders so much as vandals and disrupters.

+ *The geographic location and scale* of a resource will dictate a particular type of management. A village well requires different management rules than a regional river or a global resource like the oceans. Smaller-scale commons are easier to manage than large-scale or planetary common-pool resources such as the atmosphere.

+ *The experience and participation of commoners matters.* Indigenous communities that have centuries-old cultural traditions and practices will know far more about their resource than outsiders. Long-time members of free software networks will be more expert at designing programs and fixing bugs than newcomers.

+ *Historical, cultural and natural conditions* can affect the workings of a commons. A nation that has a robust civic culture is more likely to have healthy commons institutions than a nation where civil society is barely functional and distrust is rampant.

+ *Reliable institutions* that are transparent and accessible to the commoners matter. The most responsive institutions tend to be informal self-organized commons of smaller scales, but one can imagine state-sanctioned commons institutions acting as conscientious trustees for commoners.

Ostrom's impressive body of work earned her the Nobel Prize in Economics in 2009 (along with Oliver Williamson). I like to think that the Nobel Prize committee was spooked by the 2008 financial crisis and wished to shine a light on the profusion of alternatives to markets—*nonmarket forms* of provisioning and resource management that are nonetheless productive, stable and sustainable.

Besides providing a powerful analytical platform for studying commons more rigorously, Ostrom's most lasting accomplishment may be her role in building a global network of commons scholars. Hundreds of academics from around the world have produced a vast social sciences literature, mostly about natural resource commons in Asia, Latin America and Africa. Much of the seminal academic thinking about the commons was incubated, debated or refined at the Workshop in Political Theory and Policy Analysis at Indiana University, which Ostrom co-founded with her husband in 1973. Elinor Ostrom also founded the Digital Library of the Commons and the International Association for the Study of Common-Pool Resources ("Commons" was later substituted for "Common-Pool Resources" in the organization's name), an academic network of hundreds of scholars and practitioners.

It is now easy to see that Ostrom's great strength in studying economic activity was her distance from the economics profession. As an outsider to the guild, she could more readily see that free-market theories fail to explain many things of economic importance, such as our keen interest in working with others and assuring fairness within a group. As a woman in a male-dominated field (in the 1960s and 1970s, when sexism ran rampant in academia), Ostrom was also more attentive to the *relational* aspects of economic activity—the ways in which people interact and negotiate with each other to forge rules and social understandings. And so, while operating within the premises of neoclassical economics, Ostrom helped enlarge the scope of analysis to include many humanistic and social dynamics that the numbers-oriented mandarins of the field scorned.

Interestingly, her prominence in the field came mostly *after* she was awarded the Nobel Prize in 2009. In the previous decades, the study of CPRs and common property was decidedly outside the perimeter of interest of "serious" economists. Indeed, some prominent economists had no idea who she was when she was awarded the Nobel Prize. To outsiders and market-oriented economists, the commons was perhaps of little interest because it seems to focus on "subsistence," which they interpret as bare survival. But subsistence is not necessarily just about survival; it is about providing for one's household needs. The goal is not to maximize market gains and amass money, but to make sure that one's family has enough. The commons, properly understood, is about the practice and ethic of sufficiency.

I had the good fortune to meet Lin Ostrom a few times before her death in June 2012. What I most remember is how remarkably gracious, open and down-to-earth she was. This observation is not just a personal sidelight; I think it was what made her such a fertile thinker: she was open-minded and willing to engage with people and phenomena on their own terms, unencumbered by the deep prejudices of economic theory. Yet Ostrom nonetheless operated within the standard economic framework and its assumptions about "rational actors" and "rational design" in the construction of commons. She dealt only glancingly with macro-economic dynamics and even less with politics and power. Ostrom also tended to approach commons in a functional, behavioralist way, and had less interest in the intersubjective, psychological dynamics that might animate commons. Still, the "Bloomington School" of commons scholarship deserves enormous credit for rescuing the commons from the tyranny of the "tragedy" myth.

What is fascinating is the parallel development, outside of academia, of an eclectic, transnational corps of activists and project leaders who have embraced the commons as an organizing principle for their campaigns for social change. This, arguably, is what is making the commons a significant force in politics, economics and culture today. New movements of people worldwide are beginning to see how the commons paradigm describes their lives and their relationships to other people and resources. Software programmers, urban gardeners, indigenous peoples, academic researchers, permaculturists, Indian textile makers, Istanbul residents defending Gezi Park, the users of public libraries and parks, Slow Food activists: the affinity of these groups for the commons is not necessarily intellectual or scientific; it's personal and passionate. For many of these commoners, the commons is not a "management system" or "governance regime"; it's a cultural identity, a personal livelihood and a way of life. It's a way to revive democratic practice. It's a way to live a more satisfied life.

We will meet more of these commoners in the coming chapters. For now, suffice it to say that most commoners are trying to carve out protected, nonmarket spaces in a world that is increasingly dominated by private property and markets on a global scale. While commoners have many different self-defined goals and approaches, a great many of them aspire to build a different order of provisioning that will either build up the commons as an independent sector or blend commons and markets together in more humane, accountable ways. Some commoners focus mostly on their particular commons, whether it is a cooperative bank, a community forest or an online wiki. Others concentrate on how law and public policy might enable commons to form and maintain themselves, and how the state might play a helpful or benign role. Still others see the commons as an attractive vehicle for advancing an anti-capitalist economic and social analysis, and challenging the neoliberal state.

In short, interest in the commons, an irregular topic whose study was once mostly confined to academia, has exploded into all sorts of different arenas. Or more accurately, the language and scholarship to describe what has always existed in unselfconscious, unnamed ways is becoming more culturally visible. The commons is becoming a flourishing transnational ecosystem of activism, projects and theorizing. As the commons narrative engages various communities of practice, it is triggering an exciting cross-fertilization of ideas and partnerships as well as new understandings of commoning itself.

I like to think of this as a *vernacular movement* more than a political movement or ideological perspective. The term "vernacular" was given a special meaning by iconoclastic social critic Ivan Illich in his 1981 book *Shadow Work*. As a critic of the dehumanizing tendencies of institutions, Illich saw vernacular spaces as informal cultural zones where people naturally come to their own moral judgments and act out of their own sovereign humanity. The vernacular flourishes in the realm of householding and subsistence, and of family life and child rearing. It lives in the shared spaces of a community in which people assert their collective moral values and political interests, over and above those of the state, the corporation and other institutional powers. As one of Illich's students, Trent Schroyer, put it, the vernacular realm evokes a "sensibility and rootedness... in which local life has been conducted throughout most of history and even today in a significant proportion of subsistence- and communitarian-oriented communities." The vernacular consists of "places and spaces where people are struggling to achieve regeneration and social restoration against the forces of economic globalization."

There is a certain timelessness and mystery associated with

the vernacular, and as you have probably guessed, it has a lot to do with the commons. The commons is a fragile social institution and sensibility that naturally arises from vernacular culture, as if driven by a life force. It invariably tries to assert and maintain itself in the face of powerful institutions that have other priorities and interests. Sometimes commoners succeed in negotiating a rapprochement with those institutions, and carve out a protected zone for commoning. Urban gardens in New York City had to struggle to maintain themselves in the face of development pressures, for example. Coastal fishery commons must often struggle against large-scale industrial trawlers who swoop through their waters extracting fish for global markets rather than local consumption. Digital commoners must contend with copyright laws and corporate demagoguery that equate sharing with criminal activity ("piracy").

History has shown that the forces of market enclosure are cruel and relentless in deconstructing and destroying commons; they don't like the competition. A successful commons is a "bad example" because it bears witness to better practical alternatives. Sharing is also objectionable because it is an affront to the ideology of private property rights (with the exception of tech companies like Google and Facebook, whose business model relies upon monetizing social sharing). For their part, governments and bureaucracies are often wary of the commons as an independent, potentially threatening power base, preferring the certainties and rewards of market-based allies. Governments generally prefer to manage resources through strict standardized systems of control. To them, commoning appears to be altogether too informal, irregular and unreliable—even if the actual successes of commons refute that prejudice.

Any basic understanding of the commons must inevitably take account of the dynamics and meaning of enclosure. I turn now to that topic.

Enclosures
of Nature

W HAT HAPPENS WHEN markets become so powerful that they disrupt natural ecosystems, reorder how people conduct their lives and claim ownership of life-forms? It is sometimes difficult to step outside of our culture to take stock of the actual power and far-reaching effects of markets. But once you learn to identify the commons and understand its dynamics, it becomes quite clear that the privatization and commodification of our shared wealth is one of the great unacknowledged scandals of our time. Its pernicious effects are everywhere.

This process is often called the *enclosure of the commons*. It's a process by which corporations pluck valuable resources from their natural contexts, often with government support and sanction, and declare that they be valued through market prices. The point is to convert resources that are shared and used by many to ones that are privately owned and controlled, and treat them as tradeable commodities.

To talk about enclosure is to open up a conversation that standard economics rarely entertains—the dispossession of commoners as market forces seize control of common resources, often with the active collusion of government. The familiar debate of "privatization versus government ownership" does not really do justice to this process because government ownership, the supposed antidote to privatization, is not really a solution. In many instances, the state is only too eager to conspire with industries to seize control of common resources for "private" (i.e., corporate) exploitation. Regulation is too often a charade that does more to legalize than eradicate market abuses.

To talk about enclosure, then, is a way to point to the commons and reframe the discussion. The language of enclosure makes visible the antisocial, anti-environmental effects of "free markets" and validates commoning as an appropriate, often-effective alternative.

A few years ago, I learned of a contemporary enclosure that eerily replicated the medieval pattern of land enclosure. For more than a century, the village of Camberwell, in the fertile Hunter Valley region of New South Wales, Australia, had used part of an open flood plain around Glennies Creek as a commons. It was a place for residents to keep their horses and dairy cows, and to let their children fish, swim and ride horses. In April 2005, according to the *Sydney Morning Herald*, "a pair of officers from the Department of Lands arrived, called together members of the [Camberwell] Common Trust, and told them the Crown land would be immediately resumed and turned over to the Ashton mine that looms over the Upper Hunter village in the form of a hollowed-out hill on the other side of the creek."

The action was just another instance of government using its authority to seize common lands for corporate purposes. The secretary of the Camberwell Common Trust told a reporter, "When we go to community meetings with the mines they are always talking about what they will do 'when' they get approval. They never say 'if' they get approval." Both mining companies and government make out well from enclosures. The mining companies get cheap access to minerals and lax environmental oversight. The Australian government earned about $1.5 billion in royalties and fees at the time of the Camberwell enclosure.

Commoners are generally not so lucky. In Camberwell, blasts from the mining hollowed out the hills around the village. Parts of the commons cracked, according to the *Morning Herald*. Nearly two-thirds of the village population gave up fighting the mining companies and moved elsewhere.

The Camberwell experience is a classic example of state-assisted market enclosure. In the US, the government allows mining interests to extract mineral wealth on public lands under the Mining Act of 1872. Unchanged for more than 140 years, this law lets mining companies extract gold, silver and iron ore for five dollars an acre, period. It's been estimated that Americans have lost more than $245 billion worth of revenues over the years from this law—while ruining beautiful mountains and rivers with mine tailings and other wastes.

Similar stories from around the world can be told about timber companies raping public forests, oil companies drilling in pristine wilderness areas, industrial trawlers decimating coastal fisheries and transnational water bottlers sucking groundwater dry.

In Latin America, transnational corporations are working with neoliberal governments to impose aggressive "neo-extractivist" policies. As Argentinian professor Maristella Svampa explains, the idea is to build mega-projects that can efficiently extract and export the continent's minerals, metals, hydrocarbons, maize, soya and other raw commodities to industrial nations. Cast as the only realistic path toward progress and "development," dozens of dams, mines, highways and other neo-extractivist projects are destroying entire ecosystems, communities and indigenous cultures. Among the more notorious enclosures: the Conga mega-mining project in Peru; the Belo Monte hydroelectric dam in Brazil; and the road construction through the TIPNIS indigenous territory in Bolivia.

Enclosures are a special form of theft that attract little notice, in part because governments often play a key role in legitimizing them. But in all cases, resources that belong to all of us, or to distinct communities, are being transformed into corporate-owned properties and free waste dumps. Land, water, human tissue, public spaces, the atmosphere—all are raw feedstock for market use. Whatever wastes remain after these resources are monetized are dumped back into the commons, imposing further risks and costs on governments and citizens.

While enclosure tends to be cloaked in the language of progress, efficiency and development—the cover story—it is in fact a brutal act of appropriation, a raw power grab that often requires violent coercion. The appetite of the great corporate powers that rely upon enclosures seems to be limitless as they seize minerals from the bottom of the ocean, tap the genetic secrets of exotic flora in the global South and copyright brief snippets of musical notes, enabling them to accuse sharers of "piracy."

It is important to note that enclosures are not just appropriations of resources. They are also attacks on communities and their practices of commoning. Their primary goal may be the seizure of resources, but they also seek to impose a "regime change" on people. Enclosures convert a system of collective management and social mutuality into a market order that privileges private ownership, prices, market relationships and consumerism. The goal is to treat people as individuals and consumers, not as communities with shared, long-term, nonmarket interests.

The ultimate result of so many enclosures is a desperate dependency on business outsiders whose only loyalty is to the global marketplace. Users of Microsoft products must constantly buy the next software upgrade to keep their computers running properly. Farmers who rely upon genetically modified crops must buy new seeds every year and abide by contractual restrictions. Defenders of traditional ways of life are thrust into struggles with those who want to get rich and pursue the Western ideal of "development." "The more we depend on money and markets to satisfy our needs and follow our desire," writes commons scholar Massimo De Angelis, "the more we are exposed to a vicious circle of dependency that pits livelihoods against each other."

Not surprisingly, enclosures tend to interfere with the ability of people to self-organize and control their own governance, meet their own needs and protect their culture and way of life. A town that becomes beholden to an absentee investor or corporation quickly loses its civic sovereignty and becomes a "company town."

Enclosures also undermine traditions and identities that are intertwined with a beloved landscape, historic building or cultural work. When treasures—the designs of Australian Aborigines, the special plants cultivated by Madagascans—are shorn from their historic or natural context and reduced to a price, it is an assault on the commoners who had acted as their conscientious stewards and instilled meaning and purpose in them. Through enclosure, treasures are stripped of the qualities that make them locally distinctive and emotionally significant. They become, for better or worse, little more than inert commodities.

A Brief History of the English Enclosure Movement

The term "enclosure" is generally associated with the English enclosure movement, which occurred at various times in medieval history and through the nineteenth century. To put it plainly, the king, aristocracy and/or landed gentry stole the pastures, forests, wild game and water used by commoners, and declared them private property. Sometimes the enclosers seized lands with the formal sanction of Parliament, and sometimes they just took them by force. To keep commoners out, it was customary to evict them from the land and erect fences or hedges. Sheriffs and gangs of thugs made sure that no commoner would poach game from the king's land.

Enclosure was irresistible to the 1 percent of medieval England because it was an easy way to grab more wealth and power with the full sanction of the law. It could help struggling barons and upwardly mobile gentry consolidate their political power and increase their holdings of land, water and game. An anonymous protest poem from the eighteenth century put it well:

> The law locks up the man or woman
> Who steals the goose from off the common
> But leaves the greater villain loose
> Who steals the common from off the goose.

> The law demands that we atone
> When we take things we do not own
> But leaves the lords and ladies fine
> Who take things that are yours and mine.

> The poor and wretched don't escape
> If they conspire the law to break;
> This must be so but they endure
> Those who conspire to make the law.

> The law locks up the man or woman
> Who steals the goose from off the common
> And geese will still a common lack
> Till they go and steal it back.

As enclosures swept the villages of England, commoners suffered serious hardships. They depended upon the forest for their firewood and roof thatches, and on acorns to feed their pigs. They relied on shared fields to grow vegetables, and on open meadows for wild fruits and berries. An entire rural economy was based upon access to the commons. Barred from using their commons, villagers migrated to cities, where the emerging industrial revolution turned them into wage slaves, if they were lucky, and beggars and paupers if they weren't. Charles Dickens drew upon the social disruptions and injustices of enclosures in writing *Oliver Twist*, *Great Expectations* and his other novels about London's troubled underclass.

One important goal of the English enclosures was to transform commoners with collective interests into individual consumers and employees. Which is to say: creatures of the marketplace. The satanic mills of the Industrial Revolution needed obedient and desperate wage slaves. One of the lesser-noticed aspects of enclosures was the separation of production and governance. In a commons, both were part of the same process, and all commoners could participate in both. After enclosures, markets took charge of production and the state took charge of governance. The modern liberal state was born. And while the new order brought about vast improvements in material production, those gains came at a terrible cost: dissolution of communities, deep economic inequality, an erosion of self-governance and a loss of social solidarity and identity. Governance became a matter of *government*, the province of professional politicians, lawyers, bureaucrats and monied special interest lobbies. Democratic participation became mostly a matter of voting, a right limited to men (and at first, property owners). Enclosure also isolated people from direct encounters with the natural world and marginalized social and spiritual life.

During the course of a hundred and fifty years, from the late 1600s to the mid-1800s, about one-seventh of all English common land was carved up and privatized. As a result, deep inequalities took root in society and urban poverty soared. The foundations of the modern market order were being laid, and the masters of this new world had no need for the commons. The hallmarks of the new order would be individualism, private property and "free markets."

Karl Polanyi was an economic historian who studied this unique transition in human history—the end of the commons and the rise of markets and enclosures. In his underappreciated 1944 classic, *The Great Transformation*, Polanyi noted that for millennia, people had been bound together through community, religion, kinship and various other social or moral ties. All economic systems had been based on systems of reciprocity, redistribution or householding, and people were induced to produce things by way of "custom and law, magic and religion."

Then, as enclosures proceeded in the seventeenth through nineteenth centuries, production and profit became the central organizing principles for society. Instead of focusing on household use within a stable social context, production became reoriented toward private gain and accumulation. This required that numerous resources—especially land, labor and money—be redefined as commodities. Polanyi called these "fictional commodities" because human life and natural ecosystems cannot really be broken into fungible, substitutable units. But markets require that nature's gifts, labor and money be treated as commodities if they are to be assigned prices and made suitable for trade and speculation.

These commodity fictions quickly expanded to other realms, making virtually everything subject to purchase and sale. Food, water, fuel, firewood and other necessities of life—once available as a matter of right through the commons—could now only be acquired through the market, at a price.

Polanyi characterized the history of enclosure as "a revolution of the rich against the poor." "The lords and nobles were upsetting the social order," he wrote, "breaking down the ancient laws and customs, sometimes by means of violence, and often by pressure and intimidation." As the market economy gained the upper hand, it imposed its commodity logic on everything—nature, labor, social life—and gave everything a price.

Karl Marx, of course, had a great deal to say about the dynamics of capital accumulation and how they shaped the workplace, colonized social life and exploited public resources. Much of his political and economic critique is about the fierce private enclosures of the commons. However, Marx had relatively little to say about the commons itself as a locus of resistance or as a generative source of production and social reproduction. This was surely because the most significant development of his time was the sheer power of capitalist modernization. He saw modern workers' collectives as the most promising vehicle for creating new forms of commons.

The Massive International Land Grab

Many people believe that enclosures are a relic of the past—something that happened in medieval times, but not now. Not so. Vast portions of Africa, Asia and Latin America are currently reeling from a fierce international land grab. Investors and national governments are snapping up millions of acres of land that traditional peoples have used for generations. These commoners rarely have formal property deeds; as lawyers might put it, they have only "customary usage rights." The enforceable property rights belong to the government, which in theory acts as a trustee for the people. But in reality, most autocratic and troubled states find it quite profitable to ignore their public trust duties and sell off vast swatches of "unowned" lands to foreigners. By brokering deals and legalizing title to the land, governments can reap new tax revenues. Well-connected officials can quietly pocket handsome bribes. In theory, "development" and prosperity will follow.

In practice, not so much. Some investors use the land to produce biofuels or commercial crops that are exported to world markets. Others are speculators who leave the land idle, hoping to cash in as land prices rise. Saudi Arabia has spent a billion dollars to buy seven hundred thousand hectares in Africa. India is assembling investment pools to buy up farmlands. South Korea and China are also active players.

The scale of enclosure of customary lands is massive—and so is the displacement of commoners. An estimated 90 percent of the people in sub-Saharan Africa, or some five hundred million people, do not have statutory title to their lands and are at risk of eviction. Citizens of the Democratic Republic of the Congo, Northern Sudan, Ethiopia and Madagascar are especially vulnerable. Worldwide, some two billion people have only customary usage rights to their lands—some 8.54 billion hectares (or 21.1 billion acres). Once their lands are seized, commoners can no longer grow and harvest their own food, draw water or hunt wild game. Enclosures are shattering their communities and cultures.

By the light of free-market economics, turning land into private property and trading it in the market will enhance its productivity. This process is said to encourage owners to produce more food and develop the land so that it will be more valuable. Collectively used lands without property titles, by contrast, have historically been called "wastelands." That's because, in the eyes of the law, no one owns the land or takes care of it.

But look behind the curtain of free-market fables and you see thousands of stable, sustainable commons that provide basic subsistence to millions of people. Not surprisingly, the land grabs are producing the familiar pathologies associated with enclosure: ecological abuses, the decimation of community, hunger, inequality and migrations to cities in search of jobs and food. Evicted commoners find themselves displaced, dispossessed and thrust into a world of flashy modern consumerism and shanty-town poverty: an ugly replay of English commoners at the dawn of the Industrial Revolution.

"In light of the fact that most allocations to investors are in the form of renewable medium-term leases of up to 99 years," writes Liz Alden Wily, a specialist on land tenure rights, "it may be expected that loss of common properties will remove these lands from meaningful access, use and livelihood benefit for at least one generation and potentially up to four generations."

This is a recipe for decades of famine, poverty and political turmoil. At one time, imperial nations asserted direct military control over people and resources in order to exploit them. The neocolonial process has become more refined. With the sanction of law, foreign investors and speculators simply negotiate deals with friendly, self-dealing governments that welcome the plunder of native lands. What could be more lucrative than the private sale of the public's equity assets at bargain prices?

The Privatization of Water

Water is another resource that has been targeted for enclosure by many transnational corporations. Most people expect their drinking water to be a public service provided by governments or at least managed by communities. But many transnational companies see water as a valuable private commodity that can be a rich source of profits. This has prompted many companies and investors to buy up groundwater aquifers, extract large quantities of fresh water from public lands for minimal or no payments and privatize municipal water systems.

Sometimes water enclosures are achieved indirectly. Companies may choose to build expensive water purification, treatment or desalinization systems, for example, even though conservation and preventive regulation are cheaper and could yield more reliable results (but, alas, no return on investment to private investors). The fierce international land grab now underway is often just another name for "water grabbing."

The opening salvo in an ongoing series of "water wars" began in 2000, when the World Bank, working in cooperation with an international consortium led by the transnational engineering and construction firm Bechtel, pressured Cochabamba, then the third largest city in Bolivia, to privatize its water system. The official policy rationale was to provide incentives to private companies to improve the water infrastructure and so improve people's access to water. But such "market solutions" are more about boosting profits than providing access. After gaining control of Cochabamba's water supplies, Bechtel raised prices by 50 percent or more and even prohibited the collection of rainwater from roofs. Water in Cochabamba was strictly regarded as private property under the control of Bechtel.

A grassroots protest movement arose overnight. Thousands of ordinary people took to the streets with the battle cry, "Water is life!" The Coordinadora for the Defense of Water and Life called on the government to cancel its forty-year contract with Bechtel and return the water to municipal control. The protests also called for the "social re-appropriation of wealth"—that is, sovereign control of the water system and its collective management by water users. Coming only months after the Seattle anti-globalization protests in 1999, the Cochabamba insurrection vividly confirmed that the globalization of commerce has more to do with stoking corporate profits than with meeting basic human and environmental needs fairly and sustainably.

Protesters ultimately prevailed in Cochabamba, forcing cancellation of the Bechtel contract and galvanizing new calls for self-determination and commons-based control throughout Latin America. More than ten years later, the Cochabamba protests are still remembered as one of the first major triumphs against the privatization of water. It's a war that will not end any time soon. Billionaire T. Boone Pickens has spent more than a hundred million dollars acquiring groundwater aquifers in the Texas High Plains, which could make it very expensive for many communities there to survive as water becomes a private, proprietary product. Transnational water companies continue to appropriate groundwater supplies throughout the world in order to bottle it—even though public water systems can provide a thousand gallons of tap water for the same price as one bottle of branded water.

The Corporatization of Food

Sometimes enclosures involve things that a community only owns morally or inherits, such as the biodiversity of nature. These are common-pool resources, not actual commons (because the social systems to manage them remain aspirational, not actual). CPRs are particularly vulnerable to enclosure because there is no organized community to resist the seizure, so they are seen as "free for the taking." Markets become the structural force for redesigning nature.

A good example is the enclosure of apples in the US. A century ago, Americans ate more than six and a half thousand distinct varieties of apples. People could choose from an exotic array of cultivars with names like Scollop Gillyflower, Red Winter Pearmain and Kansas Keeper. When it came to cooking and eating, everyone had their favorites, usually local. People used different varieties for making pies, cider and apple sauce.

All that has changed dramatically. As US food companies built national markets in the twentieth century, eclipsing local production and distribution, the natural diversity of apples has essentially disappeared. Some varieties were abandoned because their thin skins and susceptibility to bruising made them unsuited for shipping. Others were too small or served only a tiny niche of the market. Red Delicious probably prevailed in the marketplace because it was so big and shiny (thanks in part to wax coating).

The point is that the shrinkage of varieties of apples was engineered by a commercial agriculture system intent on building national and international markets. Driven by large-scale efficiencies and corporate consolidation, it had no interest in idiosyncratic or diverse fruits. And so a bland homogeneity of apples was deliberately engineered in order to boost sales. Today, writes farmer-journalist Verlyn Klinkenborg, "only 11 varieties make up 90 percent of all the apples sold in this country [the US], and Red Delicious alone counts for nearly half of that."

Nature's dazzling diversity of apples has been culled and diminished. Most of the remaining varieties are easy to grow and cheap to distribute and sell in large quantities. Only older people realize that apples used to be delightfully varied and locally grown—and tastier. The rest of us have been trained to accept our narrow range of choices as "the way things are." A popular fruit has been made to conform to regimented, highly commodified markets.

Fortunately, the local food movement in its many aspects— Slow Food, community supported agriculture, organic farming, permaculture and beyond—is starting to resurrect many "heirloom" seed varieties that have fallen into disuse. These efforts are motivated not only by the interesting tastes and easier cultivation of locally adapted seeds, but by a realization that genetic biodiversity is an important form of ecological "insurance." Even though there are more than a thousand banana varieties worldwide, for example, the fruit industry has cultivated the Cavendish cultivar for 99 percent of the export market. Thanks to such monoculture farming, the world's supply of bananas may be decimated by a soil-borne fungus that attacks Cavendish bananas.

The fate of the apple and banana mirrors the fate of American food more generally. As Mark Kurlansky documented in his book *The Food of a Younger Land*, the diversity of cuisine in the US used to be far greater before the rise of the grocery superstore, the national highway system and the fast-food restaurant. Chain restaurants brought uniformity and low quality, displacing food that was seasonal, fresh, regional and traditional. When food was rooted in local cultures, it shaped people's character, attitudes and identities. Before American food habits fell under the sway of national markets, Kurlansky writes, there were food traditions such as "the southern New England May breakfast, foot washings in Alabama, Coca-Cola parties in Georgia, the chitterling strut in North Carolina, cooking for the threshers in Nebraska, a Choctaw funeral, and a Puget Sound Indian salmon feast. It also had old traditional recipes such as Rhode Island jonny cakes, New York City oyster stew, Georgia possum and taters, Kentucky wilted lettuce, Virginia Brunswick stew, Louisiana tête du veau," among dozens of others.

As the global reach of US corporations grew in the postwar period, so did the enclosure of countless food traditions around the world. As Western brands and fast-food chains have expanded from Bangkok to Bogota and from Mumbai to Moscow, modern heavily marketed foods have supplanted "backward" traditional cuisines. Everyday diets have become more homogenized—and less nutritious. No surprise that the diseases associated with Western diets—diabetes, obesity, heart disease—have also proliferated.

LAND, WATER, APPLES, LOCAL FOODS. These are only a few of the significant enclosures of nature perpetrated over the past several generations. The theft of natural wealth has been little noticed because it has been so incremental—and because it is generally portrayed as a sign of economic and technological progress.

The range of enclosures of nature is vast. They extend from the global (the atmosphere, the oceans, outer space) to the regional (groundwater aquifers, fisheries, forests) to the local (native foods, hometown traditions, independent businesses). Enclosures include living things (cell lines, genes, genetically engineered mammals) and infinitesimally small things (microorganisms, synthetic substitutes for nano-matter).

One of the most audacious new enclosures of nature involves the *financialization* of natural resources. Rather than treat land, water and local ecosystems as resources that should abide by the imperatives of nature, hedge funds and other investors are starting to develop clever financial instruments to "securitize" the revenues that can be generated by renewable natural systems, such as flows of water, harvestable timber and fish stocks.

Antonio Tricarico of the Italian group Re:Common reports that the financial industry is now trying to create a futures market and derivative financial instruments for water, similar to those that exist for oil. This would radically increase the pressure on governments at all levels to regard their water, forests and fisheries as financial assets that must be monetized and sold, or used as collateral for loans. By the lights of finance, natural resources that go unexploited are underleveraged assets; the presumption is that everything should produce revenue.

Needless to say, the financialization of nature would heighten pressures to disrupt and deplete many natural flows, intensifying stresses on the carrying capacities of natural systems. If water were to become a commodity traded in an integrated global marketplace, for example, it could devastate local ecosystems and make this vital resource unaffordable for many people.

Tricarico writes that the financialization of nature will only grow in coming years as the financial industry seeks to displace public finance and build its own large infrastructure and extractive projects in order to benefit private investors. The industry wants to develop financial markets that treat more aspects of food, land, electricity, metals, forests and other resources not just as commodities, but as financial assets suitable for global trade and speculation. Considering how little we understand about the macroeconomic and macrofinancial implications of such enclosures—not to mention the ecological disruptions that would ensue—these plans are a recipe for disaster.

I could easily cite dozens of additional types of enclosure. But let me confine the scope of our inquiry to providing a closer look at how enclosures work. I turn now to two classes of enclosures that don't get that much attention: the private takeover of urban spaces and infrastructure (Chapter 4) and the many appropriations of knowledge and culture (Chapter 5). You can tell that enclosure has reached troubling extremes when businesses claim ownership of words, colors and smells!

4

Enclosures of Public Spaces and Infrastructure

T HE CITY IS ONE of the most fiercely contested arenas for market enclosures. Public squares, parks, walkways, sports arenas and the very face and identity of a city are being taken over by a cozy alliance of corporations, politicians, developers and professional architects and planners. "Development" and "progress" are the watchwords—or perhaps more accurately, PR codewords—for the supremacy of corporate needs and market growth over all else.

In many big cities, corporate branding has taken over public spaces that used to be "no-sell" havens in our culture. One of the most notorious is the selling of naming rights to sports stadia. There is Coca-Cola Stadium in Xi'an, China; Land Rover Arena in Bologna, Italy; and Mr. Price King Park Stadium in Durban, South Africa. Beloved playing fields that used to have charming and cherished histories—Candlestick Park (San Francisco) and Mile High Stadium (Denver)—now bear icy corporate names that will never inspire lyrical sports lore. Sometimes arenas need to be renamed because the corporation goes bankrupt (3Com) or gets embroiled in a scandal (Enron).

The implications of selling naming rights or digitally imposing logos onto playing fields (an increasingly common practice) may seem trivial to some, but they are symptomatic of a more troubling trend: the "hollowing out" of our social identity. The shared experiences that over time give a city soul are seen as yet another commodity to be bought and sold. At a more subtle level, national franchises and branding have the same effect on how we experience our own culture; they quietly eliminate all that is distinctive, idiosyncratic and charming. The irregular textures of a specific place and its public life are flattened out to maximize commercial appeal.

Starbucks' enclosure of the coffee shop experience in the US is revealing. Originally inspired by the lively cafe culture of Italy, Howard Schultz, the chairman of Starbucks, was distressed in 2007 to see how his company's success in "branding the customer experience" had eroded the social charm and conviviality of its thirteen thousand coffee shops. In an internal corporate memo, "The Commoditization of the Starbucks Experience," Schultz lamented how the company's fierce expansion and efficiency measures had "lead to the watering-down of the Starbuck's experience, and, what some might call the commoditization of our brand." He cited how Starbuck's new automatic espresso machines—an efficiency measure that allowed faster service for more customers—meant that customers could no longer watch baristas make coffee by hand. Schultz complained that this had "removed much of the romance and theater" of the Starbuck's experience. Similarly, store clerks are "no longer scooping fresh coffee from the bins and grinding it fresh in front of the customer" because the coffee now came in flavor-locked packaging. Customers no longer experienced the tangy smell of coffee from the bins.

Schultz fretted: "Clearly we have had to streamline store design to gain efficiencies of scale and to make sure we had the

ROI [return on investment] on sales to investment ratios that would satisfy the financial side of our business. However, one of the results has been stores that no longer have the soul of the past and reflect a chain of stores vs. the warm feeling of a neighborhood store. Some people even call our stores sterile, cookie cutter, no longer reflecting the passion our partners feel about our coffee. In fact, I am not sure people today even know we are roasting coffee. You certainly can't get the message from being in our stores."

Call it the pathos of enclosure: Schultz cannot quite acknowledge that his branding aspirations eliminate the slack pace and local oddities that made coffee shops so attractive in the first place. He cannot quite admit that branding is precisely about creating a monoculture—the commodification of experience: the exact opposite of what a commons provides.

The market colonization of public spaces—and our consciousness—has become so extreme that many gas pumps and hotel elevators are now equipped with video screens that force us to watch or listen to ads. As public schools and universities suffer from budget cutbacks, corporations often step up to "help" by buying advertising space on school buses, highway toll booths, even municipal vehicles. In many cities, even the empty spaces above buildings have been turned into a special type of private property—"air rights"—that can be bought and sold as entitlements to build skyscrapers in empty spaces now redefined as legal property.

Commoners, of course, have a more expansive, egalitarian idea of what cities should be. Pulska Grupa, a group of architects and urban planners from Pula, Croatia, put it in this way in their Kommunal Urbanism Social Charter: "We imagine city as a collective space which belongs to all those who live in it, who have the right to find there the conditions for their political, social, economic and ecological fulfillment at the same time assuming duties of solidarity. This concept of the city is blocked by capitalist dialectic based on difference in public and private good. From these two poles State and Market emerge as the only two subjects. We want to escape this dialectic, not to focus on eventually 'third subject,' but on a group of collective subjectivities and the commons that they produce."

Pulska Grupa uses the language of the commons to help reassert a moral entitlement to public spaces. Such language helps claim the right to access and use public spaces and create new spaces with one's own tools and imagination, especially in the face of bureaucratic systems that ignore basic human rights and social needs. In a rudimentary sense, that is what the Occupy movement was all about, too. Commoners took over public spaces as a physical protest against oppressive enclosures that deny basic rights and dignity. That is also the goal of many "right to the city" movements around the world that are striving to reclaim cities whose design and operations have been captured by developers, industry and the very rich.

It is important to remember that access to open, uncontrolled public spaces is directly related to the vitality of democratic culture. It was no accident that following Generalissimo Franco's death in Spain, the city of Barcelona created all sorts of new public squares. These spaces are crucial to the ability of citizens to express themselves as a collective in public—and to challenge government abuses of power. We have seen how the existence of Tahrir Square in Cairo was critical to the public protests that toppled President Mubarak. That was surely a key reason why Turkish president Tayyip Erdogan in 2013 sought to transform Istanbul's Gezi Park in Taksim Square into a shopping mall, and then used violence to expel peaceful protesters. Public, physical spaces are important in enacting democracy.

The enclosure of public spaces is essentially an anti-democratic act. When shopping malls supplant our public squares and corporate brands seize control of our parks and our promenades, we lose our capacity to see each other as a people. We can't socialize and speak publicly, and it becomes harder for individuals to identify and empathize with each other. The erosion of public space means that it is much harder to *be* commoners. Without these spaces, we are forced into playing roles dictated by the Market and the State—acquisitive consumer and quiescent citizen.

Enclosures of Infrastructure

One of the easiest ways to make serious money is to somehow engineer a private takeover of infrastructure resources. Highways, bridges, airports, telecommunications systems and the Internet are coveted prizes because any private enterprise that controls them can reap risk-free revenues by bypassing competition and charging monopoly or oligopoly prices. Owners can also leverage their control of infrastructure to shape people's habits and steer them to related products in which the company has an interest.

Microsoft shrewdly leveraged its control over 90 percent of computer operating systems (Windows) to spur sales of desktop applications (Office, including Word, Excel and PowerPoint), by pressuring manufacturers to bundle the Office program into the pre-installed Windows software on computers. This strategy enabled Microsoft to reap enormous profits, stifle competition and shape the contour of future markets. By enclosing the commons of computer technical standards—a key infrastructure resource—Microsoft was able to slow innovation to suit its own business interests and shrink the diversity of software applications. The dozens of word-processing programs that used to compete in the marketplace, for example, have shrunk to only a few. Today Word is run on more than 90 percent of all computer desktops. And lest state or local governments try to change this situation, Microsoft has taken pains to lobby aggressively against open software standards in government procurement.

Infrastructure that is kept open and accessible to all can help guarantee that there is competition and innovation in the marketplace. It can also help protect all sorts of nonmarket social concerns, such as assuring universal access to infrastructure (e.g., roads, waterways and the Internet) and protecting the needs of future generations.

The Internet may be the most significant piece of infrastructure now endangered. In many parts of the world, cable and telephone companies are trying to exploit their oligopoly power as "on-ramps" to the Internet. They want to be able to charge a premium for providing faster, higher-quality service and larger amounts of bandwidth that people can use for uploads and downloads. If such "service tiers" and differential pricing were to take root, it would open the door to a balkanization of the Internet. Large corporate users would enjoy faster, more reliable service while ordinary users and non-profits would be stuck with slower, inferior access.

Rather than allow the Internet to remain a commons that is open and nondiscriminatory in how it transmits data, cable and telephone companies want to be able to censor or slow down types of network traffic that might compete with their own business interests. So, for example, if cable and telephone companies don't want the Internet phone service Skype or video-streaming services competing with their own services (or those of their partners), they could choose to shut them out or slow them down.

This is why so many public-interest advocates around the world are insisting on so-called net neutrality policies for the Internet. Imagine if the dominant telecom providers had been allowed to discriminate against Google when it was a startup fifteen years ago. It never would have gotten off the ground. Imagine if cable companies had been allowed to screen out or slow down YouTube videos when that company was just launching. Imagine all the innovative competition that would be stifled if Internet service providers could say "yea" or "nay" to the sorts of Web traffic they would allow on "their" wires. They could veto what future technologies or services we could enjoy.

Historically, regulatory policies known as "common carriage" have assured open, nondiscriminatory access and pricing to telephone lines. Such rules have been adopted precisely to prevent dominant companies from stifling competition. Net neutrality follows in that tradition. It is an essential tool for assuring the Internet's infrastructure is treated as an accessible, nondiscriminatory commons, and not simply as a proprietary corporate asset. Without such rules, Internet users could lose their most basic online freedoms.

These attempted enclosures of the Internet parallel what has happened with the broadcast airwaves in many countries. In the US, the electromagnetic spectrum used for broadcasting belongs to the public. In return for being allowed free use of an essential public infrastructure, the airwaves, broadcasters were originally required to act as "public trustees" of the airwaves with legal requirements to serve the "public interest, convenience and necessity."

For decades, broadcasters "paid" for their spectrum by adhering to a handful of modest regulatory requirements to air local news, children's shows and educational programming. But these rules were eliminated during a massive round of deregulation under President Ronald Reagan in the 1980s and President Bill Clinton in the 1990s. Free-market deregulators simply rescinded the industry's side of the bargain and brazenly declared that market-driven broadcasting *is* the public interest. Broadcasters enjoyed a sweet deal: exclusive legal control over a valuable public asset worth billions of dollars, at no cost to them!

The corporate takeover of the airwaves infrastructure (assisted by liberals, it should be noted) has meant that market values dictate the type and quality of programming being aired. This accounts for the endless stream of reality shows, sexual titillation, vulgarity and violence on American TV—not to mention as many as twenty minutes of commercials per hour and "product placement" during shows.

A new frontier in the enclosure of infrastructure is Wall Street's attempts to buy roads, bridges and airports that generations of taxpayers paid for. Investors want to acquire equity ownership or long-term leases on civil infrastructure so they can reap guaranteed high rates of return and enjoy low risks.

In Indiana, for example, investors have now acquired a 99-year lease on a long stretch of the Interstate 90 highway as well as the Chicago Skyway road, both of which they have turned into toll roads. The City of Chicago now lets a private company owned in part by Morgan Stanley manage its thirty-six thousand parking meters, a deal that has tripled parking rates, introduced meters where they previously didn't exist and reduced the quality of service. The City's inspector general later found that the $1.15-billion privatization deal was undervalued by $974 million. And now the public and government have even *less* public influence over how the system is run.

Political leaders often favor such deals because they allow them to avoid raising taxes or making public spending commitments to pay for infrastructure. But privatization also means that the public loses control over infrastructure for which it has already paid billions. Private companies that manage public infrastructure are allowed to skim the cream from the operation while cutting quality, reducing employees' wages and shifting costs to future generations.

This familiar dynamic is why "public/private partnerships" often amount to hidden scams that bilk taxpayers. The government assumes the risk of business failure while guaranteeing healthy profits no matter what happens to the business. Variations on this theme of corporate socialism—in which profits are privatized and risks are socialized—can be seen in government dealings with the water, energy, highway construction and financial industries. Sometimes the hidden subsidy takes the form of loan guarantees, with the government guaranteeing to pay debts if companies default. Sometimes the subsidy takes the form of regulatory schemes that guarantee profits to electricity and water suppliers while quietly reducing their infrastructure costs, legal liabilities and operating risks. In the US, governments have given industry tax-exempt bonds totaling more than $65 billion over the past ten years to reduce the financial risks of private investors. Among the beneficiaries: a North Carolina winery, a Puerto Rican golf resort, a car museum in Kentucky and Goldman Sachs and Bank of America, which both got subsidized office buildings.

THE NOVELIST WILLIAM FAULKNER once said, "The past is never dead. It's not even past." So it is with enclosures. They are not distant and forgotten episodes of history; they and their social and ecological harms continue. They remain a deep imperative of our modern capitalist economy. An incestuous Market/State alliance—not "free markets"—is the order of the day. The magnitude and mendacity of this alliance was laid bare in the aftermath of the 2008 financial crisis as the federal government bailed out banks and financial institutions while letting them evict millions of Americans from their homes.

Of course, the methods of enclosure have changed a great deal since the Middle Ages. Instead of stone walls and hedges, modern-day enclosures are achieved through international trade treaties, property law, lax regulation and corporate asset purchases. But the handmaidens of enclosure—stealth, complexity and persuasive cover stories—remain all too familiar. The lords and ladies fine continue to take things that are yours and mine—while working mightily to divert our attention from the disruptive injustices of their enclosures.

ENCLOSURES OF KNOWLEDGE AND CULTURE

IF YOU'VE EVER SUNG "Happy Birthday" at a restaurant or park, you are—in the entertainment industry's sense of the word—a "pirate." That's because the Warner Music Group owns the copyright to "Happy Birthday." The song was written in 1858 by two sisters, Mildred and Patty Hill, who were inspired by Negro folk songs and a tune called "Good Morning to All." Amazingly, their piece of mid-nineteenth-century music, originally intended for schoolchildren, will remain a piece of private property until it enters the public domain in 2030—172 years after its "original" creation.

In the meantime, the Warner Music Group rakes in about $5,000 a day in royalties from "Happy Birthday," or nearly $2 million a year. Copyright lawyers don't seem to notice that the only reason this song has any commercial value at all is because it has circulated freely for generations in people's households, a tenacious host of folk culture that exists *outside* of the marketplace.*

---

* The song's copyright may not even be valid, according to scholar Robert Brauneis. As he writes, "There are serious questions about whether a court would find 'Happy

The "Happy Birthday" story is no aberration, alas. It is just one of countless contemporary enclosures of the cultural commons. In the early 2000s, after hearing too many of these stories, I cofounded a Washington, D.C., advocacy group, Public Knowledge, to stand up for the public's stake in copyright and Internet policy. The experience prompted me to write a book, *Brand Name Bullies*, documenting some of the most outrageous examples of overreaching by entrenched media industries that use copyright and trademark to claim proprietary control over all sorts of our creativity and culture.

I find dark amusement in the greed of the American Society of Composers, Authors and Publishers (ASCAP), the music-licensing body that threatened dozens of children's summer camps with legal action in 1996. The summer camps' big crime was to sing copyrighted songs. By ASCAP's reckoning, commercial summer camps that organize children to sing around the campfire and dance in the dining hall are hosting "public performances." And, as copyright law clearly states, public performances of copyrighted songs require payment to copyright holders. ASCAP reportedly sought $1,200 per camp per season as an opening offer. The organization's chief operating officer told a reporter at the time, "They [camps] buy paper, twine and glue for their crafts—they can pay for the music, too."

Once the public and press learned of these outrageous demands, the barrage of public criticism became so intense that

---

Birthday to You' to still be under copyright, due to difficulties with proving authorship of the song, with potentially improper copyright notice upon first publication, and with renewal applications that seem only to cover particular arrangements of the song rather than the song itself." Yet because no one has a big enough financial incentive to challenge the copyright in court, says Brauneis, and because copyright law offers no easy way to invalidate a dubious copyright, "Happy Birthday to You" remains private property. In June 2013, filmmaker Jennifer Nelson, who is making a film about the song, filed a lawsuit against Warner/Chappell Music, Inc. to try to affirm that the copyright to "Happy Birthday to You" is invalid.

ASCAP backed off. Mercifully, kids in summer camps were allowed to sing and dance to "Puff the Magic Dragon" and "Row, Row, Row Your Boat." It bears noting, however, that singing copyrighted songs at camp remains an ASCAP-granted indulgence, not a legal entitlement.

These examples may seem extreme, but they point to one of the great transformations in culture over the past century. You and I may consider music, film and photographs to be the glue that bind a society together. In truth, this is only a secondary effect. In the eyes of the law, such creative works are little more than marketable units of "intellectual property." For film studios, record labels and book publishers, culture = product. Creative works = private property.

This a fairly audacious inversion of the history of human culture. From time immemorial, human beings have freely shared their creativity with each other. Culture has always been about imitating, extending and transforming earlier creative works. Art has always been a communal, intergenerational act of borrowing. The Greek legend of Pygmalion was the basis for a George Bernard Shaw play of the same name, and later for the musical *My Fair Lady*. The musical *West Side Story* is clearly based on Shakespeare's *Romeo and Juliet*, and Shakespeare himself did his fair share of recycling from Ovid and other ancients. Mark Twain's *Huckleberry Finn* owes a huge debt to Homer's *Odyssey*, which itself draws heavily upon oral traditions. Culture cannot thrive without a commons of shared creativity.

It is impossible to imagine the development of jazz, the blues or hip-hop if musicians had not been able to freely borrow from each other. The great American folk singer Woody Guthrie proudly acknowledged that his folk music was cobbled together from the bits and pieces of old blues masters, hillbilly singers and cowboy music. Taking aim at the commercial ethic that was already beginning to dominate music in his time, Guthrie wrote,

"This song is copyrighted in US...for a period of 28 years, and anybody caught singin' it without our permission, will be mighty good friends of ours, cause we don't give a dern. Publish it. Write it. Sing it. Swing to it. Yodel it."

The 28-year period of copyright protection that prevailed in Guthrie's time has since been extended several times and now lasts for an author's lifetime plus 70 years. This is ostensibly the length of monopoly control that an author needs to be motivated to create. According to the logic of copyright law, I would not be sufficiently motivated to write this book unless I could enjoy copyright protection until the year 2100, more or less.

There have been many obscure changes to copyright law over the past century that have expanded the rights of copyright holders. Few have been as consequential as the 1976 change to US law that made *all* creative works—including scribbles on a piece of paper and casual chords recorded on a tape recorder—automatically copyrighted. No longer did an artist or her publisher have to affirmatively register a work to get copyright protection; all works created since the 1976 law are automatically *born* in an envelope of private property rights. Most countries of the world—165 by 2012—have adopted this standard by ratifying the Berne Convention, an international copyright treaty that prohibits formal registration requirements for copyright protection.

This sweeping change in the scope of copyright law has been followed by intensive PR campaigns by the entertainment industry to persuade us that music, film and books must be seen as "intellectual property" that is as sacrosanct as your home or car. Likening culture to private property has been insidiously effective—if misleading—because it has allowed industry to claim that any unauthorized use of creative works constitutes a theft. Our natural human impulses to imitate and share—the essence of culture—have been criminalized.

That, in a nutshell, is the problem we face today. Copyright and trademark law—with help from new types of "technological locks" that encrypt DVDs and ebooks—are privatizing more and more of our shared culture so that large companies can squeeze more money from it. As we will see below, this is limiting the freedom of creators in all media. It is also homogenizing culture, erecting legal barriers to new creativity, scientific research and free expression.

Copyright scholar James Boyle wrote a famous essay declaring that we are in the midst of a "Second Enclosure Movement." The first was, of course, the English enclosure movement, described in the next chapter. The second one, now underway, is the over-privatization (i.e., corporatization) of creative works, information and knowledge.

This trend has been going on for several decades, but it has accelerated with the arrival of new electronic technologies: video recorders, satellite and cable television, personal computers, the Internet, smartphones, ebook readers and countless others. Before these devices, words were affixed to sheets of paper, film images were frozen in celluloid and music was embedded into vinyl. It was technically difficult to extract the "content" from the medium and costly and cumbersome for ordinary people to copy and share copyrighted works fixed on paper, celluloid or vinyl. But as one medium after another has gone digital, and as the Internet became a universal communication medium, it has become far easier to copy and share creative works. To industry's chagrin, it has also become increasingly difficult to control creative works as private property. Digital bits are just too fluid and portable. That's what Stewart Brand, the countercultural futurist, meant when he famously said that "information wants to be free."

The real issue is that the new technologies are undermining the deeply entrenched, profitable business models that

Hollywood, record labels and publishers have relied upon for nearly a century. These large corporations don't like how new technologies are enabling newcomers to outcompete their antiquated business models by selling "content" in new and cheaper ways. Hollywood once regarded the arrival of television, cable TV and the videocassette recorder as profound threats to its core business—the theatrical exhibition of films—only to discover that each invention opened up lucrative new markets for it. In this tradition, studios are now incensed that people dare to use excerpts of films and television shows noncommercially and without authorization—a right explicitly protected under the "fair use" (or in some countries, "fair dealing") doctrine of copyright law.

For the entertainment industry, the problem is not just a constant stream of new technologies that make it easier to copy, disseminate and remix cultural works. It's that people can now create and share their own works. They don't necessarily have to *buy* anything. In a sense, creativity generated *outside* of the marketplace, via digital commons, is becoming a robust new kind of competition to market-based culture.

Hollywood and the record labels have therefore run to legislatures around the world to seek special legal protections. They have also joined forces with other media industries to seek stronger international treaties that expand their rights and punish "pirates" (defined very broadly). Their primary weapons are stronger copyright laws, draconian legal penalties for unauthorized uses of their works and new technology locks such as "digital rights management" on music CDs and DVDs of theatrical films. It all amounts to a cultural lockdown.

One of the most outrageous examples was the Walt Disney Company's fierce campaign to extend the terms of copyright protection by twenty years. In the mid-1990s, the company was worried that its flagship character, Mickey Mouse—first depicted in a 1928 cartoon short, "Steamboat Willie"—would enter the public domain in 2004. Pluto, Goofy and Donald were destined to become public-domain characters five years later. To protect its cartoon characters from becoming freely available, Disney mounted an aggressive lobbying campaign to enact the Copyright Term Extension Act. It flexed its political muscle by giving campaign contributions to most of the congressional sponsors of the legislation.

In 1998 Disney succeeded in extending the length of copyright terms by twenty years. As a result, an estimated four hundred thousand books, movies and songs due to enter the public domain will remain under private ownership and control until at least 2018—a windfall to copyright holders worth tens of billions of dollars.

The irony is that copyright is intended to stimulate new creativity by rewarding creators. But it's literally impossible for this legislation to induce George Gershwin, Joseph Conrad, Robert Frost, Lewis Carroll or F. Scott Fitzgerald to create additional works. They are all dead. The extension of copyright terms was a crude political case of corporate protectionism. In order to protect the 3 percent of their works from the 1920s and 1930s that still have some commercial value, Disney and its allies succeeded in locking up *all* works from that period, including the 97 percent that are not even commercially available.

Trademark law is another tool that is being abused to shut down the cultural commons and protect markets. Trademark law governs names and logos used to identify companies and brand-name products. It has the legitimate goal of preventing consumer fraud and confusion in the marketplace. But big companies are increasingly using trademark law to control their public images and prevent ordinary people from criticizing or making fun of their products.

For example, Mattel has been quick to sue anyone who uses images of Barbie dolls or the Barbie name in unauthorized ways, even for social commentary or parody. A few years ago, the company went after a photographer who had mounted a photo exhibit depicting Barbie in a variety of silly and sexual positions. Mattel once pressured a small publisher to change the subtitle of its book about anorexia and eating disorders because it used the word "Barbie."

McDonald's has threatened legal action against dozens of restaurants that had names like "McVegan," "McSushi" and "McMuffin." The company once prevailed against a motel chain known as "McSleep" for trademark infringement. With some thirty thousand outlets in a hundred countries, McDonald's essentially claims that it has global ownership of the prefix "Mc" as applied to restaurants and related businesses.

Such trademark abuses are common. The *Village Voice* newspaper in New York City once tried to stop the *Cape Cod Voice* and other newspapers from using the word "Voice." There are actually trademarks for smells, such as "the smell of freshly cut grass on tennis balls." The US television network NBC owns a trademark on three musical notes played on a chime—"ding, dong, ding!" One wonders if Andy Warhol would have been able to create his Campbell Soup silkscreen if today's trademark laws were in force fifty years ago.

The Marketization of Universities and Their Research

It may not seem obvious, but as professors Michael Madison, Brett Frischmann and Katherine Strandburg put it, the university is a "constructed cultural commons." The university system uses the commons paradigm to help many different people work together to generate new knowledge. It manages the flows of knowledge as a living system, and devises ways to store knowledge, improve it and introduce it to new generations. The university is a complex ecosystem of many smaller-scale commons, such as the graduate and undergraduate college, the school, the department, the library, the archive, the lecture hall and the seminar room.

Anyone who lives within academia knows that the language of property rights and market transactions is quite alien to its ethos. A university does not buy and sell knowledge; it nurtures ongoing relationships of trust and reciprocity. It promotes sharing and collaboration in advancing knowledge. Well-regarded professors peer-review their rivals' papers, for instance, without ever thinking of charging money for this service, one they also benefit from many times over. Of course, academia is also an arena of competition and rivalry, but there is a presumption within scholarly circles that knowledge should not become a proprietary product. It should be openly shared and preserved.

In fact, that is how academia helps assure the integrity of its research—through open scrutiny and debate. The community is the proper steward of the knowledge. Hoarding knowledge as a privately owned good is not only hostile to the community, it defeats the value-proposition of scholarship. The goal of scholarship is not to maximize profits but to advance the search for truth and root out error. People feel a responsibility to patrol the boundaries of the academic commons in order to identify anyone who might poison the truth with falsified research or plagiarism. That is the real value of the commons in academia: its effectiveness in nourishing ethical scholarship. It is always prepared to identify and punish the sloppy or deceitful researcher, and has historically frowned upon the entrepreneur who would privatize a research community's work by patenting it for private gain.

The big story of the past thirty years has been the erosion of this ethic. The privatization and commodification of academic knowledge and scholarly relationships are now well advanced. The year 1980 was a major turning point in the history of the modern university, at least in the United States. That was the year that Ronald Reagan and Margaret Thatcher both won election and inaugurated new policy regimes based on an aggressive market fundamentalism. It was also the year that the US Supreme Court issued its famous *Chakrabarty* ruling, which opened the door for the patenting of bacteria, genes, living tissue and both natural and bioengineered life-forms.

Harvard University now owns patents for the so-called oncomouse used for laboratory research for cancer studies. It also owns patents on 23 synthetic nano-scale substitutes for elements of the periodic table. Patents on treatments for the AIDS virus mean that public funds are often used for developing medicines that later become privately owned and expensive to buy. Big Pharma thrives; indigent AIDS patients are more likely to die.

One of the most significant forces driving this new market ethic in biomedical research, among other fields, is the Bayh–Dole Act, a US law passed in 1980 and emulated around the world. Enacted at the behest of large pharmaceutical, chemical and biotech companies, the law authorizes universities to privatize publicly funded research by patenting it themselves, often in collaboration with corporate funders. The law encourages companies to see universities as sources of (cheap, publicly financed) research and development that it can colonize and corrupt to serve their short-term market needs. Not surprisingly, this has transformed many scholarly protocols and ethical standards. University administrators have intensified their search for ways to monetize scholarly and scientific research, launching "tech transfer" offices to court large corporations to fund major research institutes.

This is fine so far as it goes—but it also opened the door to corruption and serious ethical conflicts of interest. Universities and corporations have sought to claim patents in publicly funded research and privatize the profits. Even though taxpayers finance the most important drug breakthroughs, the patents are often owned by corporations and universities and the drugs are sold at high prices. US taxpayers have financed research that produced treatments for genetic disorders, depression and diabetes, and have invested in the research for Vasotec and Capoten for hypertension; the antiviral drug Zovirax; Prozac and Zantac for depression; Taxol for cancer; and Xalatan for glaucoma. But the patents for these drugs belong to corporations and their shareholders, not us.

Corporate partnerships with universities can corrupt university research priorities, often to the detriment of long-term basic research that would benefit the public. For example, instead of studying organic farming techniques and integrated pest management, a university biology department eager to secure corporate funding will find it more attractive to take money from Monsanto and study genetically modified crops. Instead of studying GNU/Linux and open source software as a tool that could help people in marginalized countries (and also reduce its own academic software bills), a university beholden to generous Microsoft research partnerships will find it attractive to steer students toward Microsoft's proprietary software projects. This simply enlarges Microsoft's customer and developer base while thwarting open innovation and competition.

Big Pharma has systematically corrupted the integrity of medical education in the United States, as Dr. Marcia Angell, a lecturer at Harvard Medical School, has documented in numerous articles. Top teaching physicians enjoy all sorts of cozy consultancies and junkets paid for by pharmaceutical companies. Not surprisingly, the country's medical profession emphasizes the virtues of drug-based therapies over cheaper, sometimes better alternatives. In the US, nearly half of all continuing education for doctors is financed by drug companies. This expenditure of money has had predictable influences on the objectivity of medical research and clinical recommendations.

The enclosure of the academic commons has had all sorts of more subtle cascading effects. One is a decline in the spirit of collaboration and sharing. After universities enter into corporate partnerships, many professors are not *allowed* to share their research. It's proprietary. Corporate sponsors often insist upon the power to suppress research results that might prove embarrassing to their business interests. Academic scientists and university administrations—having chosen in effect to become junior partners of large corporations—can get caught up in ethical conflicts of interest. Should they serve the public good or the private interests of corporate funders? Should academic norms of openness and sharing trump the proprietary terms of corporate research contracts?

As more academic knowledge becomes owned, it is creating what is called "patent thickets"—dense sets of patent rights that make it difficult to identify who owns rights and who is authorized to use them. Law professor Michael Heller calls this problem the "tragedy of the anti-commons"—the fragmentation of property rights such that it becomes harder for researchers to clear patent rights and collaborate without risking a lawsuit. Research into breast cancer was discouraged for years by the patents that a Utah biotech company claimed on "breast cancer susceptibility genes." Many academic scientists were fearful of doing work that might run afoul of these gene patents. Fortunately, a landmark ruling by the US Supreme Court in June 2013 invalidated the patents by declaring that human genes cannot be patented. Still, patent thickets remain a serious impediment to discovery and innovation.

Corporate partnerships with universities have still other troubling effects. They can throw a cloak of secrecy over research methods and delay the timely publication of research results. Sometimes new research findings are delayed so that the sponsoring company can get a patent before competitors learn of the research. This can result in other academics doing duplicative or unnecessary research. There are many cases of researchers who have lost their jobs or had their research suppressed because their work proved embarrassing to a university's corporate partners.

Historically, the State has treated academic research as a commons by building public universities, funding important research and respecting academic independence. This experience shows that the state and commons can work constructively together. But over the past generation, this ethic has eroded dramatically as the State and Market have enclosed the academic commons so that its resources can be used to spur short-term economic growth. No only do market innovation and competition suffer, the long-term, nonmarket costs are incalculable.

The Many Costs of Enclosure

Our brief survey of enclosures is meant to highlight the dangers of alienating nature, culture and social relationships for market purposes. Let me stress: it is entirely possible for markets and commons to "play nicely together." But if the market system presses its demands too far; if it insists upon monetizing things that should not be given a price; if the scope of property rights are expanded too far; if companies insist upon privatizing access to basic resources that everyone needs; if monopoly ownership rights are allowed to squeeze out competition and nonmarket values then enormous harm can result. Ecosystems are damaged. Commoners are dispossessed of vital resources. The character of the social order changes. The benefits for future generations are squandered. The freedom, autonomy and conviviality of commoners are eroded. A system that values inclusiveness and the meeting of basic needs is turned into a system of exclusion regulated by one's ability to pay—a system that privileges large corporations over all others. Left unchecked, such enclosures will destroy the generative powers of academic commons.

This is one reason why the language of the commons is so useful. It helps us confront the pathological tendency of markets to force people, communities and nature to become "fictional commodities" in the market system. It helps us understand how the commons is a system that in fact creates enormous value. Much of this value would require vast expenditures if the Market or the State were to undertake similar efforts on its own terms. Consider how Linux, blood banks and Wikipedia oversee the production of valuable work with great speed, efficiency and trustworthiness. The more significant point, which will elude most economists and politicians, is that the commons is rich with all sorts of unmeasured, qualitative and particular types of value. Our most urgent challenge is to find better ways to protect the integrity of the commons and the value that they quietly produce.

6

THE ECLIPSED
HISTORY OF THE
COMMONS

ONE OF THE MOST insidious things about enclosures is how they eradicate the culture of commons and our memory of them. The old ways of doing things; the social practices that once bound a people together; the cultural traditions that anchored people to a landscape; the ethical norms that provided a stable identity—all are swept aside to make room for a totalizing market culture. Collective habits give way to individualism. Cherished traditions fall victim to whatever works now or saves money today. The colorful personalities and idiosyncratic lore of a community start to fade away.

Karl Marx memorably described the commoditizing logic of capitalism, saying, "All that is solid melts into air." Enclosures eclipse the history and memory of the commons, rendering them invisible. The impersonal, individualistic, transaction-based ethic of the market economy becomes the new normal.

If we are to understand the commons, then, it is useful to learn more about its rich, neglected history. Capitalist culture likes to think that all of history leads inexorably to greater progress, if not perfection, as society climbs toward the present moment, the best of all possible worlds. The complex, overlooked history of the commons tells a different story. It is an account of how human beings have learned new and ingenious ways to cooperate. It is a story of building new types of social institutions for shared purposes despite systems of power (feudalism, authoritarianism, capitalism) with very different priorities.

Commons tend to be nested within other systems of power and institutional relationships, and therefore are not wholly independent. There is often a deep "creative tension" between the logic of the commons and the imperatives of its host environment (whether feudal lords, technology markets or national laws). This is why many commons thrive in the interstices of power, in "protected zones" tolerated or overlooked by Power, or accidentally remote from it.

The stark reality is that commons tend not to be dominant institutional forms in their own right. This subordinate role can be seen in the flourishing of medieval land commons under feudalism; in mutual associations under socialism and communism; and, in our time, in gift economies such as academia and civic associations under capitalism. Such commons were (and still are) nested within larger systems of power and rarely functioned as sovereign forces.

Still, human reciprocity and cooperation go back millennia. With the dawn of civilization, legal traditions were invented that sought to protect the shared interests of the many and of future generations. The human impulse to cooperate is rarely expressed in purely altruistic forms; it tends to work in creative tension with individualism and power. Even though we like to contrast "individualism" and "collectivism" as opposites, in the commons they tend to blur and intermingle in complicated ways. The two are not mutually exclusive, but rather dynamic yin-and-yang complements.

In this chapter, I want to review some of the more salient themes of the commons throughout the centuries. Historical small-scale commons belie the claims made by contemporary economists that humans are essentially materialist individuals of unlimited appetites, and that these traits are universal. Quite the opposite. The real aberration in human history is the idea of *Homo economicus* and our globally integrated market society. Never before in history have markets organized so many major and granular elements of human society. Never before has the world seen so many societies organized around the principles of market competition and capital accumulation, which systematically produce extremes of selfish individualism, inequalities of wealth and crippling assaults on natural ecosystems.

This is worrisome on its own terms, but also because of the instability and fragility of large-scale, market-based systems. Six years after the 2008 financial crisis, the great powers are still scrambling to reestablish trust, credibility and social stability to many global and national markets. Whether through crisis or choice, it is virtually inevitable that the human race (or at least the industrialized West) will need to rediscover and reinvent institutions of human cooperation.

What Evolutionary Sciences Tell Us About Cooperation

Given their premises about individual self-interest, it is not surprising that economists consider the world a nasty, competitive place that will degenerate into anarchy unless the State steps in to restrain bad actors and mete out punishment. A formidable set of political philosophers—John Locke, David Hume, Thomas Hobbes—set forth this worldview in the eighteenth century; in the words of Hobbes, life was "solitary, poor, nasty, brutish and short." Upon its principles of universal selfishness and individual "rationality," entire systems of law and public policy have been built.

But what if this is mostly a "just so" story—a partially accurate fable that does not really describe the full empirical realities of human nature? What if it could be shown that human cooperation, reciprocity and non-rational behavior are just as significant forces as "competitive rationality" and "utility maximization"?

This is the startling conclusion of much contemporary research in the evolutionary sciences, especially brain neurology, genetics, developmental and evolutionary psychology, biology, organizational sociology and comparative anthropology. These sciences are confirming that social reciprocity and trust are deeply engrained principles of our humanity. They may even be biologically encoded.

One of the first scientists to explore this possibility was the Russian zoologist Petr Kropotkin in his 1902 book, *Mutual Aid: A Factor in Evolution*. Kropotkin surveyed the animal kingdom and concluded that it "was an evolutionary emphasis on cooperation instead of competition in the Darwinian sense that made for the success of species, including the human." Animals live in association with each other and mutually aid each other as a way to improve their group fitness.

Mainstream science in the twentieth century took a very different direction, however. It has generally embraced models of rational self-interest to explain how organisms behave and evolve. In the evolutionary sciences, natural selection has traditionally been seen as something that happens to individuals, not to groups, because individuals have been considered a privileged unit in the biological hierarchy of nature. Thus evolutionary adaptations have been thought to happen to *individuals*, not to collectivities or entire species. Scientists have generally dismissed the idea that biological traits that are "good for the group" can be transmitted and evolve at the group level.

Over the past decade, however, there has been an explosion of new research by respected scientists such as Martin Nowak, E. O. Wilson and David Sloan Wilson, who argue that group-level selection is a significant force in human and animal evolution. Empirical evidence suggests that evolutionary adaptations can and do occur at all levels of the biological hierarchy, including groups. The basic idea is that while cooperation and altruism can be "locally disadvantageous" for individuals, they can be highly adaptive traits for groups. As E.O. Wilson and David Sloan Wilson put it, "Selfishness beats altruism within groups. Altruistic groups beat selfish groups. Everything else is commentary." In short, reciprocal social exchange lies at the heart of human identity, community and culture. It is a vital brain function that helps the human species survive and evolve.

Controversy still rages, of course, but it would appear that human beings are neurologically hardwired to be empathic and cooperative, and to connect emotionally with their fellow human beings. As author and essayist Rebecca Solnit showed in her book *A Paradise Built in Hell: The Extraordinary Communities That Arise in Disaster*, members of communities beset by catastrophes such as the San Francisco earthquake of 1907, the German Blitz of London during World War II and the 9/11 terrorist attacks generally show incredible self-sacrifice, joy, resolve and aching love toward each other. The communities such disasters create are truly "paradises built in hell." Her book is an answer to the economists and political leaders who believe that the world is made up of isolated, selfish individuals who must be governed through authoritarianism and fear.

"Perhaps the most remarkable aspect of evolution," writes Harvard theoretical biologist Martin A. Nowak, "is its ability to generate cooperation in a competitive world," adding, "Thus, we might add 'natural cooperation' as a third fundamental principle of evolution beside mutation and natural selection." It bears noting that the popularity of "individual selection theory" during the latter half of the twentieth century coincided uncannily with the heyday of market culture and its ethic of competitive individualism. A case of culture affecting scientific observation?

What is notable about the more recent findings of evoluitionary science is the recognition that individual organisms function within a complex system of interdependence. This means that individual self-interest and group survival tend to converge, making the supposed dualism of "self-interest" and "altruism" somewhat artificial. Anyone who participates in useful online communities will recognize this feeling; individual and group interests become more or less aligned and self-reinforcing, if occasionally disrupted by disagreements and external jolts.

As a social scientist, Professor Elinor Ostrom studied hundreds of cases around the world in which communities were able to self-organize their own systems of commons-based governance and develop a cooperative ethic. Her research unearthed an ethnographic reality: that commons can persuade individuals to limit their narrow self-interests and support a larger collective agenda. The gratifying news is that evolutionary scientists are confirming these claims at the more elemental level of genetics, biology, neurology and evolutionary psychology.

The Forgotten Legal History of the Commons

The subterranean life of the commons in evolutionary science— which is only now being recognized—parallels its legal history. The law of the commons has also been largely ignored, and yet it actually goes back to ancient Egypt and the Roman Empire, and is stitched like a golden thread throughout medieval history in Europe. Landmarks of commons-based law—such as Roman legal categories for property and the Magna Carta and its companion Charter of the Forest—are deeply embedded in Western law.

Given the market orientation of contemporary law, however, the legal principles that originated and evolved in the commons over centuries have mostly been eclipsed. This is partly because the Western tradition tends to see law as a written system of rules and sanctions administered by civic institutions like legislatures, courts and presidents. The modern liberal polity has trouble recognizing or enforcing collective interests (except those of investors, via the corporation) because the liberal State is a formal, government-managed system that focuses on individual rights.

If we are to understand the law of the commons, we must start by expanding our notion of law itself. Law is not just formal, written and institutional; it is also informal, oral and social. The law of the commons represents something of a threat to formal law because its substance and legitimacy derive from the always-shifting social practices of the community. "Commoning" is often experienced as more responsive and morally legitimate than state law, particularly when the state itself is rigid, corrupt, incompetent or captive to corporate influence.

Of course, state law can play many constructive social and economic roles, particularly in confronting corporate abuses or antisocial behaviors such as racial or gender discrimination. And informal communities may have their own odious attitudes and criminal tendencies. My only point is that a formal system of statutes, court rulings and state enforcement will become a source of tyranny if it does not connect with and respond to "the street." It must have robust feedback loops to help formal law reflect the evolving sentiments of people.

In a brilliant essay, "The Life of the Law Online," legal scholar David R. Johnson likens law to a biological organism. He sees law as more closely resembling life than a machine; in this sense, it has a life and history of its own. "Law is a story we tell each other about justice and shared social values," writes Johnson. "We have to retell this story every day—it replicates and persists only insofar as we do that."

That is essentially how the law of the commons works. A given community creates its own body of (informal, social) law to suit its needs, then replicates it through everyday social activities. This is how commons devoted to open source software, Wikipedia and academic disciplines arose—as self-organized communities with their own self-enforced rules and social ethics. Sometimes commoners may actually succeed in formalizing their law through conventional systems of state law (statutes, regulations court rulings), but this is rare. As historian Peter Linebaugh has put it, "Commoners think first not of title deeds, but of human deeds: How will this land be tilled? Does it require manuring? What grows there? They begin to explore. You might call it a natural attitude."

Custom is therefore a vital element of the law of the commons. It functions as a cultural code that provides a unifying social ethic to a community. It is a shared narrative that links the community to earlier generations, and to a repository of wisdom about local resources and how best to manage them. As property scholar Carol Rose puts it, custom is "a medium through which a seemingly 'unorganized' public may organize itself and act, and in a sense even 'speak' with the force of law."

This corresponds to David Johnson's claim that law amounts to a "self-referential, organizational identity" that belongs to the people who make it. "If law has a life of its own," he writes, "and in some sense causes its own form of order and persistence, we should be studying its biography rather than pretending that we can design and repair its mechanisms from the outside." In other words, we must understand the *subjective, socially internal dynamics* of commons and recognize that this is where law originates.

When law is seen in this perspective—not just as a series of formal constitutions and statutes but as a self-organized system that a community creates to manage itself and its resources in orderly fair ways—it is easy to see that the commons itself is a living embodiment of law. It amounts to an evolving social contract. Individuals come together to negotiate the rules and norms that will govern their community. They specify how members may access and use shared resources. They set about making rules for managing land, water, fish and wild game, and for monitoring usage and punishing vandals and free riders. In this broader sense, the law of the commons extends into the mists of time and precedes formal written law by many millennia.

From the outside, the law of the commons as embodied in an indigenous culture may seem static and slow moving, even frozen. But in truth, "commons law" constantly adapts to changes, often in small incremental ways. It is especially mindful of local realities: its signature strength. The tensions arise when formal, written law is not roughly congruent with such "commons law" and does not leave space for commoning. Is formal state law too strict and rigid—or is it open to change through peaceable politics and due process? Does it so insist upon market relationships and norms such that real citizenship is not possible?

Throughout history, state law has occasionally recognized the "vernacular law" of commoners—or at least, larger public needs—by formalizing such principles within the legal apparatus of the state. One of the earliest such instances of this occurred in the Roman Empire, which recognized explicit categories of law for property, including common property. In 535 AD, Emperor Justinian gave the first legal recognition of the commons when he enshrined *res communes* in his Institutes of Justinian body of law. "By the law of nature these things are common to mankind—the air, running water, the sea and consequently the shores of the sea.... Also all rivers and ports are public, so that the right of fishing in a port and in rivers is common to all. And by the *law of nations* the use of the shore is also public, and in the same manner, the sea itself. The right of fishing in the sea from the shore *belongs to all men*." (emphasis in original).

This legal principle—that neither the State, commerce nor citizens could make proprietary claims on resources that belong to everyone—has survived in what is known in American law as the "public trust doctrine." This doctrine formalizes the idea that the State has an affirmative duty to protect natural resources for present and future generations; it cannot sell or give away land, water or wildlife to any private party. The public trust doctrine has traditionally been applied to rivers, oceans and the coastal shoreline, and is invoked to protect the right of the unorganized public to use those waters for fishing, navigation and recreation. Versions of the public trust doctrine can also be found in most legal systems of the world and in many of the world's major religions. It stands for the principle that certain resources belong to everyone, morally and legally, and that the State cannot abrogate this right.

It is significant that *res communes* is a separate category from *res publicae*, another legal category that describes public things that belong to the state. *Res communes* is not simply "state-owned" property, but a class of property that lies beyond the power of the state. Not surprisingly, heads of state are not generally pleased to have to recognize the commons as a separate sphere of resources with its own moral authority and legal protection above and beyond their control.

Consider King John. In thirteenth-century England, a series of monarchs began to claim larger and larger plots of forest lands for their personal recreation and use, at the expense of barons and commoners. By threatening the basic livelihoods of commoners who depended on the forest for their food, firewood and building materials, these royal encroachments on the commons provoked prolonged and bitter civil strife. Livestock could not roam the forests; pigs could not eat acorns; commoners could not gather timber to fix their homes; boats could not navigate rivers upon which dams or private causeways had been built.

After years of brutal armed conflict, King John in 1215 formally consented to a series of legal limitations on his absolute power and stipulated that other members of society, including commoners, were entitled to due process, human rights and subsistence, among other rights. This was the great Magna Carta, one of the foundations of Western civilization. The rights of *habeas corpus*, trial by jury, the prohibition of torture and the rule of law all derive from the Magna Carta. All these legal principles have since found expression in modern constitutions around the world as the fundamental rights of citizens. They are also affirmed by a number of leading human rights conventions.

A near-forgotten document, the Charter of the Forest, also bears mention here. Signed two years after the Magna Carta and later incorporated into it, this charter recognized the traditional rights of commoners to use royal lands and forests. Thus commoners formally enjoyed the rights of pannage (pasture for their pigs), estover (collecting firewood), agistment (grazing) and turbary (cutting of turf for fuel) on royal properties. As a practical matter, the Charter of the Forest gave commoners basic rights to subsistence. It also protected them against state terror as waged by the king's sheriffs in their defense of the king's enclosures.

As this brief history suggests, the law of the commons points to a different *type* of law—one that originates from the lived experience of commoners; one that tends to be informal, situational and evolving rather than fixed and written; and one that encourages social mutualism and equality over commercial goals or state authority. Peter Linebaugh is instructive on this point: "Commoning is embedded in a labor process; it inheres in a particular praxis of field, upland, forest, marsh, coast. Common rights are entered into by labor. They belong to experience, not schooling.... Commoning, being independent of the state, is independent also of the temporality of the law and state. It's much older. But this doesn't mean that it's dead, or premodern, or backward."

Commoning remains vitally important as a bulwark against the abuses of formal law because it represents one of the few ways that formal law can be made accountable to the people. Formal law can be more easily corrupted and betrayed because it has identifiable access points—legislatures, courts, heads of state—where bad actors can traduce it, whereas vernacular law is deeply rooted in the daily lives of people and their culture and is therefore harder to manipulate or corrupt.

As welcome as the Magna Carta was to commoners, its guarantees could only be assured through constant vigilance. Commoners were skeptical, and understood the necessity of fighting back. This is one reason why kings repeatedly republished the Magna Carta over the years, ritualistically affirming that the basic human rights of commoners were indeed being upheld. Of course, a piece of paper has proved to be of only limited value in stopping the abuses of state power. As we've seen in our own times, the US government has, in the name of fighting terrorism, ignored with impunity the rights of *habeas corpus*, due process, the prohibitions on torture and other principles of the Magna Carta.

So, too, in the sixteenth to nineteenth centuries, the Magna Carta did little to impede enormous new enclosures of land. In 1536, King Henry III eliminated Catholic monasteries, unleashing a fierce round of enclosures by lords and nobles—a "massive act of state-sponsored privatization," as Linebaugh calls it. Authorized by four thousand acts of Parliament over several centuries, a rising class of gentry seized roughly 15 percent of all English common lands for their own private use. These enclosures destroyed many commoners' social connection to the soil and trampled their social identities and traditions, paving the way for their proletarianization.

As enclosures intensified, women who tried to maintain their old ways of commoning—who asserted their rights to common, if only because they had no other way to subsist—often found themselves accused of being witches. Silvia Federici explores these themes in her feminist history of the medieval transition to capitalism, *Caliban and the Witch*. She writes: "The social function of the commons was especially important for women, who, having less title to land and less social power, were more dependent on them for their subsistence, autonomy and sociality."

The Eclipse of the Law of the Commons

"Enclosure meant a shift away from lives guided by customs preserved in local memory toward those guided by national law preserved in writing," observed commons scholar Lewis Hyde. "It meant a shift in the value of change itself, once suspect and associated with decay, now praised and linked to growth. It meant a change in the measurement and perception of time" (as factories began to rationalize and measure time and direct people's activities based on it).

As people's access and rights to land were separated from social custom, a new type of person arose—the individual, someone who was not visibly a member of a collective and whose worldview became oriented around personal wages, technological progress, social progress and material gain. The new market order, writes Karl Polanyi, created people who were "migratory nomadic, lacking in self-respect and discipline—crude, callous beings." All of this followed when the "bundle" that constituted the commons—resources, commoners and social practices— was disassembled and commoditized to serve the needs of the new industrial market order.

Of course, enclosure had some positive effects, such as doing away with the master/commoner relationship, transforming vassals into freeholders. But this new "freedom" cut both ways: while it liberated people to pursue new identities and social freedoms, it also destroyed the social cohesion of the commons, a person's assured subsistence, ecological sustainability and the stabilizing linkages between identity and resource use.

The history of socialism and political liberalism can be seen as attempts to ameliorate some of the worst structural problems created by the dissolution of the commons. European socialism in the nineteenth and twentieth centuries introduced new sorts of social mutualism and bureaucratic systems to try to meet the needs of former commoners in the new circumstances of industrialized society. Bottom-up innovations such as consumer cooperatives, social security systems and municipal water supplies were invented. The idea was to meet the basic needs of commoners in a very different historical context, that of the Market/State.

These innovations were certainly an improvement over the *laissez-faire* order, and indeed, many of the early socialistic or utopian projects more or less functioned as commons, perhaps because they still had a lively memory of traditional commons. But as workers' collectives adapted to the requirements of state law, bureaucracy, corporations and market forces, the practice of *commoning*—and the vitality of commons—slowly disappeared.

State regulation has been another means to compensate for the problems introduced by "free markets," namely the displacement of costs and risks onto the environment, communities and the human body. The regulation of environmental practices and the safety of food, drugs, medical devices, chemicals, autos and consumer products can be seen as attempts to use the cumbersome apparatus of formal law, science and bureaucracy to enforce the social and ethical norms of commoners. Given the scale of commercial dealings and the power of transnational corporations, state regulation is absolutely necessary; conventional commons are too small, unorganized and lacking in resources to assure socially responsible outcomes.

On the other hand, regulation has not worked so well. The centralization and formalization of law made it easier for regulated industries to capture and corrupt the process—no surprise given the power of the Market/State and the depth of its overlapping interests. It remains something of an open question how governance might be restructured to rein in the chronic social and environmental abuses generated by markets.

Just as state regulation has a very uneven record, so the state's role as a trustee of common assets is uneven and often dismal. We easily forget that many resources managed by the state *belong to the people*. The state does not "own" the air, water, public lands, coastal areas or wildlife, and cannot do what it pleases with them. It is authorized to act only as an administrative and fiduciary agent of the people. Under the public trust doctrine, it cannot give away or allow the destruction of these resources. To emphasize the state's stewardship obligations, I like to call large-scale, state-mediated commons *state trustee commons* (discussed at length in Chapter 9).

Unfortunately, the state often neglects its responsibilities to "intervene" in markets because it fears that it might inhibit economic growth and violate widely believed fictions about "free market" principles. Safety regulations and public-service requirements, for example, tend to stabilize society, prevent serious harm and assure a rough social equity. But in our neoliberal times, even these goals are seen by most governments as an unacceptable burden on capital and corporations, and as a drag on economic growth.

To be sure, many grassroots movements have developed a modest independent sector of cooperatives and mutual association. Unfortunately, these alternative provisioning systems have generally failed to reach a meaningful scale. Similarly, while many important regulatory protections have been won over the years, they have failed to keep pace with the relentless stream of new problems generated by markets. In addition, regulation is generally dominated by legal proceduralism and scientific expertise, so that the views of local residents or individual consumers do not carry as much weight in decision-making as those of lawyers, credentialed technical experts and corporate officials. Commoners often find themselves delegitimized as participants in the governance process, or simply unable to afford the costs of participating.

In practice, the very institutionalization of the process, ostensibly intended to assure fair, equal and universal participation, also tends to disenfranchise commoners. This can be seen when social democratic states have taken over the administration of projects (social security) and when state communism has marginalized collective initiatives (co-ops). It is no surprise that the success of commoners in developing adequate protections for themselves and their resources through the legal systems of the nation-state has been highly irregular and limited.

Some of the most astute commentators on these problems are autonomous Marxists such as Massimo De Angelis, editor of *The Commoner* website; George Caffentzis, founder of the Midnight Notes Collective; Silvia Federici, an historian who concentrates on the feminist implications of the commons; Peter Linebaugh, author of *The Magna Carta Manifesto* and other histories of English commons; and Michael Hardt and Antonio Negri, the political theorists and authors of *Multitude, Empire* and *Commonwealth*. Each in different ways has noted that the core problem of unfettered capitalist markets is their tendency to erode the authentic social connections among people (cooperation, custom, tradition) and to liquidate the organic coherence of society and individual commons. Capital breaks commons into their constituent parts—labor, land, capital, money—and treats them as commodities whose value is identical with their price.

This has caused a persistent moral and political crisis because market capitalism cannot answer the questions, What can bind people together beyond the minimal social and civic ties needed to participate in market exchanges? Can a market-based society survive without the commons?

7

THE EMPIRE OF
PRIVATE PROPERTY

A SHIP IS ON A CRUISE sailing from port to port. Laid out on the upper deck are deck chairs; there are three times more passengers than chairs on board. During the first few days of the cruise, the deck chairs have a constant change of occupants. As soon as someone gets up, the chair is considered free; no one accepts the idea of placing handkerchiefs or other objects on chairs to indicate that they are being used. This is an expedient arrangement to allocate the limited number of deck chairs.

But once the shift sails into port and a large number of new passengers come on board, this arrangement breaks down. The newcomers, who all know each other, follow a different social convention in using the deck chairs. They draw the chairs toward themselves, and, from then on, lay exclusive and continuous claim to them. As a result, the majority of other passengers cannot use any chairs at all. Scarcity reigns, fights are the order of the day, and most of the guests on board find themselves less comfortable than before.

The "allegory of the deck chairs," as described here by German sociologist Heinrich Popitz (and brought to my attention by Silke Helfrich), illustrates just how malleable the idea of property really is. While formal laws may declare what property rights people may have in given circumstances, our *social norms* are at least as important a force—and those are highly adaptable.

The cruise ship passengers had a choice. They could treat the deck chairs as their exclusive individual property even though it meant that many passengers would have to do without—or they could treat the chairs as a shared resource that would more or less meet everyone's needs. How we define property rights matters because they influence the sorts of personal and social entitlements we may enjoy, affect the kind of social relations we will have and have enormous effects on our sense of well-being (or alienation).

In a much-quoted definition, the eighteenth-century jurist William Blackstone described property rights as "the sole and despotic dominion which one man claims and exercises over the external things of the world, in total exclusion of the right of any other individual in the universe." He implied that property rights belong solely to individuals. But of course property need not be defined this way. As the cruise ship passengers showed, they could choose to exercise temporary individual "use rights" to the same resource instead of exclusive possession. (To be technical, the cruise ship owner is arguably the "owner" of the deck chairs, but the passengers possess them for limited periods of time and in this case are free to set their own rules.)

Different property rights schemes have very different implications for how people's needs are met (or not met). Such choices influence the nature of the social order and the general attitudes among people. This may be the real point of the allegory of the deck chairs—that property rights are more malleable than most people suspect; that their design can be altered; and that such choices have far-reaching effects on how we relate to each other and how we use resources.

People like to think of property as a fairly self-evident category. By default they tend to see it as a *private* right to exercise exclusive control over physical objects such as land, cars and smartphones. A landowner typically sees his plot of land as a fixed, individual parcel of inert soil over which he may do whatever he wants. But the conceit that "property" has no social or ecological implications is a fantasy of modern life. In reality, a piece of land is a living part of a living ecosystem. Even as a commodity, its value is dependent upon the character of adjacent pieces of land and the larger ecosystem. A country home with sweeping views of the surrounding countryside alive with chirping birds and friendly neighbors is more valuable than an identical house located next to a factory and a belching smokestack.

In this sense, land is really a *fictional commodity*, as we have seen. It may be treated as private property, and we maintain the illusion that it is truly self-contained and fungible. But it is not really a bounded unit whose fullest value can be expressed by a price, in isolation from its context. Property is a kind of social fiction—an agreed-upon system for allocating people's rights to use a resource or exclude access to it. Individual property rights are by no means the only or best way to manage a resource. Land can be well managed as a trust on behalf of the public and future generations. It can be managed through cultural practices and traditions that treat it as a sacred gift of nature, as indigenous peoples often do. Specific and limited rights can be allocated to people in various ways, as farming collectives and conservation easements often do.

Libertarians and free-market champions like to argue that private property rights are a natural if not God-given entitlement. They tend to argue that theirs is the *only* legitimate system of property law, and that collective property rights are economically impractical, politically oppressive and morally suspect. A legal regime of private property is seen as a universal moral imperative.

This amounts to ideological bluster. In reality, the scope of property rights varies immensely from one culture to another, and even within one culture's history (not to mention within a culture at a given moment, because there are multiple types of property!). Let's keep in mind, too, the sly deception that the very term "private property" advances. The term often serves as a euphemism for corporate property, a far larger, more powerful and problematic creature than the personal property associated with individual households.

The Inalienable Rights of Commoners

Property rights do not arise naturally, as the great Digger leader Gerrard Winstanley noted in 1659. They are the result of conquest: "For the power of enclosing land and owning property was brought into the creation by your ancestors by the sword." A Goethe poem, "Catechism," makes this clear in a conversation between a teacher and a child. "Bethink, thee, child! Where do those gifts come from? Something from yourself alone cannot come." The child replies that they came from Papa, and that Papa got them from Grandpapa. But where did Grandpapa get them, the teacher asks. Child: "He took them all." The simple appropriation of things—perhaps with sophisticated legal doctrines to serve as justifications—is arguably the real origin of many property rights.

To be sure, sometimes people affirmatively *choose* private property regimes without a full understanding of the larger social ramifications. For example, a generation ago, many native peoples in the state of Alaska embraced the idea of administering their traditional lands and resources through "native corporations"—a shift that led to mismanagement of the resources, corruption, inequality and, in some cases, outright dispossession, as outside investors bought up lands now treated as commodities, not sacred inheritances. Similarly, the estate of Dr. Martin Luther King, Jr., run by his children, has treated his writings, images and audio recordings as commercial properties to be sold to the highest bidders, ostensibly to support the preservation of Dr. King's legacy. The King estate has even claimed a copyright in the iconic "I Have a Dream" speech and once licensed its use to a telecom company for a television and print ad campaign.

Private property rights serve all sorts of useful purposes, of course, and over the course of history have served to emancipate people from the tyranny of kings, aristocrats and authoritarians. But it is also true that private property law can be a nasty form of oppression and coercion in its own right. Taken to extremes and applied to the exclusion of other moral, social and ecological concerns, it is a singularly useful tool for achieving enclosures.

Many property theorists note that the actual scope of property rights has changed significantly over the centuries to meet new economic, technological and social circumstances. The rise of railroads and the Internet disrupted settled understandings of the scope of property rights and the duties of owners, for example. Newly built railroads often threw off sparks that started fires on adjacent farmland, raising questions about whether railroads should be held liable for the resulting harm to landowners. (US courts ruled that this was an inescapable price of economic progress.) Similarly, as the Internet and digital technologies have made it easier to copy and share books, film and records, they have triggered major political battles over the proper scope of copyright laws.

As such stories suggest, the modern tendency to assert absolute individual property rights is a libertarian fantasy. One person's property rights invariably end up affecting another person's property rights; everyone's freedom cannot be limitless.

Indigenous peoples help us see that Western conceptions of property reflect some deep-seated cultural attitudes toward nature and social relationships. We moderns presume that humans can commoditize water, land, genes and other elements of nature as if they are inert objects that can be isolated from their natural context and owned as chattel.

Private property rights are not necessarily hostile to functioning commons. Indeed, I believe the two can be mutually compatible and even work hand in glove. Examples include land trusts ("private property on the outside, commons on the inside"), digital texts and music (copyrighted by the creator but made legally shareable via fair use rights and Creative Commons licenses) and cooperatives (market enterprises owned and managed by co-op members for their own benefit).

The problem is that dominant market-based forms of law usually privilege individual rights and ignore collective rights and needs. Law does not usually recognize the commons as an institutional form, so it can be difficult to achieve a collective purpose while working within the straitjacket of individual property rights. That's why protecting commons from enclosures has generally required legal ingenuity, at least within the context of the modern liberal state: the commons exists within a lexical void, rendering it unnamed and inscrutable.

It's important to see that private property and commons are not simply mirror images of each other. The commons is not simply "non-property," as some have claimed. "Non-property" amounts to the "free-for-all" or "no-man's-land" that Garrett Hardin mistakenly regarded as a commons. No: the commons is not simply another variant of property. Its character is quite different.

First, the commons is less about *ownership* as we usually understand it than about *stewardship*. Ask indigenous peoples if they "own" the land and they will reply that the land owns them.

To talk about ownership brings to mind the "sole and despotic dominion" over a resource that Blackstone described. A commons implies a more personal engagement with a resource and a longer-term perspective. It also implies a richer ongoing set of ethical and cultural relationships than private property normally entails.

A commons is about the shared management of a resource by many—something that may or may not require formal property law to achieve. In the case of the deck chairs, for example, the "legal system" that governed how people could use them was entirely social. People tacitly negotiated and observed a certain set of rules. There was no formal statute or private contract spelling out how a passenger must behave. The system was all based on a social understanding, an instance of *vernacular law*, as described above. A coffeehouse or bar may be privately owned, but its social character and tone are largely defined by the customer/commoners, not the owner.

It is entirely natural for people to organize and enforce their own rules informally, or to follow unwritten etiquette as a matter of custom. Most Americans implicitly understand that if you want to buy movie tickets at the box office or hot dogs from a sidewalk vendor, you queue up in line. That's considered the fair and orderly way to gain access to certain limited resources. "First come, first served"—a rudimentary principle of social protocol for certain everyday circumstances—is particularly effective because it is self-organized and self-enforced.

And what if money and private property rights interfere with the socially negotiated consensus? That's essentially what happens in some high-volume amusement parks. Disneyland actually sells rich people tickets giving them the right to go to the front of the line. People who can't afford VIP tickets have to wait. Is *that* fair? Our intuitive sense of social fairness says No—but it does illustrate what happens when private property rights are asserted as the default entitlement. One reason that private property rights are so highly valued is because they can be bought and sold. Wealthier people naturally tend to favor the broadest, least restrictive private property rights, as these allow them to buy their way to the front of many kinds of lines.

The commons asks us to consider a different paradigm of social and moral order. It asks us to embrace social rules that are compatible with a more cooperative, civic-minded and inclusive set of values, norms and practices. The commons bids us to reject *Homo economicus* as the default ideal of human behavior. It asks us to entertain the idea that certain rights should be *inalienable*—that is, not for sale—and to elevate certain social values over private property rights.

This is the challenge faced by so much of the human rights movement—to recognize human dignity, respect, social reciprocity and social justice as elemental human needs that law must protect. Traditionally, human rights have been seen as an abstract, universal norm selectively enforced by the nation-state (depending upon political circumstances). The commons proposes a more local, "on the ground" reconceptualization of human rights: a way for communities to meet basic needs more directly and, quite possibly, more reliably.

John Locke's Logic of Property Rights

Buried deep within any theories of property are visions of what human beings are. Such theories do not just describe; they subtly *prescribe* what we should be. Centuries after his death, the theories of the seventeenth-century political philosopher John Locke continue to hold sway over our imaginations. His writings provide a powerful moral logic and legal justification for individual property rights—and for market enclosures.

Locke starts with the idea that human beings are isolated individuals with sweeping rights of personal entitlement to resources based upon the labor they invest in developing them. This is Locke's "labor theory of value." It was his attempt to emancipate people from kingly dominion. He wanted to empower a growing class of businessmen to have greater freedom in commercial and civic matters. The idea was to delegitimize the power of monarchs and aristocrats, and justify the power of individuals to exercise absolute dominion over "their" property through the marketplace.

Locke's theory of property merits our attention because it still sets the framework for how we see and justify property rights. If the labor that we expend in discovering or improving a piece of land entitles us to own it, then land that is "undeveloped" belongs to no one and is therefore free for the taking. This was a convenient idea for eighteenth-century European explorers eager to seize the riches of the New World. By the logic of Locke's philosophy, such lands should be considered *terra nullius*, or empty land (sometimes referred to as *res nullius*, or a nullity), because land becomes valuable only as individuals apply their labor and ingenuity to it (by improving it, making it marketable, etc.).

It is Locke's conceit that nature is an inert object that can be privately owned without regard for its connections to its existing inhabitants or larger natural ecosystems. Thus even though indigenous peoples and peasants have managed land, water, fisheries, forests and other natural resources as commons from time immemorial—without formal legal titles—Western imperialists have taken comfort in the legal fiction that *the land doesn't belong to anyone—so we can march right in and take it!* In this way, Locke's theory of private property deliberately ignores the prior use rights and customs of indigenous peoples, the rights of future generations and the inherent needs of nature itself. Using Lockean logic, it has become customary to talk about oceans, outer space, biodiversity and the Internet as if they too are resources that belong to no one. The logic of *res nullius* justifies unchecked private plunder.

Tellingly, Locke added a brief qualification to his theory stating that any private appropriation is limited to "at least where there is *enough, and as good, left in common for others*." He raises an awkward issue that is too obvious to ignore: the exercise of private property rights may encroach on and even destroy resources that belong to everyone. In other words, there is an unresolved tension between private property and the commons.

This "Lockean proviso," as it is often called, is mostly treated as a symbolic, throwaway gesture, however. Philosophers and legal scholars may invoke it to show their intellectual rigor, but in practice politicians and the investor class don't care a whit about honoring it. Transnational bottling companies are still sucking groundwater supplies dry without leaving enough, and as good, in common. Agriculture–biotechnology (ag-biotech) companies are still marketing proprietary genetically modified crops that destroy sustainable seed-sharing. Industrial trawlers are still overexploiting ocean fisheries to the point of exhaustion, dispossessing small coastal fishing communities. Whatever one makes of his proviso, Locke's singular intent was to justify private property, not assure the longevity of the commons.

In this tradition, private property laws today continue to ignore or criminalize commoners who use resources in a collective fashion. Nonmarket subsistence commoning is not seen as "adding value" in a Lockean sense; by this logic no one is entitled to property rights protection. This is how the "freedom" of private property is used to dispossess and violate commoners, as seen in the international land grab of customary lands in Africa.

It is important to understand the Lockean analysis because it has become the central moral justification of modern capitalism and its enclosures. As a number of commons scholars, such as Wolfgang Hoeschele and Roberto Verzola, have noted, capitalism is about the *engineering of scarcity*. To maximize profits and market share, businesses deliberately create scarcity by finding novel ways to limit supplies or access to resources. Copyright and patent law, for example, take resources that are cheap and easy to reproduce—information and knowledge—and deliberately give limited-term monopolies to authors and inventors whose creativity is presumed to be wholly novel and original. The ag–biotech industry likes to create sterile seeds so that farmers have to keep buying them year after year—converting natural bounty into artificial scarcity.

By contrast, commoners deliberately strive to engineer *a system of abundance*. By "abundance," Hoeschele and Verzola do not mean unlimited supplies for unlimited human appetites—the premise of market economics—but rather, plentiful, renewable supplies for what we really need. A prime example is permaculture, which emulates ecosystems by growing self-regenerating crops that help each other flourish and produce little if any waste.

Rousseau famously wrote, "The first man who, having enclosed a piece of ground, bethought himself of saying *This is mine*, and found people simple enough to believe him, was the real founder of civil society.... Beware of listening to this imposter; you are undone if you once forget that the fruits of the earth belong to us all, and the earth itself to nobody." The Lockean proviso shrewdly nods at this undeniable truth, but the Lockean theory of property rights in effect overrides it. The proviso virtually guarantees that in real life, beyond the reach of windy chambers of philosophical debate, there will *not* be enough, and as good, left in common for others.

The Measure of Wealth

Once a resource is legally recognized as property, the door swings open for markets to set its price. This is considered a great advance, because markets consider *price* to be the supreme indicator of value and prices as the fairest way to identify the true value of things. People are said to maximize their individual, rational self-interests through the price system and market exchange; the collective good then naturally manifests itself through the Invisible Hand. Markets are presumed to be more efficient and fair in allocating wealth than governments—so the best strategy for managing natural resources, according to the economic orthodoxy, is to privatize and marketize them.

The truth is that this system of market-based governance is a disaster in the real world. The price system typically fails to take account of all sorts of value that are external to the marketplace. For example, price cannot easily represent types of value that are subtle, qualitative, long-term and complicated—precisely the attributes of nature. What's the market value of the atmosphere? Of a clean river? Of babies born without pollution-induced birth defects? Markets have trouble answering such questions because there is no meaningful market price for such things.

Price only measures *exchange value*, after all; it doesn't really measure *use value*. And so the grand narrative of conventional economics celebrates Gross Domestic Product as the height of human progress by totaling the value of all market activity. It doesn't really care if that activity is beneficial to society or not—in fact, it doesn't even ask that question! Instead it just measures if money has changed hands, which is its moronic definition of wealth creation. By this reckoning, the Gulf of Mexico oil spill and the Fukushima nuclear disaster should be considered good, because they ended up stimulating economic activity.

Ida Kubiszewski, Robert Costanza and a team of other economists vividly demonstrated the shortcomings of GDP in a 2013 study of the net social benefits of economic activity in 17 countries, representing 53 percent of the world's population. Using a new index, the Genuine Progress Indicator or GPI, they explicitly took into account dozens of factors that GDP ignores, such as negative activities like crime, pollution and social problems as well as positive nonmarket activities such as volunteering and household work. Their conclusion? The economists found that the costs of economic growth globally have outweighed the benefits since 1978! This year was also the point at which the global ecological footprint of human activity exceeded global biocapacity. And despite a three-fold global increase in GDP since 1950, life satisfaction in nearly all 17 countries surveyed had not improved significantly since 1975.

John Ruskin called the unmeasured, unintended harms caused by markets "illth." The problem with the price system, as yoked to private property, is that it generates as much illth as wealth—but hardly any of this illth gets counted. It's off the books. A company's bottom line and a nation's GDP reflect only the monetized wealth generated by markets; they deliberately omit the nonmarket illth. This damage is borne mostly by commons as markets *take* what they can from nature, for free, without acknowledging its actual value (because nature is seen as *res nullius*). Once profits have been taken and privatized, the market then *dumps* its wastes and disruptions back onto the commons, leaving commoners and governments to mop up the mess.

As mentioned earlier, this might be called the "tragedy of the market"—the unmetered, hidden subsidies and costly "externalities" that markets, in the service of private property, impose upon the commons. This should not be surprising in a society that looks to price as the highest, most reliable metric of value. If a resource does not have a price or property rights, it naturally will be regarded as "not valuable" or "free for the taking."

No wonder normal market activity frequently rides roughshod over ecological values; nature's wealth does not come with price tags. Prices for fish or timber will generally not reflect the actual value of lower-order organisms and natural systems, for example, even though the invisible, non-marketable dimensions of nature are essential to growing fish and timber. Market externalities are easy to ignore, too, because they tend to be diffused among many people and across large geographic areas. No individual or locality can take effective action against air pollution, say, or against pesticide residues in food. Externalities also tend to lurk on the frontiers of scientific knowledge (Does this vaccine cause autism? Do cell phones cause brain cancer?), which means that identifying and confirming negative externalities can be scientifically difficult. And industries actively resist the scientific verification of harmful externalities, lest unwelcome news triggers angry political responses and costly reparations.

For all these reasons, a system of stewardship, not ownership, is more likely to take conscientious precautions to prevent harms. In a commons, the structural pressures to earn money are reduced and the incentives to take into account subtle, long-term factors are greater. As a social institution, a commons is also more likely to care about the long-term sustainability of a resource than a market, because the very identities and cultures of commoners are wrapped up in the management of the resource. Markets tend to care primarily about financial returns, and see everything else (working conditions, product safety, ecological concerns, etc.) as secondary. The basic problem is that the signals communicated by prices are too crude and impersonal to alter management practices.

Commons as a Form of Governance

The unresolved question is how to devise adequate systems to protect the commons from market encroachments. What steps can commoners take to protect the things they love? This is an urgent issue so long as private property and price are the default definitions of value in public policy, because as we have seen, the price system, however valuable in certain contexts, overrides most ecological, social and moral values.

How can commoners assure protection for human dignity and respect, over and above that enabled by private property rights? How can they secure the right to engage in nonmarket social exchange—gift economies, informal collaborations, new forms of collective action—whose value is barely recognized by the modern liberal polity? How can commoners uphold social justice and human rights as inalienable values that may have to trump corporate property rights?

These very large questions lie at the heart of the challenge facing the contemporary commons movement. I cannot answer them all in this book, but I do want to point to ways that might help our search for answers. Understanding the role of property law is an important part of the equation. But it is important to understand that securing the commons is about far more than property rights and formal legal rules. As we will see in the next chapter, social governance—values, practices, norms, culture—lies at the heart of the commons.

8

The Rise of the
Digital Commons

If conventional institutions of power remain stubbornly resistant to change and tethered to conventional property rights, cyberspace has been a very different story. Since it became widely available in 1994, the World Wide Web has been an exciting arena for innovators, idealists and iconoclasts precisely because there are no legacy institutions to displace. Anyone is free to start something new. No need to ask for permission or pay expensive fees. To be sure, copyright law still applies, but as digital commoners have learned, it is the social practice as much as law itself that tends to call the tune.

And so it has come to pass that the Web, and all other networked digital technologies generally, have become preferred spaces for experimentation. Perhaps the biggest surprise has been the unparalleled capacity of the Internet to foster social cooperation and sharing. While tech and media corporations have struggled to invent new online markets, ordinary Internet users have realized that it is fairly easy to create their own digital commons. Build a website; start a new online community. As if by spontaneous combustion, entirely new species of creative production have arisen on the Internet that are neither market-based nor state-controlled.

The first, most astonishing set of revelations about online commoning came with the emergence of free software, also known as open source software. Open source programs include Perl (a programming language), Sendmail (a mail program), Apache (the most used server program on the Internet, which powers critical "backend" functions) and Linux (a major computer operating system that rivals Windows). The surprising power of distributed networks was quickly followed by the rise of the blogosphere, social networking and Wikipedia, a living, pulsating Web encyclopedia that has become a digital republic unto itself, with more than seventy thousand volunteers working in 285 languages.

There is also the flourishing genre of open-access scholarly publishing, which has enabled academic disciplines and universities to bypass parasitic commercial publishers and reclaim control over their research literature. Working along the same lines, the open educational resources (OER) movement has pioneered the cooperative development of open textbooks, curricula and course materials.

Many of these commons-based innovations have been possible only because of Creative Commons licenses. These are a suite of six basic licenses and other legal instruments that let copyright holders invert copyright law's default rules of strict private control and instead authorize legal sharing. Creators can build commons of shareable content by asserting defensible legal limits on the private appropriation or commercialization of their content. Over time this has produced an unprecedented global sharing economy of software code, research studies, photo archives, blog posts and other creative works.

To be sure, many people share lots of content on social network platforms like Facebook, YouTube and Twitter without the use of Creative Commons licenses. Such sites are governed by corporate "terms of service" that users accept upon registering; they resemble commons in many respects but with a significant difference: corporate management and investors ultimately call the shots. That's why sharing on for-profit websites has been compared to "digital sharecropping" on corporate plantations. A user's body of stored content and links is vulnerable to the whims of shifting corporate policies and investor pressures. A shift in corporate revenue models may mean that you forever lose your blog or photo collection, or are suddenly bombarded with pop-up ads. Corporate platform owners also tend to sell users' mountains of personal information and Web habits to advertisers.

Such are the perils of open platforms governed as corporate fiefdoms and not as user-accountable commons. An open platform may enable collaboration but not necessarily open sharing, user participation or long-term, user-accountable governance. Money-minded corporate executives call the shots.

The Commons Sector, as I like to call it, is far more developed on the Internet than in any other sphere, perhaps for the very reason that it has become such a powerful and independent economic and cultural force there. Prior to the rise of the Web, commons were usually regarded as little more than a curiosity of medieval history or a backwater of social science research. "What we are seeing now," wrote Harvard law professor Yochai Benkler in his landmark 2006 book *The Wealth of Networks*, "is the emergence of more effective collective action practices that are decentralized but do not rely on either the price system or a managerial structure for coordination." Benkler's preferred term is "commons-based peer production," by which he means systems that are collaborative, nonproprietary and based on "sharing resources and outputs among widely distributed, loosely connected individuals who cooperate with each other."

Much of the political and social struggle over the terms of copyright law (as described in Chapter 5) can be traced to the disruptions caused by open Web platforms accessible to anyone. The Internet provides an infrastructure that enables innovation and sharing to occur in ways that are simply impossible or too expensive on conventional mass media. That's why its rise has been so disruptive. The social logic of online cooperation (cheap and easy social interaction among distributed users) can trump the economic logic of conventional markets (which require large amounts of capital, centralized corporate management and professional control). Online commons require little more than a shared software platform, personal computers and Internet access. Unorganized individuals can easily come together to create and curate their own bodies of "user-generated content," challenging the lowest-common-denominator economics and centralized control of mass-media TV shows, films, books and magazines. The result: a profound global cultural revolution whose full disruptive potential is still ahead.

It All Began With Free Software

The first significant type of digital commons was free software. This software is not necessarily free in the sense of "no price," but free in the sense that the code is open and accessible. Anyone can freely examine, tinker with, improve and share the software without violating the creators' copyrights.

In the early 1980s, when software development for personal computers was still a budding community art, the legendary MIT hacker Richard Stallman was one of the first to recognize that proprietary software could significantly limit an individual's freedom to access and reuse software, and thus to innovate. Stallman was disturbed to learn that companies were using copyright law to prohibit others from fixing nasty bugs, improving the code or sharing it with friends and colleagues. Software—once developed through the open, collegial social process of a hacker community*—was becoming a highly lucrative and proprietary product. A shared community resource was being converted into private property.

This enraged Stallman because it meant that a basic human freedom—creativity—was being stifled. He was also concerned that the market ethic and copyright law were stifling the hacker ethic of sharing and mutual support. His solution was an ingenious legal innovation known as the General Public License or GPL, first released in 1989.

The GPL, sometimes referred to as "copyleft" (with a reverse "c" symbol inside of a circle), is widely celebrated today as a landmark "hack" around copyright law. Instead of locking the code up as private property, it ensures everyone the freedom to copy, modify or distribute a software program as they see fit, including to sell it at a price. (Hence the misleading term "free software." Stallman tried to clarify the confusion by famously saying that the software should be "free as in freedom, not free as in free beer." Europeans use the term "libre," which does not have the same double meanings as "free.")

A copyright holder who affixes the GPL to his or her software program is legally committing that code to the commons. The license accomplishes this goal by insisting upon one simple legal requirement—that any derivative work, such as a modified software program, must *also* be licensed under the GPL, so that it too is shareable. Any further derivations of the secondary work, in turn, must also be licensed under the GPL, and so on indefinitely. In this way the GPL cleverly makes software sharing viral and legally protected. To make things even more secure, no user can modify the terms of the license.

* Contrary to press accounts that falsely conflate hackers with criminals, the term has traditionally referred to programmers who are ingenious in solving difficult technical challenges with a playful, community-minded ethic.

The genius of the GPL is that it ensures that a commons of GPLed software code will forever remain a commons. The code created by a given group of commoners will stay within the commons and can never be privatized. Future users can *sell* the code (there are a number of commercial vendors of the open source Linux program, for example), but the point of the GPL is that no one can legally withhold access to the code or prevent its reuse. This made hackers willing to freely contribute their talents to building a software commons because they knew that the fruits of their labors would remain forever accessible.

In the 1980s, Stallman's obsession with "software freedom" seemed like a quixotic mission. Stallman himself—shaggy, sometimes barefoot, imperious—looked like an Old Testament prophet. As the World Wide Web took root in the mid-1990s and Linus Torvalds created the kernel of an amateur computer operating system, the GPL suddenly became historically significant. Torvalds licensed his program, Linux, under the GPL. When combined with other bodies of code, including many that Stallman had written, a commons of code for a complete computer operating system became possible. Linux (GNU Linux, to Stallman) went on to become one of the most powerful and respected software programs in history.

Free software, as licensed under the GPL, soon gave birth to a legally similar body of code known as open source software. The chief difference between "free" and open source software is that the backers of the latter try to steer clear of the word "free," which not only is confusing (does it mean "no price" or "free to use"?) but connotes low quality. Open source advocates wanted to make community-made software more attractive and credible to large corporate and institutional users. They were less concerned with the political dimensions of Stallman's free software movement than they were eager to highlight the practical utility of shareable software.

Open source software has gone on to become a powerhouse of the tech economy despite (or thanks to?) its no-cost access and use. Large companies like IBM, Oracle and Hewlett-Packard have built lucrative businesses by providing technical support to and customized extensions of open source programs. Linux is now used on millions of Web servers, and world-class computer users and corporations around the world (NASA, Pixar, IBM) rely on it for mission-critical tasks.

In the late 1990s, the GPL's importance was not lost on Harvard law professor Lawrence Lessig, who was keenly aware that copyright law was also stifling creativity. Lessig convened a small team of law professors, computer scientists, artists, authors and activists to invent a series of six standardized public licenses that could be placed as "tags" on copyrighted content. A copyright holder could use one of these "CC" (Creative Commons) licenses to indicate that her work is available for sharing and reuse under specified terms.

For example, a website's content could be tagged as freely shareable but not entitled to commercial usage without permission (the "NonCommercial" license); or it could be tagged freely shareable but with a prohibition against derivative works such as photo-cropping or text translations unless permissions were obtained (the "No Derivatives" license). One CC license, the "ShareAlike license," emulates the GPL by requiring that any derivative work also be shareable under the same license. This means that the work and all of its "progeny" will forever be accessible. This book is licensed under a Creative Commons BY-NC-SA license (Attribution-NonCommercial-ShareAlike) because I want to authorize copying of it so long as credit is given to me as the author (BY) and no commercial reuses are made without my permission (NC). Any derivative uses of this book, including translations, new printings and excerpts, must also be legally shareable (SA).

All works carrying a CC license have to credit the original author (the "Attribution License"), but beyond that, copyright holders themselves may specify how their work may or may not be used by others (without abridging "fair use" rights under copyright law, which guarantee certain types of sharing for non-commercial purposes).

Both the GPL and the CC licenses have been hugely significant in enabling all sorts of digital commons to take root and flourish. They constitute a kind of legal infrastructure that protects the commons from enclosure because works are made permanently shareable. The licenses have also inspired a range of other legal innovations for making other bodies of content legally shareable, such as databases and physical specimens used in laboratories.

In certain fields, especially education, academic research and government services, the CC licenses have helped advance the presumption that works from public institutions should be freely available. All sorts of museums, archives, government agencies and educational institutions around the world now use CC licenses to make sure that their Web documents and digital files are freely accessible to anyone.

The Open Access Revolution

At one time, commercial publishers offered the best way for scientists to move from a system of private correspondence about their discoveries to a system of widely distributed, peer-reviewed journals. But with the arrival of the World Wide Web in 1994, it became far cheaper and easier to reach a global readership instantly. Thus began a long struggle—still underway—to shift scholarly publishing toward a more accessible genre of publishing: the open-access (or OA) journal.

While commercial journal publishers have provided certain valuable services like production and distribution, they have also become parasites on academic knowledge commons by insisting on owning the copyrights to research articles. This has enabled publishers to gain control over knowledge that was, in fact, funded by a long chain of others, including governments, foundations and universities. These very same commercial journals have often used their copyright control—and the prestige associated with certain journal titles—to charge university libraries exorbitant subscription fees. Between 1986 and 2004, journal publishers raised subscription rates to American universities by 273 percent.

It took universities years to heed calls for reform and mount a concerted counterattack. In 2012, Harvard University finally declared that it had had enough. It publicly advised its faculty to avoid publishing in journals that required paid access. The move helped persuade many research libraries and colleges across the US and the world that it was time to begin a more aggressive transition to OA publishing models. Harvard's motivation was largely financial; its annual budget for journals was approaching $3.75 million. It was paying some journal publishers as much as forty thousand dollars per year. The average US university library was spending about 65 percent of its budget on research journals, with more than half of that sum going to three major publishers: Elsevier, Springer and Wiley.

The OA scholarly publishing movement first began to organize itself in 2001 with the goal of making academic research free and openly available to anyone in perpetuity. In retrospect, this seems like an unassailable initiative, considering that taxpayers were funding billions of dollars in research. No matter: the OA movement has had to struggle for years to overcome opposition from publishers and uninformed politicians as well as the sheer inertia of academic communities. It has had to develop new revenue models and administrative structures for scholarly journals, and disrupt some long-standing traditions within academic publishing. For example, because many tenure and promotion decisions are based on the quality and prestige of the academic journals in which faculty publish their work, junior faculty members are often reluctant to publish in lesser-known OA journals rather than in high-profile periodicals like *Nature* and *Science*. The OA movement has been impeded, too, by fierce resistance from the large academic publishers, which have balked at efforts by national governments to require that all taxpayer-funded research be published under OA protocols.

Notwithstanding such resistance and misleading excuses, by late 2013 there were nearly ten thousand open-access scholarly journals being published. Like the GPL and CC licenses, OA journals are making knowledge more freely available to everyone without the contrived scarcity that publishers like to impose through copyright restrictions and "digital rights management."

I called my book about the rise of free software and free culture *Viral Spiral* because the evolution of one commons-based innovation typically inspires many others, and then others. The GPL led to the CC licenses, which then gave rise to OA publishing. From there, in 2009 and after, a wide array of open educational resources, or OER, emerged as the next turn of the viral spiral. All levels of education and learning communities—not just scholarly publishing—got wise to the fact that proprietary control of knowledge is antithetical to their core values: to learn and grow through participation and sharing. Academia is a commons.

Community colleges were dismayed to learn that many students were dropping out or delaying their educations because they could not afford their textbooks. It is not unusual for textbook publishers to bring out new editions every two or three years simply to make the existing used books "obsolete" and promote new textbook purchases. Some farsighted OA educators have responded by forming the Community College Consortium for Open Educational Resources, which helps identify and publicize open textbooks. Such books are CC-licensed and available for the cost of a print-on-demand copy. This has reduced students' expenses by hundreds of dollars apiece.

The Massachusetts Institute of Technology (MIT) pioneered open educational resources in 2001 when it produced the first major body of curricular materials—syllabi, readings, videos, datasets—for free online use. MIT's innovation has profoundly influenced the teaching of physics and other scientific fields in China as well as many small countries with isolated rural populations. It has also spawned the OpenCourseWare Consortium, which now has more than 120 member universities and educational institutions worldwide.

The viral spiral that started with free software and the CC licenses continues to expand. The very term "open source" has become a widely used cultural meme to celebrate production that is open, participatory, transparent and accountable. Open source principles now animate a robust "open design" movement that invites anyone to help design clothing, furniture, computer components, even automobiles. A group called Arduino now designs and produces scores of printed-circuit boards and computer components, which enable cheap and easy customization by techies. An Open Prosthetics Project invites anyone to contribute to the design of prosthetic limbs—or to the specifications for limbs that ought to be designed even if the designer doesn't know how to do it herself. Among the designs: prosthetic limbs for rock climbers and a prosthetic arm for fishing.

One of the more fascinating open-network projects is Wikispeed, a Seattle-based automotive prototyping and manufacturing start-up project that has collaborators in fifteen countries. Its goal is to use open source principles to design and build a modular, lightweight race car that can travel a hundred miles on a gallon of gasoline.

Community networks like Open Source Ecology are now building shareable, low-cost equipment for off-the-grid "resilient communities." One of its prime projects is the LifeTrac, a low-cost, multipurpose open source tractor whose components are modular, inexpensive and easy to build and maintain. In other words, *not* complex, expensive or proprietary. Open source design and manufacturing of physical things has reached a large enough scale that the community of innovators have formed their own association, the Open Hardware and Design Alliance.

Digital commons now pop up in the most unlikely places. A self-organized group called Crisis Commons is a network of tech volunteers who provide humanitarian aid in response to natural disasters. Following the Haiti earthquake of 2009, thousands of volunteers associated with Crisis Commons swiftly built Web-based translation tools, people finders and maps showing routes to empty hospital beds.

There is also a range of what I call "eco-digital commons," in which Internet technologies are being used to help monitor and manage the environment. Some websites now invite individuals to use mobile phones, motion sensors, GPS tracking and other electronic systems to monitor local sightings of birds, butterflies and invasive species, or to monitor pollution levels in a local body of water. These "participatory sensing" projects aggregate highly dispersed bodies of data and, in so doing, improve the quality of government policymaking and enforcement.

The City of Linz, Austria, population 190,000, has embarked upon one of the most ambitious digital commons plans for an urban region. It plans to turn the greater Linz region into an open information commons. The City already provides free wifi hotspots and email accounts to every citizen and Web hosting for non-commercial content. Now it is trying to get the entire region to embrace open source software, Creative Commons licenses, open data platforms, open street maps and open educational resources. City officials believe that a regional information commons will stimulate innovators to produce locally useful information tools while encouraging greater civic engagement and more robust economic development.

The future is likely to see a continued proliferation of digital commons, if only because of their efficiencies, usefulness and social appeal. The commercial world understands this and is positioning itself to exploit digital commons, or at least to host open platforms. A telling bellwether of this shift can be seen in the business world's burgeoning interest in the "sharing economy" fuelled by new Web-assisted business models for car-sharing, overnight apartment rentals and other forms of "collaborative consumption." (Whether these businesses will actually function as commons is another matter entirely.)

Tech companies realize that open networks naturally foster cooperation and sharing—yet their conventional business models are based on "monetizing" communities, not necessarily on serving their long-term or nonmarket interests. Thus, while Facebook and Google provide many useful services "for free," they are also aggressively data-mining people's personal information and selling highly personalized ads to markets that want to invade our minds as we browse the Web. Through its book digitization project, Google is also establishing itself as a privileged, proprietary gatekeeper for access to public-domain materials, to the detriment of competitors and the public. As such examples show, corporations only support "sharing" if they can make money from it. That's not commoning.

Still, the people who participate in online sharing communities are part of an important cultural vanguard. They are bringing their social practices and expectations—and their distaste for excessive private property rights—to other areas of their lives. It is one reason why the Swedish-based Pirate Party has spawned dozens of other national Pirate Parties that are fielding candidates for political office. And why a major international copyright treaty, the Anti-Counterfeiting Trade Agreement, was defeated in 2012 by a coalition of free culture advocates, free software hackers and open-platform businesses.

Now that so many people have tasted the freedom, innovation and accountability of open networks and digital commons, there is no going back to the command-and-control business models of the twentieth century. Among the "born digital" generation, many conventional ideas about private property rights—the exclusivity of control, commercial motives and indifference to the common good over the long term—seem decidedly old-fashioned, if not antisocial. It is too soon to know what sweeping legal or political changes the ethic of commoning might translate into, but if one is to judge from the Internet-assisted movements of the past several years—the Arab Spring; the Spanish *indignados*; the Occupy movement; the landmark 2012 defeat of ACTA, the secretly crafted anti-piracy treaty—it is clearly infectious. In the next chapter, I want to show how varied and robust the commons paradigm truly is, transcending even these developments in cyberspace.

9

Many Galaxies of Commons

W HILE DIGITAL COMMONS are fresh and contemporary, at least to us in the West, a broader perspective is in order. Indigenous peoples were there first. They refined the art of commoning long before hackers began to share software code and social scientists developed complicated theories about the commons. And let's not forget the long history of medieval English and European commons; of subsistence commons in rural settings around the world; and of urban spaces and community projects managed as commons. Human societies have produced a glorious cavalcade of commons throughout the ages.

In this chapter, I'd like to explore some salient classes of commons more deeply. The point is to help us develop a richer mental map of commons "in the field," and not just as an abstraction.

First, a methodological warning: some people seem to think there is a natural, logical classification scheme for commons. I seriously doubt this—or at least, I believe that any classification system will necessarily reflect the analyst's cultural biases. An African would have a very different mental map of the commons than a European, and both would have different perspectives than an American. Classification schemes tend to impose an overly tidy, regularized and intellectual understanding of commoning, which I believe is ultimately *experiential* and *historically situated*.

Rather than strive to over-theorize, therefore, I think it's better to simply recognize general clusters of commons that represent certain general characteristics. A commons may arise whenever a group of people decides that it wishes to manage a resource in a collective manner, with a special regard for equitable access, use and long-term stewardship. Still, it helps to have a crude mental map to orient us to the galaxies of commons that do exist. So let's begin with a quick survey of subsistence and indigenous peoples' commons, social and civic commons, state trustee commons and businesses embedded in commons. (We already surveyed prominent digital commons in Chapter 8.)

Subsistence Commons

Traditional commons—the familiar commons of history and the ones most studied by contemporary academics—usually revolve around natural resources: water, forests, fisheries, arable land, wild game. These resources are gifts of the Earth that must be actively managed for the survival and well-being of all.

The recurring question is *How* should access and use of shared resources be managed? How can free riding and abuse of a commons be prevented? What governance systems work best? Specific communities and bioregions have explored such questions through trial and error and active stewardship over long periods of time. That, after all, is the point—to develop a socio-ecological system that blends social customs and practices with the natural dynamics of a river, forest or farmland. It is not surprising that certain general patterns of commoning have emerged.

In New Mexico, native Hispanic-Americans have managed community-based waterways known as *acequias* since the 1600s. This "biocultural" institution has shown how, even in a very dry region such as the American Southwest, a commons can align community usage of water with ecological limits. Remarkably, *acequias* have the sanction of New Mexico state law. But it is the community itself that manages and protects the water supply. All *acequia* members are expected to participate in maintenance responsibilities such as the annual cleaning of the water ditches. While nearby towns in New Mexico are plagued by unchecked suburban development and voracious demands for water, the *acequias* have succeeded in allocating their water allotments to meet people's needs fairly while conserving soil and water, recharging aquifers and preserving wildlife and plant habitat.

Subsistence commons strike the modern mind as backward and premodern. But in many respects, that is the very point—to reach back to pre-market social norms that once placed vital limits on market activity. To commoners, maximizing market value is not the supreme purpose; community needs and ecological stability take precedence. Subsistence commoners take only what they need while protecting the resource. This is a singular achievement in modern times: to develop an ethic of sufficiency.

Most economists have little interest in subsistence commons, perhaps because they see them as small, isolated and disconnected from markets. How boring! And because the value of subsistence commons cannot be expressed in numbers, they don't show up in GDP statistics. The conventional economic framework has no way of comprehending the importance of community self-determination, ecological resilience, social equity or cultural connection to a place. Yet subsistence commons, operating outside of market system without private property rights or money, are vitally important to an estimated two billion people worldwide, according to the International Association for the Study of the Commons.

It's worth emphasizing that subsistence commons vary a great deal and are not without their problems. Many need better management; others are poorly managed and could be improved; still others struggle in unsupportive political environments. Yet they remain an important means of everyday sustenance and dignity that strive to respect ecological limits. That's an impressive accomplishment that markets and states have trouble emulating.

Indigenous Peoples' Commons

A decade ago, Peruvians created the Potato Park as a "landscape conservation commons" so that indigenous tribes of the Andes could have full stewardship rights over a tremendous diversity of native potato species and varieties. This was a major achievement because transnational ag-biotech firms were eager to acquire patents on some of the nine hundred genetically valuable potato varieties that Andean tribes had developed over thousands of years.

Officially known as an Indigenous Biocultural Heritage Area, the Potato Park authorizes seven thousand villagers from six indigenous communities (Amaru, Chawaytire, Cuyo Grande, Pampallaqta, Paru-Paru and Sacaca) to jointly manage their communal land for their collective benefit. The point is to let these peoples legally protect their livelihoods and ways of life from "development" (especially international patents and trade) while conserving the agro-ecological landscape. On the one hand, the Potato Park is quite unusual because its alignment of community values and practices with the regional ecosystem has been formally and legally recognized. On the other hand, such commons-based stewardship is typical of indigenous peoples' commons.

Indigenous peoples' commons vary a great deal, of course. The Aboriginal Australians have long fought to protect their sacred places, cultural knowledge and striking artistic designs from outside appropriation, especially by commercial interests. India and Southeast Asia are home to many "traditional knowledge commons" (or "TK commons") that protect and use highly specialized types of knowledge about local plants and medicinal treatments. Some transnational companies are attempting to appropriate this knowledge in order to patent it for genetically engineered crops or drugs—a type of enclosure often known as "biopiracy." In India, there have been several notorious cases in which transnational companies tried to patent neem seeds and turmeric. Madagascar's rich biodiversity has also been a prime target of companies in search of patentable genetic knowledge. Such commercialization poses a serious threat to TK commons because people may be reluctant to contribute to a commons if they fear that their knowledge could be taken private and sold for money. "One man's gift must not be another man's capital," as the anthropologist Marcel Mauss warned.

Corporate enclosures of TK commons have prompted some innovative responses. Commoners in India have compiled a Traditional Knowledge Digital Library, a database of public-domain medical knowledge, to help challenge patent applications that would privatize the knowledge. A South African lawyers' group called Natural Justice has developed a legal instrument known as "biocultural community protocols" (BCP) that is a novel attempt to protect cultural traditions and practices from appropriation by outsiders. BCPs set forth the specific values and customary procedures that a community has chosen to manage its natural resources. The protocols also spell out the procedural and substantive rights of commoners to participate in decision-making, and to demand free, prior and informed consent to specific public policies that might be imposed on them. The BCPs also ensure that people can monitor and evaluate the impact of projects in their community.

It is difficult to overgeneralize about indigenous peoples' commons because they embody so many different types of landscapes, tribal cosmologies and cultural practices. Still, legal scholar Rebecca Tsosie has noted striking similarities among indigenous systems of knowing and interacting with the natural world. Indigenous peoples' commons tend to reflect "a perception of the earth as an animate being; a belief that humans are in a kinship system with other living things; a perception of the land as essential to the identity of the people; and a concept of reciprocity and balance that extends to relationships among humans, including future generations, and between humans and the natural world."

Indigenous peoples have developed remarkably stable socioecological models precisely because they focus on long-term social *relationships*, not irregular market *transactions*. Westerners often dismiss indigenous peoples' commons out of hand because they are not based on strict individualism, private property rights and market notions of "value" (i.e., a price for everything). As N. Bruce Duthu, a leading scholar of Native American law, has written, "The idea of 'property' in the Western tradition... implies an orientation toward the Market use of resources without special regard for the long-term ecological consequences or the social meanings of nature to people; the price system presumes a basic equivalence among like-priced elements of nature. Societies that have a more direct, subsistence relationship to nature may therefore find property- and market-based sensibilities alien and even offensive."

Not surprisingly, the industrialized nations of the world scoff at Bolivia's proposal that the United Nations recognize "nature's rights," an idea that lies at the heart of so many indigenous peoples' commons. Honoring "Mother Earth"—as the

Pachamama movement in Latin America advocates—is seen by the industrialized world as ridiculous, impractical nonsense, but this prejudice simply illustrates the West's alarming cultural myopia. It cannot even imagine the commons.

Social and Civic Commons

Human beings' natural propensity to cooperate is a powerful source of innovation that has given rise to a rich variety of social and civic commons. A great example is the international "time banking" movement. Time banking (sometimes known in the US as "time dollars") is a system that lets people earn "time credits" for providing services to others in their communities. Examples of services include mowing lawns, babysitting, providing household help or driving someone to a medical appointment. People can then spend their time credits for other services provided by members of the community. Often administered by churches and non-profits, time banking has proven to be a boon to many elderly and poor people who have more time than money. They can turn their time into a "currency" (time credits) that lets them meet basic needs that cannot be met through markets. Interestingly, many participants regard time banking more as a system for making social connections than as a surrogate market.

Blood and organ donation systems are another exemplary social commons. While body parts and plasma are sometimes treated as commodities, voluntary systems persist because we like to regard donations of intimate bodily substances (tissue, organs, blood, body parts) as a social gift. Blood banks have often been likened to a "gift economy" in which people give with no expectation of direct personal benefit, but out of a sense of social duty or as a tribute to loved ones. Some famous studies show that gift economies for blood and organs are more likely to avoid the ethical conflicts that can plague markets and, moreover, elicit higher-quality blood and organs. The people most likely to sell their blood or organs are alcoholics, drug users and those in poor health.

As discussed in Chapter 5, academic disciplines are a significant, highly productive social commons. Researchers do not generally use cash or legal contracts to exchange knowledge; their universities and disciplines amount to hosting infrastructures for gift economies. Scholarship and instruction are considered "contributions" to the field, not "products." A discipline advances through a community ethic of sharing, open debate and peer review, not cash purchases among individuals.

Because it nurtures inner commitments and peer support, a social commons helps avoid the ethical problems that tend to be associated with markets. Markets usually do not nourish elevated ethics because they typically focus on transactions, not long-standing relationships. The focus is on the "cash nexus," and relationships tend to be impersonal, fixed-term (or one-time) in nature and based on a strict "even-steven" exchange of value. The boundaries separating individuals and their interests are kept quite clear.

In gift economies, however, as Lewis Hyde noted in his classic book *The Gift*, social boundaries are blurred or even eradicated through gift exchange. There is no self-serving calculation of whether the value given and received is strictly equal; the point is to establish ongoing social relationships and sympathies. The subtitle of Hyde's book—*Imagination and the Erotic Life of Property*—captures this idea nicely: gifts bring people closer together, especially when the exchange is indirect and staggered over time. So long as gifts continue to circulate among people, without a clear reckoning of what one is "owed," the social commons thrives.

Social commons are proliferating, especially on the Internet, because they often radically lower the transaction costs that markets require, such as the costs of advertising, legal contracts, paid employees and so forth. It is often cheaper, easier and more reliable to coordinate an activity through a trusted community. This is surely one reason that "collaborative consumption" is growing as a new hybrid sector of the market economy; artfully designed Web systems let people coordinate the (cash-based) "sharing" of cars, commuting rides, bikes and tools.

One of the more remarkable Internet-based gift economies is CouchSurfing, a free, informal system of overnight hospitality used by travelers (and the people who host them) in more than ninety-seven thousand cities and towns around the world. Cash exchange between host and visitor is explicitly prohibited. CouchSurfing is a vast Wed-mediated gift economy that helps more than five million strangers a year give and receive hospitality in each other's homes, often forging new friendships in the process.

Social commons are seemingly as spontaneous and diverse as life itself. They include community gardens and town festivals, civic associations and amateur sports leagues, ecovillages and co-housing and community-supported agriculture.

Cities are an especially fertile environment for social commons because of the great diversity and density of people there. San Francisco has been something of a leader. After a local organization, *Shareable* magazine, issued a policy paper, "Policies for a Shareable City," Mayor Ed Lee appointed a Sharing Economy Working Group to explore ways to encourage a "shareable city." Among the ideas: resource-sharing among citizens (e.g., ride sharing), coproduction assisted by the city government (urban agriculture) and mutual aid among citizens (eldercare). In Naples, Italy, Mayor Luigi de Magistris has appointed an Assessor of the Commons to take account of local commons systems and has rallied municipal officials throughout Italy to improve city government support for local commons.

In Rome, Italy, the former employees of a grand public theater and former opera house, Teatro Valle, took over the premises in 2011 after the city government had failed to support it, and managed it as a self-organized commons. The protest was part of a larger complaint about the government's failure to maintain civic and recreational spaces even as it privatizes cherished public properties, leading to higher rents and evictions. The occupation of Teatro Valle, still underway, has inspired other citizen groups to mount direct action protests that have reclaimed other buildings and spaces. Instead of simply fighting privatization, aggrieved Romans have come to realize that they need active, ongoing self-governance *beyond* representative government.

There are other more ambitious initiatives to try to promote social commons in urban areas. Urban designers Nikos A. Salingaros, Federico Mena-Quintero and others are seeking to apply the principles of peer-to-peer production to urban environments. "P2P Urbanism," as it is called, seeks to make city design and daily life more hospitable to ordinary people. Instead of the dehumanizing monumentalism that "starchitects" have inflicted on many cities, P2P Urbanism proposes collaborative design and user participation in urban planning, drawing upon the wisdom of pattern theory guru and architect Christopher Alexander. The initiative also seeks to make urban design more adaptable to local conditions and individual needs in the style of open source software and peer production.

Businesses Embedded in Commons

As a matter of principle, some commoners regard the ethic of the money economy to be fundamentally hostile to the ideals of commoning. Other commoners are more open to pragmatic relationships with markets so long as these do not undermine the commons. So can market activity and commons coexist happily? The question is a controversial one among some commoners.

My own view is that few commons can operate in total isolation from the rest of society. Virtually all commons are hybrids that depend in some measure upon the State or the Market. The important point, therefore, is to assure that commons can have as much autonomy and integrity of purpose as possible. If commons are to interact with markets, they must be able to resist enclosure, consumerism, the lust for capital accumulation and other familiar pathologies of capitalism.

Finding a sustainable rapprochement between commons and markets is a complicated challenge. It helps to understand that markets are not necessarily the same thing as capitalism. Markets can be entirely local, fair and responsive to community needs if they are sufficiently embedded in communities and accountable to them. However, in contemporary life, commerce is so often integrated with vast national or global markets and driven by the "divine right of capital," as Marjorie Kelly puts it. Capital-driven markets tend to produce enormous structural disparities of power that disenfranchise consumers, workers and communities. They plunder nature with little concern for the long-term consequences.

The good news is that it is becoming easier for many communities to assert greater control over the structure and behavior of markets. For example, community-supported agriculture (CSAs) and local farmers' markets have a deep stake in their communities. These social relationships and the local accountability of markets mean that a community can meet many needs while avoiding the rapacious ethic of global capitalism. Markets need not be predatory and socially corrosive; they can become socially integrated into a community and made locally responsive. Other examples include cooperatives, the Slow Food movement and mutual businesses (owned by their member-consumers), all of which try, in different ways, to incorporate larger social values with market activity.

One of the most successful commons-based business enterprises I have encountered is Cecosesola, the Central Cooperative for Social Services of Lara, in Venezuela. For more than forty years, this self-organized, self-financed project has run over eighty cooperatives—banks, farms, factories—as well as civic associations and organizations. Cecosesola deliberately avoids hierarchical relationships and bosses by moving tasks and production among its 1,200 associate workers. Deliberations take place in assemblies that strive for consensus—a process that requires a great deal of mutual education, communication and dialogue. Prices at Cecosesola's five local food markets are not based on demand but on "fairness." All vegetables are sold at the same price per kilo, for example. Cultivating trust, commitment to the common good and the courage to take risks—all within a flexible, evolving organizational structure—lie at the heart of Cecosesola's improbable success.

The trick in melding commons and markets, to my mind, consists in nourishing a distinct culture of commoning while devising "defensible boundaries" around the commons so that it can maintain its basic autonomy. In medieval times, commoners would often "beat the bounds"—walk the perimeter of their forest or piece of communal land—as part of an annual community celebration that doubled as an occasion to patrol the boundaries of their commons. If they came upon a private fence or hedge that had enclosed the commons, the commoners would knock it down, re-establishing the integrity of their land. Community enforcement of the "perimeters" of commons is essential.

Our task today is to devise modern-day equivalents of beating the bounds. Two successful examples in cyberspace are the General Public License for software and the Creative Commons licenses. Both ensure that commoners can retain control over the fruits of their shared labors by prohibiting private appropriations of code and digital content, respectively. The biocultural protocols developed by the South African advocacy group Natural Justice have a similar purpose—to prevent transnational corporations from appropriating the specialized ethnobotanical knowledge and agro-ecological practices of indigenous peoples.

Commoners today "beat the bounds" when they devise formal rules and ethical norms as ways to preserve their commons. The elaborate governance rules of Wikipedia editing, the customs that Maine lobster fishers have negotiated among themselves, the rules for New Mexican *acequias*—all have the goal of preserving the resource and the community while excluding outsiders who have not invested their energies in cultivating the commons or who may act as vandals or free riders.

Equipped with self-devised rules and governance systems, commoners achieve something else as well: they can pressure markets to be more responsive to the consumers who must rely upon them. One might call these "commons-based markets"— coherent communities with enough power to influence and tame markets. Such markets are more prevalent on the Internet, where social communities (or loose networks) can self-organize as passionate affinity groups before turning to markets to meet certain needs.

In his book *Democratizing Innovation*, MIT professor Eric von Hippel describes numerous communities of "extreme sports" enthusiasts—bicyclists, surfers, rock climbers and so forth—who are the source of pioneering ideas that business enterprises then develop and commercialize. Of course, many commoners question why any profit-driven business is needed to play this role when, in principle, commoners could produce what they need themselves, directly, cheaply and perhaps more responsively. It's a fair point, but for now, the practical ability of commoners to implement the necessary, often complicated business functions (raising capital, managing complex supply chains) in the context of a commons remains limited. But this could change in the near future.

There is great debate among commons advocates about how to adequately protect the commons from capitalist exploitation. How can the commons be structured so that its logic is decoupled from that of capitalist markets—and yet still be able to interact with markets as needed? For my colleague Silke Helfrich, the key is to ensure that a commons has the capacity to protect and reproduce itself. The commons must have within its very structure the capacity to assure its own longevity and self-protection. It must be able to protect its resources and community norms.

This could be achieved through legal rules that prevent outsider appropriation or interventions. It could be achieved through social practices and norms that constitute commons governance. It could be achieved through geographic isolation from markets or through technological barriers (fences around a resource; digital "gates" for authorized commoners). Without such protections, commons are vulnerable to capitalist appropriations, a problem that can be seen in the Google Books Library Project, Facebook and other open platforms. In such situations, commoning becomes another type of "market input" that can be alienated from commoners and privatized. It is therefore important that commons develop the means to protect the fruits of their labor and reproduce themselves and other commons.

What we need, says Helfrich, is "a shift from commons-based peer production to *commons-creating* peer production." Ultimately, she insists, "the commons is not about organizational form or property rights. It's about the *purpose*. If commoning ends with a sale on the market, then what happens to all the other people who have a stake in the process of commons-based production?" "Open" systems give no guarantee that the long-term social or ecological interests of contributors will be respected or protected.

State Trustee Commons and Global Commons

Many of our shared resources are so large that they require government to take care of them properly. These common-pool resources, or CPRs, include large-scale entities such as national parks, federally funded research, public lands, the airwaves and the atmosphere. (Remember: CPRs = the resources, without commoners. Commons = resources + community + the rules and norms for managing them.) It is impossible to manage large CRPs in the same way as a small village commons. A larger set of institutional systems and legal rules—a "commons infrastructure"—is needed.

The *state trustee commons* is one way to manage a large common-pool resource. This is not just another word for state management of resources; it is a way of emphasizing the state's important role in facilitating commoning. Instead of conceiving government as "just taking care of things," we need to think about how state bureaucracies can host a wider, more robust citizen role in policymaking and enforcement.

It helps to get the state's role right in the first place: the state must act as a *trustee* for commoners. It must conscientiously maintain and protect shared assets from enclosure. It must ensure that those assets are accessible to everyone on fair, non-discriminatory terms, and that commoners have the authority and space to engage in genuine commoning. I like to call government-run programs *state trustee commons* to emphasize that the resources belong to the people, not the state. As a trustee, the state has affirmative obligations to assure maximum possible transparency, participation and stewardship at the lowest level of governance possible ("subsidiarity").

A state trustee commons can take many forms. It can oversee the rentals of government-managed assets. It can sanction independent commons trusts to act with their own delegated authority. It can use online tools such as social networking to elicit useful citizen participation in government proceedings. Here are some examples.

In the US, the federal government leases grazing rights on public lands to cattle ranchers (at rock-bottom rates). It sells the right to mine gold, silver and other metal ore on public lands for $5 per acre and no standing royalties. The government also auctions off parts of the electro-magnetic spectrum for use in telecommunications (recouping some measure of their value). The issue for a state trustee commons is how to ensure that it acts as a conscientious steward of the land and a fiscally responsible agent of leases. This idea needs to be "baked into" the legal structure, operations and accountability mechanisms of government bodies that manage public resources for the public benefit.

One ingenious model is the stakeholder trust. A classic example is the Alaska Permanent Fund, an independent trust fund established by the state legislature to collect a portion of royalties for oil extracted from state lands. The trust then disperses a dividend, usually on the order of a thousand dollars to every household in the state each year. Because the fund is independent of the government and charged to act as a fiduciary trust on behalf of specific beneficiaries (the citizens of Alaska), it helps assure that a modest portion of oil revenues directly benefit taxpayers, providing them with a welcome source of non-wage income. As described in a recent book (*Exporting the Alaska Model* by Karl Widerquist and Michael W. Howard), this model could be adapted to manage many other types of natural resources, in the US and around the world. Commons activists in Vermont have in fact proposed a common assets trust fund that would act as a fiduciary and steward of the state's wildlife and fish, forests, groundwater, minerals and other natural resources. Thanks to innovations in social networking, it is now possible to imagine the state providing a greater role to citizens through online platforms. They can do more than "participate" in a preordained (rigged?) government agenda; they can initiate new ideas of their own devising and assume real responsibilities that matter.

Earlier I mentioned a number of "eco-digital commons" that are inviting citizens to help collect environmental data or assist NASA in classifying craters on Mars. Another example is the U.S. Patent and Trademark Office's Peer to Patent project, which invites people to submit instances of "prior art" for inventions. This is a way to improve the quality of patents by helping to identify prior innovations that might call into question a patent application claiming ownership of a novel invention. The wiki-style crowdsourcing helps prevent the government from giving out unwarranted patent monopolies that could inhibit future innovation. Given the proper support, citizen-commoners with expertise and interests in given fields could evolve into active constituencies that act as agency watchdogs. They could come up with their own innovations and pressure government agencies to fulfill their missions better.

A new frontier for state trustee commons is devising institutional forms and legal principles that can improve the governance of CPRs that are regional or global in scope. It is clear that the existing nation-state and international treaty organizations are not going to set enforceable limits on global carbon emissions, for example, or prevent the destruction of fisheries, coral reefs and biodiversity loss, all problems that span political jurisdictions. These issues have been festering for decades; the Market/State just can't bring itself to set meaningful limits on the commercial activity that's exacerbating them.

In our book, *Green Governance: Ecological Survival, Human Rights and the Law of the Commons*, my colleague Burns H. Weston and I tried to imagine new sorts of minimalist, flexible policy structures that could encourage the work of commons at all levels—local, regional, national, transnational and global.

This takes us beyond the state trustee commons to entirely novel modes of state support for commons. The goal is to unleash the great self-reinforcing energies of commons as a valuable form of governance without stifling them through top-down microman-agement or political interference. The design challenge is to find a way to govern CPRs at the lowest levels feasible—a principle often known as "subsidiarity"—and with multiple centers of authority. Levels of commons would be diversified and "nested within" higher levels of governance—the concept of "polycen-tricity," an idea that Elinor Ostrom explored in her work.

While skeptics may scoff at such ideas as too speculative and far-fetched for dealing with global environmental problems, it is surely more utopian to think that centralized state institu-tions of limited competence and declining social trust will be able to *force* people to adopt changes that the Market/State it-self does not really wish to implement in the first place. By con-trast, commons have shown their capacity to energize people to take direct responsibility; set limits on market activity; model a new vision of human development; and nurture an ethic of suf-ficiency. However the new global commons are structured (and this is a longer discussion than we can deal with here), the new state-mediated systems will have to open up new spaces that let commons-based governance flourish. That, at least, is the vision that Burns Weston and I propose.

Such global commons are indeed a departure from the clas-sical notion of a commons. I see them as a logical extension. They are surely related in spirit to classical commons, yet they set forth a new "policy imaginary" for preserving our shared eco-logical gifts. The first step down this path is for the state to rec-ognize the commons as a quasi-independent sector in its own right. Commons have provisioning capacities and a social legiti-macy that state bureaucracies will never have.

These ideas clearly require a bold reconceptualization of the neoliberal Market/State. My colleague Michel Bauwens has proposed that we reimagine the State and the Market as a "triarchy" that shares governance authority with the commons—the *Market/State/Commons*. The goal is to realign authority and provisioning into new, more socially beneficial configurations. The State must shift its focus to become a "Partner State," as Michel Bauwens puts it, and become more than a colluding partner of the Market sector.

As a member of a triarchy, the State would remain important in managing resources that cannot be easily divided into neat parcels (the atmosphere, oceanic fisheries, the human genome). It would also manage resources (petroleum extraction, minerals) that may generate large amounts of money on a regional basis. But it would have to devise better ways to manage public lands, national parks, wilderness areas, state-sponsored research and civil infrastructure in conscientious, effective ways. Government agencies—long accustomed to doling out subsidized assets and infrastructure to voracious corporations—must be structured to act as conscientious and transparent administrative and fiduciary trustees of common assets.

Purists may object that government-managed systems for shared resources cannot truly be considered commons. But we should remember that even commons such as open source software or academic research depend upon government and markets in all sorts of *indirect* ways. Government funding supported the development of the Internet and still funds a vast amount of academic research; most personal computers are still acquired through commercial vendors; and so on. The question is not so much *whether* markets or governments have some role in commons but rather to what degree and under what terms. The preeminent challenge is to assure the greatest integrity of commons, so that the fruits of commoning are not siphoned away by clever, covetous businesses and governments.

For now, the idea of a state-authorized Commons Sector may seem politically quixotic. After all, the state is generally indifferent or hostile to most collective enterprises except corporations. Thus a serious ongoing challenge for commoners is to self-organize themselves into quasi-sovereign collectives—a wiki, a seed-sharing collective, a water commons—committed to building and protecting their various resources and to insisting that the State recognize and respect them. We need new federations within the Commons Sector that can mobilize politically. We must devise legal innovations that can give the commons real standing in law. Until such things are achieved, the empire of capital will continue to impose its suffocating logic as widely as possible.

THIS SURVEY OF prominent classes of commons cannot truly do justice to the variety of commons in the world. But I hope that it conveys the range and complexity of commons, as well as some of their deep "similarities amidst difference." This truly is one of the enduring hallmarks of commons—their capacity to surprise.

The Commons as a Different Way of Seeing and Being

To Andreas Weber, a theoretical biologist in Germany, the commons is not simply a matter of public policy or economics. It is an existential condition of life in all its forms, from cellular matter to human beings. "The idea of the commons provides a unifying principle that dissolves the supposed opposition between nature and society/culture," he writes. "It cancels the separation of the ecological and the social." According to Weber, the commons provides us with the means to reimagine the universe and our role in it.

If we are to truly transform our economic and political systems, Weber argues, then we must also address some unquestioned, deeply embedded premises of those systems. In effect we must reassess the nature of reality itself. As creatures immersed in the liberal political paradigm and the principles of Darwinian evolution, most of us implicitly see life as a fierce, competitive struggle and the economy as a kind of machine in which countless individuals strive to maximize their personal wealth and advantage. Competitive triumph is all. We also see, implicitly, a Newtonian universe in which large abstract forces buffet the inanimate particles of nature. In this view, human consciousness and meaning are insignificant if not moot in the cosmic scheme of things.

Our tacit metaphysical commitments, argues Weber, are the very basis for our "free market" economic and political structures. What's so intriguing is that many scientists are starting to see the natural world and evolution through a different metaphysical prism, one that sees life as a system of cooperative agents constantly striving to build meaningful relationships and exchange "gifts." Competition still exists, of course, but it is interwoven with deep, stabilizing forms of cooperation.

In this new theoretical scheme, the subjective experiences of an organism *matter*. That's because, in the emerging scheme of biological thought, all organisms are "meaning-making" living systems. Life is seen as an evolutionary process in which embodied subjects interact with their environment and other living organisms to create meaningful relationships. Subjectivity is not an illusion or an inconsequential side-story, as our existing metaphysics claims; it is not a mere bubble of ephemeral, trivial feelings in an empty universe. Rather, subjectivity is the centerpiece of a new "existential ecology" whose primary concern is *subjects*, not objects alone. Human beings are not isolated atoms adrift in a vast indifferent universe. Our human subjectivity is not separate from a nature that exists as an alien, unfathomable "other." The subjective and the objective, the individual and the collective, blur into each other—just as in a commons!

Weber, speaking as a scientist, calls his new evidence-based theory "biopoetics." It is both a metaphysics and a biological theory that can explain "the deep relationship between felt experience and biological principles." Weber argues that the "science of life" as traditionally studied is no longer an adequate methodology for understanding living things. Conventional science fails to address the realities of consciousness and subjectivity in living organisms; indeed, these topics have been more or less banished from the field of study. But, as Weber writes, "only if we understand organisms as feeling, emotional, sentient systems that interpret their environments and do not slavishly obey stimuli, can we ever expect answers to the great enigmas of life." For him, biopoetics has the potential to provide "a new holistic account of biology as the interaction of subjects producing and providing meaning and hence laying the ground for understanding the meaningful cosmos of human imagination."

The commons is central to this vision. Only through commoning do we start to reintegrate ourselves with nature and with each other. Our challenge, Weber contends, is to bring about a new "Enlivenment"—a new type of rebirth to succeed the three-hundred-year-old Enlightenment. Our calling is to enact a vision of the universe that honors our subjective identities and need for meaning as biological necessities. We can do this by engaging in "the rituals and idiosyncrasies of mediating, cooperating, sanctioning, negotiating and agreeing, to the burdens and the joy of experienced reality," says Weber. "It is here where the practice of the commons reveals itself as nothing less than the practice of life."

While Weber's biological theories, like the commons, remain outside of the mainstream, to me they help explain the deep visceral appeal of the commons paradigm. They confirm that the commons is no PR gambit or "messaging" strategy, but rather a prism for seeing the world anew, and more profoundly: in its totality. In all its diversity. With a realistic understanding of humanity as it works on the ground. Weber's analysis situates the individual as a conscious, subjective agent in the world. It recognizes the role of actual history, local circumstances, culture and individuals in shaping human evolution and in creating commons.

To see the commons—*to really see the commons*—we need to escape the highly reductionist mindset of market-based economics and culture. We have to learn to see that a cooperative logic can animate human institutions, and that, with the right social structures and norms, this humanistic ethic actually *works*. Market culture has insidiously narrowed our imaginations. By privileging the interests of private property, capital and markets as governing priorities, our very language marginalizes the idea of working together toward common goals.

In this chapter, I want to touch on some of the ways in which the commons cuts deeply into our received notions of "reality" and invites us to reorient our thinking. The commons helps bring to the fore new perceptions and perspectives, and opens up new solution sets for vexing problems. To be sure, it is perfectly possible to talk about the commons in conventional terms and not raise any bothersome questions about the prevailing frameworks of knowledge or worldview. Economists do it all the time. They conflate the commons with "public goods," treating them as *things* and ignoring the social practices and relationships that animate those things. NATO talks about outer space and oceans as "global commons"—meaning, collections of mute resources—failing to appreciate that it is really talking about free-for-all, open-access regimes, not commons.

Taking the commons seriously, however, means changing some of the ways that we see the world. Our choices are not confined to being employees, consumers, entrepreneurs or investors seeking to maximize our personal economic well-being. We can begin to imagine ourselves as commoners. We can begin to become protagonists in our lives, applying our own considerable talents, aspirations and responsibilities to real-life problems. We can begin to act as if we have inalienable stakes in the world into which we were born. We can assert the human right and capacity to participate in managing resources critical to our lives.

The Metaphysics of the Commons

It is impossible in this short chapter to deal with all the complex metaphysical and epistemological issues raised by the commons. And in truth, these issues remain somewhat shrouded in mystery, at least to those of us immured within the Western modern, scientific worldview. Our culture and language do not equip us to see the humanistic and spiritual roots of the commons. It is nonetheless possible to glimpse some very different ways of seeing, acting and being in the world.

Proposing a new metaphysics of the commons—and new epistemological categories of knowledge—raises some disruptive questions about the basic assumptions of market economics and liberal democracy. Are human beings really capable of behaving rationally, independently and with informed consent in the marketplace and political sphere? Is it possible for human beings to be utterly autonomous and self-made, and to live in some zone outside of history and social particulars, as liberal universalism implies?

The commons challenges some of the myths that lie at the heart of liberalism, market economics and modernity. It rejects the idea that technological innovation, economic growth and consumerism will inexorably improve our lives if only we try harder and give ourselves more time. As noted earlier, normal economic activity arguably generates as much *illth* as it does wealth. In this sense, the commons dares to challenge the commodity logic that enshrines price as the supreme arbiter of value and material progress as the linchpin of all progress.

Commons scholar James Quilligan helps us understand this when he writes: "The notion of 'goods and services' in traditional economics is a reduction of the social relations among individuals—and of the individuals themselves—into commodifiable and fungible things. But *a commons-based economics raises the possibility of experiencing value through the practical relationships that arise among individuals, the resources of the world, and that which exists between people and the world*" (emphasis in original).

To talk of the commons is to validate this social coproduction as a constructive, satisfying activity. It also questions the social order and relationships implied by private property rights. "Commoning must be entered into," writes the historian Peter Linebaugh. "Whether on high pastures for the flock or the light of the computer screen for the data, the wealth of knowledge, or the real good of hand and brain, requires the posture and attitude and working alongside, shoulder to shoulder. That is why we speak neither of rights nor obligations separately."

The power of a commons comes from the actual social practices that animate it. But these practices—the complex rules and methods for how a forest may be used; for how Wikipedia entries are accepted and revised; for how irrigation waters are maintained and allocated in New Mexico—are highly specific, local and contextual. Norms cannot be easily generalized or made universal. This is precisely why it is so difficult to commodify the fruits of the commons without destroying the commons; its value is socially embedded and not readily converted into cash. Monetizing resources in a commons threatens to corrode the social relationships that hold a commons together.

As we saw in Chapter 9, indigenous peoples tend to have very different attitudes toward property. When a transnational corporation attempts to patent traditional knowledge or genetic material, they consider such propertization both fatuous and outrageous. No individual can claim to be the sole "author" of collective resources (as copyrights and patents imply) because these resources required generations of stewardship, inherited innovation and culture to develop and refine! No one can appropriate and sell for private gain something entrusted to a commons as a sacred trust. Hence the term "biopiracy."

It is important to note that indigenous communities can be as vulnerable to the seductions of money and power as anyone else. Some indigenous leaders have sold their traditional knowledge or resources for a pittance or entered into "benefit sharing" arrangements with Western pharmaceutical interests that end up betraying or greatly weakening their cultures. The San people of the Kalahari Desert in Africa agreed to 8 percent of the profits in a new diet drug made from *Hoodia gordonii*, a cactus the San have traditionally used as a natural appetite suppressant. Many have criticized this deal as a case of biopiracy that has injected market norms and large sums of cash into a traditional culture, with troubling effects.

Indigenous peoples generally see individuals as nested within a larger network of people; the very idea of the "self-made" person is somewhat ridiculous or even delusional. Not surprisingly, the idea of private property tends to be nonsensical for them because property is not so much a description of *a thing* as it is a description of *social relationships* with others. The idea of "sole and despotic dominion" over a resource, as Western law has come to think of property, denies our inescapable dependence on nature and our interdependence on each other.

Indigenous people tend to see their resources and knowledge as embedded in a community of reciprocal care and group stewardship. Modern industrial societies presume (incorrectly) that such arrangements are archaic and unnecessary, and that markets can provide what we need. *"Monetize the resource and split the income. What could be fairer?"* The arrival of climate change, Peak Oil and countless other environmental crises suggests the actual limits of this type of thinking and its ontological assumptions about our place in the world.

Interestingly, an emerging universe of digital commons is also revealing the inadequacies of the "monoculture of knowledge of the 20th Century," as anthropologist Marianne Maeckelburgh has put it. The knowledge generated by large centralized institutions and disciplines is too brittle, monochromatic and remote from the diverse lived realities of real people. The dominant systems of thought in our time, especially those of bureaucracies, conventional economics and scientific inquiry, have delegitimized vernacular culture—the practice-based ways of knowing and being. We need to understand ourselves as corporeal, situated human beings if we are to surmount our many ecological and social challenges.

The loss of diverse languages around the world represents a major setback in humanity's quest to come to terms with the more-than-human world. Most of Australia's two hundred and fifty aboriginal languages have disappeared, as have one hundred native languages in the area now known as California. As Daniel Nettle and Suzanne Romaine point out, "the extinction of languages is part of the larger picture of near-total collapse of the worldwide ecosystem." Native languages represent invaluable storehouses of particularized knowledge, especially about specific ecological systems. "Every language is an old-growth forest of the mind," as ethnobotanist Wade Davis memorably puts it.

The commons, taken seriously, is about honoring the new and diverse types of knowledge that are collectively constructed by commoners themselves, in their own specific circumstances. This knowledge could be about the seasonal habits of wildlife, the folkways of open source software communities or the community traditions that reward blood donations. Maeckelburgh has studied a range of activist and networked communities to identify the "alternative ways of knowing" that self-organized communities are developing. This "knowledge is collectively constructed," she notes. It is "context-specific, partial and pro-visional." And it makes a distinction "between knowing something and knowing better. At the heart of the struggle for self-determination, then, is what anthropologist Arturo Escobar calls "a micro-politics for the production of local knowledge.... This micro-politics consists of practices of mixing, re-using, and re-combining of knowledge and information."

Commoners rarely presume that there is a fixed body of canonical knowledge whose authority must be respected. They create their own (situational) types of knowledge through engagement with each other and their common resources. Why should some abstract, self-serving bureaucratic or economic framework automatically prevail when local expertise and experience-rich traditions may be more trustworthy, responsive and practical?

The Commons as a Crucible for Localism

This is, in fact, a great appeal of the commons—its promise of local self-determination. People are gravitating to the commons because they see it as a way to celebrate and protect their particular local circumstances. A community's identity is inevitably entangled in its geography and its buildings, its history and its leaders. It is the place where people learn and develop a fuller sense of humanity and ecological responsibility. Wendell Berry, the poet and ecologist, has put it this way: "Only the purpose of a coherent community, fully alive both in the world and in the minds of its members, can carry us beyond fragmentation, contradiction, and negativity, teaching us to preserve, not in opposition but in affirmation and affection, all things needful to make us glad to live." Or as Berry said on another occasion, quoting Alexander Pope, "Consult the genius of the place in all."

This approach resonates so deeply with commoners because global commerce has diminished so much that was once distinctive and fecund about individual places. A shopping mall in Bangkok is now the same as ones in Qatar, Germany and the US. Millions of people have gotten so accustomed to getting food from supermarkets, which are supplied by huge corporations with heavily advertised, brand-name foods, that it is sometimes hard to imagine that food was once filled with rich, homegrown, local variety. If you went to Nebraska, you once got Nebraska baked beans. If you went to Georgia, you might get possum and taters. Alabama kitchens would serve up oyster roasts, and Montanans considered fried beaver tail a delicacy. In the West, our relationship to the biological origins of food has been nearly lost.

The Slow Food movement is an attempt to recover some measure of local control over food production and distribution—and in so doing, to recover some of the social satisfactions and stability of living locally. The commons is often invoked in these conversations as a way to help reassert and reconstitute everyday community. The same impulse drives the so-called Slow Money movement, which seeks to make flows of finance more responsive to long-term community needs. The Transition Town movement, which aims to anticipate possible catastrophes stemming from Peak Oil and global warming, also seeks to mobilize local cooperation and citizen innovation to take steps that neither markets nor states seem capable of doing.

FORTIFYING THE LOCAL has far-reaching political implications. Again, Wendell Berry said it well: "The great enemy of freedom is the alignment of political power with wealth. This alignment destroys the commonwealth—that is, the natural wealth of localities and the local economies of household, neighborhood, and community—and so destroys democracy, of which the commonwealth is the foundation and practical means."

We should not romanticize the local as an easy or automatic

solution to the problems caused by global markets, however. The need for responsive "top-down" structures remains. Some collective-action problems can only be solved with appropriate high-level policies or infrastructures. Centralized bodies are often needed to assure a rough equality of opportunity and resources, or to oversee redistributions of wealth. It doesn't make sense for every community to replicate functions that might be performed effectively (and without harmful externalities) at a state or national level, or even by larger markets. On the other hand, a certain redundancy and inefficiency are essential to a system's long-term resilience.

For the time being, however, we don't really have a rich typology of larger-scale commons infrastructures. We don't really know how to design or build them. Such functions are usually considered the province of government. But I think it is time for commoners themselves to imagine how infrastructures and large governing protocols should be engineered. This could be politically difficult. Governments are jealous of their sovereignty and are not generally predisposed to understand and support commons. The idea of letting bottom-up, network-driven decisions emerge and prevail is threatening to traditional institutions of control. Yet that may be the only way that the energy, imagination and social legitimacy of commoners will be available to solve our myriad problems. We've already seen in countless ecological and social crises that the state and market, as constituted, are not up to the job. Let's begin to acknowledge this simple fact.

The Commons as a New Vision of Development

The capacity to honor the local through commoning suggests that there are better ways to achieve "development" than through economic growth. In this sense, the commons constitutes a new vision of human development. It begins to recognize the failures of conventional economic development strategies, and it takes seriously the idea that people can use commons-based systems to advance their long-term interests. There is currently a great deal of innovation and intellectual ferment surrounding the commons as a new development paradigm.

I mentioned earlier the role of seed-sharing in helping emancipate traditional farmers from the clutches of volatile global markets. The System for Rice Intensification—an international community of farmers who advise each other on improving yields from organic non-GMO varieties of rice—is another example. The Potato Park in Peru, mentioned above, is also noteworthy. So is the Oaxaca Commune in Mexico, which is forging new ways of communally managing land and other resources in the city of 600,000 people, and the Zapitistas' innovations in self-government in Chiapas, Mexico.

The Guassa Community-Based Conservation Area in Ethiopia, managed by the Menz indigenous people, has served as a grazing commons for more than four hundred years. The Menz still collect grass for thatching and wood for cookstoves there. Even though the region does not have any formal protection status, the Menz community has successfully combined its subsistence needs with a respectful coexistence with wildlife, including the most endangered carnivore in the world, the Ethiopian wolf.

These and many other innovations show that the commons can provide a "scaffolding" for exploring realistic alternatives to the (failed) neoliberal vision of development. Commons-based models are not just "policy mechanisms" that are inserted into a situation to "solve" a problem; they generally embody a very different vision of life than that of Western industrialization and consumerism. In Ecuador and Bolivia, *buen vivir*—"good living"—is a discourse that attempts to name a different development vision and way of being in the world. *Buen vivir* honors the ideas of community autonomy, social reciprocity, respect for natural ecosystems and a cosmic morality. In various ways, indigenous peoples, traditional cultures and commoners caught up in market systems are trying to express a worldview beyond the rational instrumentalism and economic mentality of market capitalism. In this sense, the commons is not just about managing resources; it's an ethic and inner sensibility.

This inner conviction ultimately empowers people to take responsibility for the Earth's resources and to nourish their own sense of stewardship. People discover that it is not only personally enlivening and culturally wholesome to participate in a commons; it is a way to encourage people to set and enforce sustainable limits on markets. Commoning provides a credible alternative to the growth- and consumer-based visions of development peddled by the World Bank. It provides a path for reducing inequality and insecurity in marginalized nations while highlighting the vital role of local ecosystems and commons-based governance.

Finding a Rapprochement
Between the State and Commons

The idea of commons-based development strategies naturally raises the question, What then should be the proper role of the State with respect to the commons? This, too, is a complicated question that deserves much further investigation.

Historically, the State has had very little to do with commons except to indulge their existence or work with market players (corporations, investors, industries) to enclose them. The basic problem is that the state has strong incentives to ally itself with market forces in order to advance the privatization and commodification of public resources. Enclosures + economic growth = power and tax revenues. To disrupt this logic, we must reconceptualize the role of the State so that it acts to authorize and support commons-based provisioning.

As Professor Burns Weston and I explain in our book *Green Governance*, political pressure must be brought to bear on states to recognize a number of "macro-principles and policies" to support the commons. These include recognition of:

+ commons- and rights-based ecological governance as a practical alternative to the state and market;
+ the principle that the Earth belongs to all;
+ a state duty to prevent enclosures of commons resources;
+ state trustee commons as a way to protect large-scale common-pool resources;
+ state chartering of commons;
+ legal limitations on private property as needed to ensure the long-term viability of ecological systems; and
+ the human right to establish and maintain ecological commons.

Michel Bauwens' idea of a "triarchy" that realigns authority among the State, Market and commons (as discussed earlier) is bound to be controversial and perhaps confounding. In many nations, the idea of the collective good is so fused with government that it is difficult to imagine an independent, non-governmental sector (the commons) serving that purpose. The commons, to the extent it is considered at all, is often equated with "the citizenry" or "the public," and not with distinct communities of commoners. It may take some cultural imagination, therefore, to entertain the idea of the commons as an independent sector separate from the State, with its own moral compass and political identity.

There are legitimate policy questions about how national and provincial governments can formally recognize the commons in law. It is not self-evident how the State could assure that local commons, absent intervention, would not abuse their authority or the environment, or discriminate unfairly against some people. These are serious questions, but I do not consider them insuperable. After all, the State has delegated considerable authority to corporations to perform certain functions while retaining ongoing oversight. If the State can charter corporations as a vehicle for serving the public good, in principle it ought to be able to delegate similar authority to commons. Diverse sorts of commons demonstrably serve the public good every bit as much as State-chartered corporations do (and at far less cost to the environment and public resources). And properly structured commons are generally more responsive than legislatures and State bureaucracies, which tend to be geographically remote, inaccessible to the layperson and heavily influenced by monied special interests.

The more fundamental problem may be the deep philosophical tension between the liberal polity and the commons. Through the apparatus of constitutional law and limited government powers, liberal democracies in theory seek to promote the greatest good through individual rights, universally applied, among legally equal citizens. The liberal polity generally makes few provisions for collective rights that exist beyond the individual. To be sure, various United Nations treaties and programs have a commitment to social, economic and cultural human rights, which in practice can act as a hybrid legal shelter for collective interests. But these are not collective rights as such, nor do they necessarily protect the commons. Indigenous peoples around the world have discovered this time and again; the juridical categories for protecting collective interests have scant legal and philosophical standing in the liberal worldview. The commons is thus frequently inscrutable to conventional policy-making, if not wholly incompatible.

To date, the few existing commons-based innovations that have sought the protection of formal state law—the Creative Commons licenses, the General Public License, community land trusts, protections for indigenous peoples—have had to resort to "legal hacks" around the law. The State could and should do more to recognize the authority of commons as vehicles for serving the public interest. But calibrating the level of State involvement is tricky. It is important that the State not become *too involved* in overseeing the commons lest it overwhelm the will of commoners to manage things themselves, which is the very point. Yet the State should not simply use the existence of commons to shirk its own responsibilities by withdrawing legal, administrative or financial support for them. This is a criticism made of UK Prime Minister David Cameron's "Big Society" policy gambit, which has celebrated community control while cutting public funding to assist it.

As I see it, the proper model for State support of commons should be "State policies in the service of commons formation and stewardship." The State should openly recognize that self-organized commons can perform certain functions more effectively than the State or Market, and with greater perceived legitimacy, fairness and participation. This is complicated terrain because the devil is in the details, and the details vary immensely from one commons to another. But it is abundantly clear that commoners using digital networks can now amass, organize and deploy knowledge more rapidly and reliably than large centralized bureaucracies (examples abound in the use of wikis, crisis-relief coordination, reporting via social networks and crowdsourcing of research). The real challenge may be how to find new ways for bureaucratic institutions and digital commons to collaborate. Ecosystem resources, too, are often more effectively and responsively managed by local commoners with the direct authority and responsibility to supervise their own forests, fisheries or water systems without outside interference.

Not all commons are necessarily equitable and benign, so the state may have an important role in setting minimal ground rules and performance parameters for them—and then letting the "distributed creativity" of commoners evolve the most appropriate local solutions. This model has worked famously on the Internet, as demonstrated by the TCP/IP protocols that lie at the heart of that infrastructure. The tech architects of the Internet did not seek to control or direct how people must behave on the Internet; they simply established minimal common standards (TCP/IP) for how communications should be formatted, addressed, transmitted, routed and received. This gave people enormous freedom to innovate as they saw fit within those basic parameters—a freedom that ultimately allowed something entirely unimaginable to emerge: the technical protocols for the World Wide Web.

Of course, autonomous commons in non-digital spaces are not going to simply spring up out of the blue because we stipulate a few basic parameters. Budgets and resources are needed. The state may need to help this process legally and financially, or at least provide support for self-organized, self-funded commons to establish themselves. Let's remember that most governments have created elaborate bureaucracies, legal privileges and subsidies to help businesses form and flourish. Why not similar support for commons?

Such a change would require close political oversight, however, because many governments would welcome the "offloading" of financial and programmatic responsibilities—"Just let the commons do it!"—without shouldering the burden of helping new commons succeed. Indeed, most states remain yoked to the twentieth-century mindset of centralized bureaucratic control, and so would have trouble recognizing the value of self-organized commons based on minimalist design principles. This, truly, is one of the big tensions that nation-states are now grappling with as crowdsourced Internet innovation explodes. They can't understand how distributed authority, participatory innovation and self-organized governance (outside of government) can yield effective, trustworthy results.

The problem to be overcome here comes down to how we conceive ourselves in the world, and thus how we perceive governance ought to be structured. Italian commons theorist and activist Ugo Mattei argues that if we are to understand the commons, we must

> move beyond the reductionist opposition of "subject-object," which produces the commodification of both. It helps us understand that, unlike private and public goods, commons are not commodities and cannot be reduced to the language of ownership. They express a qualitative relation. It would be reductive to say that we *have* a common good. We should rather see to what extent we *are* the commons, in as much as we are part of an environment, an urban or rural ecosystem. Here, the subject is part of the object. For this reason, commons are inseparably related and link individuals, communities and the ecosystem itself.

If Mattei's analysis is accurate—and I believe it is—then it holds rather profound implications for the future of governance and the modern liberal state. It is no secret that state power is increasingly seen as illegitimate and ineffective. The authority and efficacy of "classical-modernist political institutions," writes Dutch scholar Maarten Hajen, are waning. The idea that politics can be separated from bureaucratic implementation, and that neutral scientific expertise and centralized systems can manage complexity, is no longer credible.

Hajer argues that we are now living in an "institutional void" in which "*there are no clear rules and norms according to which politics is to be conducted and policy measures are to be agreed upon.* To be more precise, there are no *generally accepted* rules and norms

according to which policymaking and politics are to be conducted" (original emphasis). Of course, proponents of neoliberal governance believe that the rules and norms for governance
are entirely clear and generally effective. Their mantra generally
focuses on trying harder to appoint the "right people" or reliable
science to enact "reforms" that will finally prevent antisocial behaviors and "solve" unacceptable problems.

But the proliferation of political alienation and insurgency
movements around the world calls into question the blind faith
of neoliberal elites—or more to the point, the deep structural
deficiencies of neoliberal institutions. Many citizens around
the world no longer have confidence that conventional governments *can* provide solutions. They don't trust government to act
as a fair-minded host of democratic deliberation and broker of
political interests. Many disillusioned citizens are shifting their
political imaginations and energies toward their own DIY alternatives, interacting with the State only as necessary.

In the wake of the Internet, civil society has become too robust and transnational for governments to assert the kind of ter-
ritorial sovereignty they once took for granted. There are now
too many transnational networks of commoners and too many
huge flows of information and communication beyond the control of governments. Enormous wells of innovation are emerging
from the bottom up, on open networks, while the State struggles
mightily to keep up. As a practical matter, insurgent commons
may not pose an imminent political or economic threat. Global
financial capital and market forces remain extremely potent,
seemingly invincible forces. Yet the pervasive erosion of legitimacy, efficacy and credibility afflicting states around the world
(and the neoliberal paradigm more generally) cannot continue
indefinitely. At some point, a reckoning is inevitable.

Which makes me wonder: Can the old citizen/state dyad
continue to function without significant shifts of authority and

governance? Can the state solve our myriad social and ecological challenges, most notably arresting climate change, without reconfiguring itself? I doubt it.

As this analysis suggests, the challenge we face is to devise new forms of governance that will necessarily transform the nature of state sovereignty. This is uncharted territory for which the old rules and assumptions will have limited relevance. It seems clear to me that the commons—a highly versatile system of governance, resource-management and sense-making that can meet people's needs in ways that are experienced as both legitimate and effective—will likely be part of the new order.

11

The Future of the Commons

THERE IS MUCH MORE that can be said about the commons—in greater depth, with greater precision, from different cultural perspectives, and with the wisdom of historians, poets and artists. My account here is only one of many. But if I've whetted your appetite to explore further, I am satisfied. This book is only a short introduction, after all.

A question I am asked a lot is What can I do to help the commons? Or as one woman put it after a talk I had given, "How can I become more "commonable"? A wonderful coinage! I always reply that it must start with your passion and where you live—and then you must find others to help push the idea forward, however small the effort may seem at first. The famous line by Margaret Mead comes to mind: "Never doubt that a small group of thoughtful, committed citizens can change the world; indeed, it's the only thing that ever has."

If you prowl the world of commoning as covered by my blog, the Peer to Peer Foundation, the Commons blog in Germany, *Shareable* magazine, Onthecommons.org or *Stir* magazine in the UK (or many others—see the blogroll on my website), you will encounter dozens of stories of ordinary people doing some amazing work. It is tempting to patronize some commons initiatives as "too small" to be significant; conventional policy experts like to imagine bold, sweeping plans that can be decisively implemented to "solve" problems. But the truth is that commons work best when they emerge organically over time in coordination with local conditions and specialized needs.

It is surely true that the government, public policy and international law at the "higher" levels must begin to provide legal and financial support to commons initiatives. There is a need for infrastructures and platforms to let commons flourish and unleash enormously important local energies. There is a need for commons-based innovations at national and regional levels, but also at the small levels, which are often patronized as "too small" to be consequential, but which can collectively, over time, remake a society. In this regard, I think of Mark Lakeman and City Repair, an enterprising civic project dedicated to reviving neighborhood spaces in Portland, Oregon; Rajendra Singh and his Young India Association, which has reclaimed the nearly dry Arvari River by applying commons principles; and the dozens of hackerspaces and FabLabs that commoners have created to co-produce software, customized fabrication and open hardware design and manufacturing.

The point in any of these instances is not so much to "scale" the commons in a linear, hierarchical sense—that's so twentieth century!—but rather to intensify and diversify its workings everywhere at once. The process is more akin to crystallization, as my friend Silke Helfrich puts it. New "atoms" join the crystal as they resonate with its basic structures and ideas, and soon the crystal begins to take shape and grow in all directions without any traces of hierarchy or points of centralization. In this way, small changes—commons by commons—can have big cumulative effects on the whole system. (The Internet—a network or World Wide Web—has grown in much this way.)

This process is already underway. As the 2012 anthology *The Wealth of the Commons* documents, there is enormous world-wide interest in the commons as a way to reimagine a different kind of future. Some of this energy was catalyzed by the International Commons Conference in November 2010, which attracted two hundred self-identified commoners from thirty-four countries to Berlin to explore the possibilities. Another huge boost for commons activism was the May 2013 conference on economics and the commons, also in Berlin.

The fascinating reality is that scores of projects around the world are spontaneously adopting the commons discourse to frame their efforts. The World Social Forum and the alternative People's Summit at the Rio+20 environmental conference issued stirring manifestos about reclaiming the commons. Political movements in Italy have arisen to prevent the privatization of water supplies and to launch citizen-managed commons. There are now websites that provide online courses on the commons and a Commons Atlas that directs people to maps of commons. The University of Notre Dame and the School of Commoning in London now host an Introduction to Global Commons course, while Occupy activists in the US have hosted two conferences on the commons. In Istanbul, artists have gathered to discuss the connections between art and the commons. And so on.

Most commoners I know are not interested in developing a "unified field theory" of the commons as a political philosophy. To be sure, they want to develop a larger, more coherent idea of what the commons means and how it may apply to diverse circumstances. But they tend to be wary of overemphasizing ideology and abstractions. The first priority of commoners, when it comes right down to it, is to tend and protect their particular commons. They understand that they need to focus their energies on the beloved commons that are near and dear to them. To cultivate the art of commoning: this is the base for all else.

It is precisely the decentralized, self-organized and practice-based approach of the commons that makes it so hardy as a political strategy. It's harder to co-opt a movement when there is no single cadre of leadership. To put it more positively, a diversified movement rooted in on-the-ground, self-directed leadership can elicit much more energy and imagination than centrally directed initiatives can. Because it is usually based in practice, not theory, the commons can also skirt many of the enervating battles over ideological purity that often plague movements. (Not always, of course: the free software movement has had its share of battles over ideological purity, and many other commoners remain focused on the theoretical over the practical.) For many commoners. the point is less about getting the right intellectual formulation than about getting real work done. Ideas matter, to be sure, and strategic debates are important. But as the conceptual artist Jenny Holzer has pointedly noted, "Action causes more trouble than thought."

In the early pages of this book, I asked how we could confront the aging dogmas of neoliberal ideology. How might we unseat a "free market" theology that cannot deliver on its promises and yet will not allow serious consideration of alternatives? The basic answer is now fairly clear, I hope. It's important to form and expand a wider circle of actual functioning commons that can serve as "staging areas" for building a new vision for the future, a new cultural ethic, a new political constituency. This vision cannot simply be announced. A brilliant leader cannot simply declare what should be. The vision has to be negotiated and "co-enacted" by commoners themselves, over time. Appropriate strategies and solutions can only emerge from active experimentation, debate and innovation.

The commons is at bottom a cultural practice and outlook that seeks to understand the world in different terms. It is driven by a shift in perception about how human beings can actually influence the making of a better world. It is animated by personal ethics and social engagement finding new fulcrum points to leverage change. Representative democracy and law remain important vehicles for progress, but commoners tend to be realistic. The most urgent task is not necessarily to pass new laws or elect the right candidates, especially when the old system of governance is so corrupt and ineffective. The most urgent task is to devise durable and appropriate institutions for commoning. Enclosures of commons must be fought, and new defenses to protect the commons (legal, technological, social) must be built. This may or may not require state law.

A top priority, then, should be expanding the conversation about the commons. Get the cultural meme in circulation. Ground it in actual practice. This is the way that the commons will emerge as a credible, functioning reality. The more that people have personal, lived experiences with commoning of any sort, the greater the public understanding of the commons. To name it is to begin to (re)claim it.

In most societies around the world, the prospects for meaningful political change remain fairly dismal. The neoliberal project manifestly cannot deliver on its utopian promises of progress and prosperity for all, yet the traditional critics of neoliberalism and political progressives are not likely to pioneer the new paths we need. Most of them, I fear, are too intellectually fatigued, politically demoralized or compromised by their own yearning to appear relevant to the world of power and respectability.

The imaginary of the commons helps extricate us from this morass. It provides the opportunity to start anew, with a different conceptual foundation, a new framework of analysis and a more robust moral and political vocabulary. In its broad sweep, the commons offers a powerful way to reconceptualize governance, economics and policy at a time when the existing order is incapable of reforming itself. The commons offers a way to revitalize democratic practice at a time when conventional political institutions are dysfunctional, corrupt, resistant to reform or all three. It demonstrates that societies can actually leverage cooperation and bottom-up energies to solve problems. It points to new modes of governance that go beyond, or can work in constructive partnership with, representative democracy.

The feasibility of the commons to develop a new vision can be seen in the growing number of transnational commoners and the innovations they are developing. Not all of them espouse the commons discourse per se, but their various social practices certainly embody its core values: participation, cooperation, inclusiveness, fairness, bottom-up innovation, accountability. They all seek to combine production, consumption and governance into an integrated paradigm of change. These eclectic movements include the Solidarity Economy movement, the Transition Town movement, alterglobalization activists, water activists, the Landless Workers' Movement in Brazil (MST), the international movement of peasants known as La Via Campesina, the free software and free culture movements, Wikipedians, the open-access scholarly publishing world, the Open Educational Resources (OER) movement, the dozens of international Pirate Parties and the Occupy movement, among others. The budding federation of these efforts suggests the beginnings of a new sort of global movement—a loosely coordinated movement of movements.

Four Strengths of the Commons

The commons could well become a focal point for much of this energy because it has four distinct advantages. First, it is a *worldview and sensibility* that is ecumenical in spirit and analysis. It isn't a rigid totalizing ideology, but rather a template for change that is open-ended, flexible and accessible to diverse cultures and societies. It respects on-the-ground realities and practical working models.

Second, the commons has a *venerable legal history* that stretches back to the Roman Empire and the Magna Carta and its companion Charter of the Forest. This history is a great source of instruction, credibility and models for political and legal innovation today.

Third, the commons is a serious *intellectual framework and discourse* that lets us critique market culture and validate human cooperation and community. This has been an abiding limitation of political liberalism, which is too closely aligned with market ideology to take issue with its systemic flaws and limitations. It is not willing to entertain a notion of human existence that strays far from the models of *Homo economicus*. Its vision of political emancipation is also tethered to a vision of liberal universalism that cannot make good on its promises.

Finally, the commons consists of a rich array of successful *working models* for provisioning and empowerment that in many instances are out-competing the Market and State. It provides some positive, constructive alternatives that ask us to step up and show responsibility and imagination; it is not just an exercise in carping and criticism. In the commons, we are called to be active participants in building a new world, not just consumers and voters. The commons is an active verb, not just an inert noun. It is not something that we just hand off to politicians and bureaucrats.

The Commons as Both Gift and Duty

Alain Lipietz, a French political figure and student of the commons, traces the word "commons" to William the Conqueror and the Normans—not the English, interestingly. The term "commons" supposedly comes from the Norman word *commun*, which comes from the word *munus*, which means both "gift" and "counter-gift," which is to say, a duty.

I think this etymology gets to the nub of the commons. We need to recover a world in which we all receive *gifts* and we all have *duties*. This is a very important way of being human. The expansion of centralized political and market structures has tragically eclipsed our need for gifts and duties. We rely on the institutions of the Market and the State for everything, leaving little room for personal agency or moral commitment. And so we have largely lost confidence in what Ivan Illich called the vernacular domain, the spaces in our everyday life in which we can create and shape and negotiate our lives. I think we need to fortify what I call vernacular law—the law of the commons.

What I find reassuring is the deep resonance that this idea has among so many different people around the world—Filipino farmers, Brazilian remix artists, Amsterdam hackers, German co-op members, American free culture users, Italian municipalities. The explosion of commons-based initiatives popping up around the world in countless different milieus is creating powerful synergies and opening up some rich possibilities for change.

This is exciting because when theory needs to catch up with practice, you *know* that something powerful is going on. At a time when the old structures and narratives simply are not working, the commons gives us many reasons to be hopeful.

The Commons, Short and Sweet

The commons is:

- A social system for the long-term stewardship of resources that preserves shared values and community identity.
- A self-organized system by which communities manage resources (both depletable and and replenishable) with minimal or no reliance on the Market or State.
- The wealth that we inherit or create together and must pass on, undiminished or enhanced, to our children. Our collective wealth includes the gifts of nature, civic infrastructure, cultural works and traditions and knowledge.
- A sector of the economy (and life!) that generates value in ways that are often taken for granted—and often jeopardized by the Market/State.

There is no master inventory of commons because a commons arises whenever a given community decides it wishes to manage a resource in a collective manner, with special regard for equitable access, use and sustainability.

The commons is not a resource. It is a resource *plus* a defined community *and* the protocols, values and norms devised by the community to manage needed resources. Many resources—such as the atmosphere, oceans, genetic knowledge and biodiversity—urgently need to be managed as commons.

There is no commons without commoning—the social practices and norms that help a community manage a resource for collective benefit. Forms of commoning naturally vary from one commons to another because humanity itself is so varied. And so there is no "standard template" for commons, just shared patterns and principles. The commons must be understood, then, as a verb as much as a noun. A commons must be animated by bottom-up participation, personal responsibility, transparency and self-policing accountability.

One of the great, unacknowledged problems of our time is the enclosure of the commons, the expropriation and commercialization of shared resources, usually for private market gain. Enclosure can be seen in the patenting of genes and life-forms, the over-extension of copyright law to lock up creativity and culture, the privatization of water and land, and attempts to transform the open Internet into a closed proprietary marketplace, among many other enclosures.

Enclosure is about dispossession. It privatizes and commodifies resources that belong to a community or to everyone, and dismantles a commons-based culture (egalitarian coproduction and cogovernance) with a market order (money-based producer/consumer relationships and hierarchies). Markets tend to have thin commitments to localities, cultures and ways of life; for any commons, however, these are indispensable.

The classic commons are small and focused on natural resources; an estimated two billion people depend upon commons of forests, fisheries, water, wildlife and other natural resources for their everyday subsistence. But other types of commons exist in cities, at universities and as infrastructure and social traditions. One of the most robust classes of commons is based on the Internet and digital technologies, which enable commoners to create valuable bodies of shared knowledge and creative works.

The contemporary struggle of commoners is to find new structures of law, institutional form and social practice that can enable diverse sorts of commons to work at larger scales; to protect their resources from market enclosure; and to ensure the generative power of their commons.

New commons forms and practices are needed at all levels—local, regional, national and global—and there is a need for new types of federation among commoners and new linkages between different tiers of commons. Transnational commons are especially needed to help align governance with ecological realities and serve as a force for reconciliation across political boundaries. To actualize the commons and deter market enclosures, we need innovations in law, public policy, governance, social practice and culture. All of these endeavors will give rise to a very different worldview than the one that now prevails in established governance systems, particularly those of the State and Market.

The Logic of
the Commons and
the Market

A Short Comparison of Their Core Beliefs

	The For-Profit Paradigm	The Commons Paradigm
Resources	Scarcity is given or created (through barriers and exclusions).	For rivalrous resources, there is enough for all through sharing. For non-rivalrous resources, there is abundance.
	Strategy: "efficient" resource allocation.	Strategy: strengthening social relations is decisive for assuring fair shares and sustainable use of resources.
Idea of the individual	Individuals maximize benefits for themselves (*Homo economicus*).	Humans are primarily cooperative social beings.
Human relationships to nature and other people	Separation • Either/or • Individualism vs. collectivism • Human society vs. nature	Interrelationality • Individuals and the collective are nested within each other and mutually reinforcing.
Change agents	Powerful political lobbies, interest groups and institutionalized politics focused on government.	Diverse communities working as distributed networks, with solutions coming from the margins.
Focus	Market exchange and growth (GDP) achieved through individual initiative, innovation and "efficiency."	Use-value, common wealth, sustainable livelihoods and complementarity of enterprise.
Core question	What can be sold and bought?	What do I/we need to live?
Governance		
Decision-making	Hierarchical, top-down; command and control.	Horizontal, decentralized, bottom-up. Self-organization, monitoring and adjustment of resource use.
Decision principle	Majority rules	Consensus

	The For-Profit Paradigm	The Commons Paradigm
Social Relationship		
Power relations	Centralization and monopoly	Decentralization and collaboration
Property relations	Exclusive private property: "I can do what I want with what is mine."	Collectively used possession: "I am co-responsible for what I co-use."
Access to rival resources (land, water, forest...)	Limited access; rules defined by owner.	Limited access; rules defined by users.
Access to non-rival resources (ideas, code...)	Limited access; scarcity is artificially created through law and technology.	Unlimited access; open access is the default norm.
Use rights	Granted by owner (or not). *Focus on*: individual rights	Co-decided by co-producing users. *Focus on*: fairness, access for all
Social practice	Prevail at the expense of others; competition dominates	*Commoning*; cooperation dominates
Knowledge Production		
	Corporate ideology and values integrated into education and knowledge production.	Peer-to-peer, networking and collaborative allows diversity of viewpoints.
	Knowledge regarded as scarce asset to be bought and sold.	Knowledge regarded as plentiful resource for the common good of society.
	Proprietary technologies	Free and open source technologies
	Highly specialized knowledge and expertise are privileged.	Knowledge is subject to social and democratic control.
Implications for...		
Resources	Depletion/exploitation Enclosure	Conservation/maintenance Reproduction and expansion
Society	Individual appropriation vs. collective interests	"My personal unfolding is a condition for the development of others, and vice-versa." Emancipation through convivial
	Exclusion	connections

This chart, by Silke Helfrich, first appeared in *The Wealth of the Commons: A World Beyond Market and State* (Levellers Press, 2012). It is licensed under a Creative Commons Attribution-ShareAlike 3.0 license.

Further Reading on the Commons

Markets, Economics and Commons

Ackerman, Frank and Lisa Heinzerling, *Priceless: On Knowing the Price of Everything and the Value of Nothing* (New Press, 2004).

Alperovitz, Gar and Lew Daly, *Unjust Deserts: How the Rich Are Taking Our Common Inheritance* (New Press, 2008).

Barnes, Peter, *Capitalism 3.0: A Guide to Reclaiming the Commons* (Barrett–Koehler, 2006).

Bollier, David, *Silent Theft: The Private Plunder of Our Common Wealth* (Routledge, 2002).

———, *This Land Is Our Land: The Fight to Reclaim the Commons* [DVD] (Media Education Foundation, 2010).

———, and Silke Helfrich, editors, *The Wealth of the Commons: A World Beyond Market and State* (Levellers Press, 2012). Available at wealthofthecommons.org.

Frank, Robert, *One Market Under God: Extreme Capitalism, Market Populism and the End of Economic Democracy* (Doubleday, 2000).

Hardt, Michael and Antonio Negri, *Commonwealth* (Harvard University Press, 2009).

Harvey, David, *A Brief History of Neoliberalism* (Oxford University Press, 2005).

Heller, Michael, *The Gridlock Economy: How Too Much Ownership Wrecks Markets, Stops Innovation and Costs Lives* (Basic Books, 2008).

Korten, David, *Agenda for a New Economy: From Phantom Wealth to Real Wealth* (Berrett-Koehler, 2010).

Kuttner, Robert, *Everything For Sale: The Virtues and Limits of Markets* (Knopf, 1997).

Nomini, Donald, editor, *The Global Idea of 'the Commons'* (Berghahn Books, 2007).

Patel, Raj, *The Value of Nothing: How to Reshape Market Society and Redefine Democracy* (Picador, 2009).

Penalver, Eduardo Moises and Sonia K. Katyal, *Property Outlaws: How Squatters, Pirates and Protesters Improve the Law of Ownership* (Yale University Press, 2010).

Radin, Margaret Jane, *Contested Commodities* (Harvard University Press, 1996).

Rose, Carol M., *Property and Persuasion: Essays on the History, Theory and Rhetoric of Ownership* (Westview Press, 1994).

Sandel, Michael, *What Money Can't Buy: The Moral Limits of Markets* (Allen Lane, 2012).

Schroyer, Trent, *Beyond Western Economics: Remembering Other Economic Cultures* (Routledge, 2009).

Wall, Derek, *The Sustainable Economics of Elinor Ostrom: Commons, Contestation and Craft* (MIT Press, 2014).

Walljasper, Jay, *All That We Share* (New Press, 2011).

The Social and Cultural Dynamics of Commons

Benkler, Yochai, *The Penguin and the Leviathan: The Triumph of Cooperation Over Self-Interest* (Crown Business, 2010).

Bowles, Samuel and Herbert Gintis, *A Cooperative Species: Human Reciprocity and Its Evolution* (Princeton University Press, 2011).

Cahn, Edgar and Jonathan Rowe, *Time Dollars* (Emmaus, PA: Rodale Press, 1992).

Gintis, Herbert, Samuel Bowles et al., *Moral Sentiments and Material Interests: The Foundations of Cooperation in Economic Life* (MIT Press, 2005).

Hyde, Lewis, *The Gift: Imagination and the Erotic Life of Property* (Vintage Books, 1979).

Kropotkin, Petr, *Mutual Aid: A Factor of Evolution* (Boston: Porter Sargent Publishers/ Extending Horizons Books, reprint of 1914 edition).

Linn, Karl, *Building Commons and Community* (Oakland, CA: New Village Press, 2007).

Sennett, Richard, *Together: The Rituals, Pleasures and Politics of Cooperation* (Yale University Press, 2012).

The Commons in History

Alexander, Gregory S., *Commodity and Propriety: Competing Visions of Property in American Legal Thought, 1776–1970* (University of Chicago Press, 1997).

Federici, Silvia, *Caliban and the Witch: Women, the Body and Primitive Accumulation* (Autonomedia, 2004).

Hill, Christopher, *The World Turned Upside Down: Radical Ideas During the English Revolution* (Penguin, 1972).

Hyde, Lewis, *Common as Air: Revolution, Imagination and Ownership* (Farrar, Strauss and Giroux, 2010).

Linebaugh, Peter, *The Magna Carta Manifesto: Liberties and Commons for All* (University of California Press, 2008).

Polanyi, Karl, *The Great Transformation: The Political and Economic Origins of Our Time* (Beacon Press, 1944, 1957).

Wall, Derek, *The Commons in History: Culture, Conflict and Ecology* (Routledge, 2014).

Knowledge and Digital Commons

Aufderheide, Patricia and Peter Jaszi, *Reclaiming Fair Use: How to Put Balance Back in Copyright* (University of Chicago Press, 2011).

Benkler, Yochai, *The Wealth of Networks: How Social Production Transforms Markets and Freedom* (Yale University Press, 2006).

Bollier, David, *Brand Name Bullies: The Quest to Own and Control Culture* (John Wiley, 2005).

———, *Viral Spiral: How the Commoners Built a Digital Republic of Their Own* (New Press, 2009).

Boyle, James, *The Public Domain: Enclosing the Commons of the Mind* (Yale University Press, 2008).

Ghosh, Rishab Aiyer, *CODE: Collaborative Ownership and the Digital Economy* (MIT Press, 2005).

Klemens, Ben, *Math You Can't Use: Patents, Copyright and Software* (Brookings Institution Press, 2006).

Krikorian, Gaelle and Amy Kapczynski, *Access to Knowledge in the Age of Intellectual Property* (Zone Books, 2010).

La Follette, Laetitia, *Negotiating Culture: Heritage, Ownership and Intellectual Property* (University of Massachusetts Press, 2013).

Lessig, Lawrence, *Free Culture: How Big Media Uses Technology and the Law to Lock Down Culture and Control Creativity* (Penguin Press, 2004).

Ostrom, Elinor and Charlotte Hess, *Understanding Knowledge as a Commons: From Theory to Practice* (MIT Press, 2007).

Patry, William, *Moral Panics and the Copyright Wars* (Oxford University Press, 2009).

Suber, Peter, *Open Access* (MIT Press, 2012).

Vaidhyanathan, *Copyrights and Copywrongs: The Rise of Intellectual Property and How It Threatens Creativity* (New York University Press, 2001).

Natural Resource Commons

Barnes, Peter, *Who Owns the Sky? Our Common Assets and the Future of Capitalism* (Washington, D.C.: Island Press, 2001).

Buck, Susan J., *The Global Commons: An Introduction* (Washington, D.C.: Island Press, 1998).

Burger, Joanna, Elinor Ostrom et al., *Protecting the Commons: A Framework for Resource Management in the Americas* (Island Press, 2001).

Cooper, Melinda, *Life as Surplus: Biotechnology and Capitalism in the Neoliberal Era* (University of Washington Press, 2008).

Davey, Brian, *Sharing for Survival: Restoring the Climate, the Commons and Society* (Foundation for the Economics of Sustainability, 2012).

Dolsak, Nives and Elinor Ostrom, *The Commons in the New Millennium: Challenges and Adaptations* (MIT Press, 2003).

Donahue, Brian, *Reclaiming the Commons: Community Farms and Forests in a New England Town* (Yale University Press, 1999).

Freyfogle, Eric T., *The Land We Share: Private Property and the Common Good* (Island Press, 2003).

McKay, Bonnie J. and James M. Acheson, *The Question of the Commons: The Culture and Ecology of Communal Resources* (University of Arizona Press, 1987).

National Research Council, Elinor Ostrom, Thomas Dietz et al., *The Drama of the Commons: Committee on the Human Dimensions of Global Change* (National Academy Press, 2002).

Ostrom, Elinor, *Governing the Commons: The Evolution of Institutions for Collective Action* (Cambridge University Press, 1990).

Shiva, Vandana, *Biopiracy: The Plunder of Nature and Knowledge* (South End Press, 1997).

Steinberg, Theodore, *Slide Mountain, or the Folly of Owning Nature* (University of California Press, 1995).

Waldby, Catherine and Robert Mitchell, *Tissue Economies: Blood, Organs and Cell Lines in Late Capitalism* (Duke University Press, 2006).

Weston, Burns H. and David Bollier, *Green Governance: Ecological Survival, Human Rights and the Law of the Commons* (Cambridge University Press, 2013).

Special Types of Commons

Bollier, David and Laurie Racine, *Ready to Share: Fashion and the Ownership of Creativity*, with DVD (USC Annenberg School/Norman Lear Center, 2006).

Brown, Michael F., *Who Owns Native Culture?* (Harvard University Press, 2003).

Frischmann, Brett M., *Infrastructure: The Social Value of Shared Resources* (Oxford University Press, 2012).

Hallsmith, Gwendolyn and Bernard Lietaer, *Creating Wealth: Growing Local Economies with Local Currencies* (New Society Publishers, 2011).

McSherry, Corynne, *Who Owns Academic Work? Battling for Control over Intellectual Property* (Harvard University Press, 2001).

Shuman, Michael H., *Going Local: Creating Self-Reliant Communities in a Global Age* (Routledge, 2000).

Van Abel, Bas, Lucas Evers et al., *Open Design Now: Why Design Cannot Remain Exclusive* (The Netherlands, Bis Publishers, 2011), available at opendesignnow.org.

Washburn, Jennifer, *University, Inc: The Corporate Corruption of Higher Education* (Basic Books, 2005).

Leading Websites on the Commons

Bollier.org	Bollier.org
Commons Abundance Network	commonsabundance.net
Commons Atlas	commonsparkcollective.org /index.php/about/
CommonsBlog (Germany)	commonsblog.wordpress.com
The Commoner (U.K.)	commoner.org.uk
Commons.fi (Finland)	commons.fi
Creative Commons	creativecommons.org
Digital Library of the Commons	dlc.dlib.indiana.edu
FreeLab (Poland)	freelab.org.pl
Free Software Foundation	fsf.org
Global Commons Trust	globalcommonstrust.org
Int'l Assn for Study of the Commons	iasc-commons.org
Int'l Journal of the Commons	thecommonsjournal.org
Keimform (Germany)	keimform.de/category/english
Knowledge Ecology Int'l	keionline.org
New Economics Foundation	neweconomics.org
OER Commons	oercommons.org
On the Commons	onthecommons.org
Ouishare	ouishare.net
Philippe Aigrain (France)	paigrain.debatpublic.net
P2P Foundation	p2pfoundation.net
Real World Economics Review	paecon.net/PAEReview
Re:Commons (Italy)	recommons.org
Remix the Commons	remixthecommons.org
Science Commons	creativecommons.org/science
Shareable Magazine	shareable.net
Solidarity Economy	solidarityeconomy.net
Stir to Action (UK)	stirtoaction.com
Workshop in Political Theory and Policy Analysis	www.indiana.edu/~workshop
Yes! magazine	yesmagazine.org

Acknowledgments

It is no exaggeration to say that the writing of this book required the past fifteen years of my life, in which I have intensively studied the commons—its workings, political implications, cultural significance and future directions. I cannot possibly thank the hundreds of commoners around the world with whom I have shared instructive encounters. (You know who you are!) So I will single out my dear colleagues and sparring partners who have had so much influence on my thinking and enriched my life: Silke Helfrich, Michel Bauwens, Heike Löschmann and, in the US, Peter Barnes, Jonathan Rowe (1946–2011) and John Richard.

I am especially indebted to Matthieu Calame, Director of the Charles Léopold Mayer Foundation in Paris, for his keen interest in the commons and in commissioning a French translation of this book. My thanks also to Aline Duriez-Jablonka, Director of Editions Charles Léopold Mayer (ECLM) for overseeing the process and for her great patience as I navigated past other commons-related projects in my life. The gracious and erudite Olivier Petitjean of Ritimo, my editor and French translator for ECLM, provided many insightful comments that made this book smarter, deeper and subtler. Olivier, you were a pleasure to work with across the time-space divide.

I also wish to thank Karen Johnston, Charlie Cray, Ricardo Jomarron, Hervé Le Crosnier, John Richard and other readers whose careful review of my manuscript and thoughtful suggestions improved the text. Of course, I assume all responsibility for any errors or omissions.

Since any book is really part of an ongoing conversation, not the last word, I invite future commoners not only to challenge my mistakes, omissions and interpretations as seen from their vantage points, but to take this conversation into new territory that may not have occurred to me. The world of commoning is vast and expanding indeed.

— David Bollier
Amherst, Massachusetts

Index

About the Author

David Bollier has been exploring the commons as an author, policy strategist, international activist and blogger since the late 1990s. He has written or edited twelve books (sometimes with collaborators), including six on commons-related themes: *Silent Theft; Brand Name Bullies; Viral Spiral; The Wealth of the Commons; Green Governance;* and now, *Think Like a Commoner.*  The American Academy in Berlin awarded Bollier the Berlin Prize in Public Policy in 2012 for his work on the commons.

Bollier founded and edited the Onthecommons.org website (2003–2010) before cofounding the Commons Strategies Group, an international consulting project that assists the global commons movement. In 2002 he cofounded Public Knowledge, a Washington advocacy organization for the public's stake in Internet, telecom and copyright policies. Bollier now works on a variety of commons projects with international and domestic partners, and is Editor at ID³, a non-profit tech start-up that is building a "social layer" of protocols for the Internet. He blogs at Bollier.org and lives in Amherst, Massachusetts.

If you have enjoyed *Think Like a Commoner* you might also enjoy other

BOOKS TO BUILD A NEW SOCIETY

Our books provide positive solutions for people who want to make a difference. We specialize in:

Sustainable Living • Green Building • Peak Oil •
Renewable Energy • Environment & Economy Natural
Building & Appropriate Technology • Progressive Leadership
Resistance and Community • Educational & Parenting Resources

New Society Publishers

ENVIRONMENTAL BENEFITS STATEMENT

New Society Publishers has chosen to produce this book on recycled paper made with **100% post consumer waste**, processed chlorine free, and old growth free.

For every 5,000 books printed, New Society saves the following resources:[1]

18	Trees
1,654	Pounds of Solid Waste
1,820	Gallons of Water
2,374	Kilowatt Hours of Electricity
3,007	Pounds of Greenhouse Gases
13	Pounds of HAPs, VOCs, and AOX Combined
5	Cubic Yards of Landfill Space

[1]Environmental benefits are calculated based on research done by the Environmental Defense Fund and other members of the Paper Task Force who study the environmental impacts of the paper industry.

For a full list of NSP's titles, please call 1-800-567-6772 *or visit our website* at:

www.newsociety.com

new society
PUBLISHERS

Love the Harlequin book you just read?

Your opinion matters.

Review this book on your favorite book site, review site, blog or your own social media properties and share your opinion with other readers!

"Is it okay with you i

He chuckled. "We're supposed to be in love. I think you're allowed to get as close as you want without asking permission."

She stepped in and leaned her head on his shoulder. It felt good there. Felt right. As if his body remembered their intimacy. He took his hand from her waist and wrapped it around her, securing her against him, and she let out a contented sigh.

He imagined leaning down, finding her lips and losing himself in her kiss. Then taking her by the hand down the hall to her bedroom...

Except they had an audience.

And they were pretending.

This wasn't real. He couldn't let himself be lulled into falling for the very story they were spinning for the press. He released her and stepped back.

"Look, I should head home."

"I'll be in touch first thing in the morning."

He settled on the same greeting he gave his brothers' fiancées, and kissed her cheek.

Then he left the apartment. Quickly. Because the stupid part of his brain had told him to kiss her again. And this time, not on the cheek.

* * *

His 24-Hour Wife is part of the Hawke Brothers trilogy: Three tycoon bachelors, three very special mergers...

Dear Reader,

This is the third book in the Hawke Brothers series, and the last one. I can't tell you how sad I am to leave this family, but I'm also glad that Adam's story will be out in the world.

If you've missed Liam's book, *The Nanny Proposition*, or Dylan's book, *Bidding on Her Boss*, you can still get copies as ebooks and in paperback in some places, but you don't need to have read them to read this book; it stands alone.

While I was writing Liam and Dylan's stories, Adam was always lurking in the back of my mind, and I knew he'd need a very special heroine. Callie Mitchell is that heroine, and, although they have some obstacles to overcome to reach their happily-ever-after, I know that at the story's end, I've left each of them in safe hands.

I hope you enjoy Adam and Callie's journey to find a home in each other's hearts, and that you appreciate the chance to see Liam, Jenna, Dylan and Faith again as much as I did!

Cheers,

Rachel

HIS 24-HOUR
WIFE

———

RACHEL BAILEY

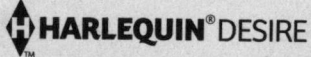

Recycling programs
for this product may
not exist in your area.

ISBN-13: 978-0-373-73419-1

His 24-Hour Wife

Printed in U.S.A.

Rachel Bailey developed a serious book addiction at a young age (via Peter Rabbit and Jemima Puddleduck), and has never recovered. Just how she likes it. She went on to earn degrees in psychology and social work but is now living her dream—writing romance for a living.

She lives in a piece of paradise on Australia's Sunshine Coast with her hero and four dogs, where she loves to sit with a dog or two, overlooking the trees and reading books from her evergrowing to-be-read pile.

Rachel would love to hear from you and can be contacted through her website, rachelbailey.com.

Books by Rachel Bailey

HARLEQUIN DESIRE

Claiming His Bought Bride
The Blackmailed Bride's Secret Child
At the Billionaire's Beck and Call?
Million-Dollar Amnesia Scandal
Return of the Secret Heir
Countering His Claim

The Hawke Brothers

The Nanny Proposition
Bidding on Her Boss
His 24-Hour Wife

Visit the Author Profile page at Harlequin.com, or rachelbailey.com, for more titles.

This book is for Charles Griemsman, who's worked on all my Desire books since 2009. Charles, you are an absolute pleasure to work with, and have such an excellent eye for story. Thank you for making my books better!

Thank you to Barbara DeLeo, Amanda Ashby and Sharon Archer for your brainstorming and suggestions. Also to Amy Andrews for my favourite line in the book. You're all amazing!

One

Callie Mitchell straightened her skirt, took a deep breath to calm the butterflies in her stomach and followed the receptionist to Adam Hawke's office on the top floor of a downtown LA office building. The central operations of his company, Hawke's Blooms, took up the entire floor and, as CEO, Adam had a corner office, which had to have killer views.

In hindsight, it had probably been a bad idea to stop on the way for a little Dutch courage—especially because it had been alcohol that had started this whole crazy mess—but she'd needed some help. It wasn't every day a woman had an appointment to see her secret husband.

In fact, she hadn't seen him once in the three months since their wedding day, so this was quite the momentous occasion. They'd met at an industry conference in

Las Vegas just over two years ago and spent an amazing night together, then had hooked up again at the following year's conference. Third time had been the charm—this year they'd added vows to their rendezvous.

The receptionist opened the door and waved her through and suddenly Callie was standing in front of him. The man she'd spent the most explosive times of her life with. The rest of the world faded away, leaving only him. The oxygen must have faded away, as well, because suddenly she couldn't get her lungs to work.

The receptionist had slipped out and closed the door behind her, leaving them alone, but Callie couldn't find a word to say. Although Adam wasn't saying anything, either.

He was as perfect as she remembered, which was a surprise—she'd been certain her imagination had embellished things, that no man could be that gorgeous. Yet here was over six feet of proof standing before her. His green eyes were as intense, his frame as broad and powerful as the image she had in her mind's eye. But he was wearing a suit with a crisp white shirt and dark blue tie. Most of her memories were of him stretched across the Vegas hotel sheets wearing nothing but a smile.

He cleared his throat. "You look different as a brunette."

She'd gone back to her natural caramel brown about three weeks ago, but instead of telling him that, she heard herself say, "You look different with clothes on."

His eyes widened, and she covered her mouth. That Dutch courage had been a very bad idea.

Then he laughed, a low rumble that seemed to fill the room. "I'm starting to remember why I married you."

"And what drove you away again," she said and

smiled. After a day spent in bed, gradually sobering up, Adam had suggested a divorce. She'd been having so much fun—and was, in all honesty, so dazzled by the Adonis who'd proposed to her—that she would have given their marriage a shot. But she'd had no rational argument for staying together, so she'd agreed.

Still, after three months, neither one of them had started those divorce proceedings. She didn't know Adam's reasons, but there was a small kernel of hope deep in her chest that maybe he wasn't quite ready to cut all ties with her yet.

He indicated two upholstered chairs near the windows, which, sure enough, offered a premium view of Los Angeles below. "Take a seat. Can I get you a drink?"

She knew he probably meant coffee or tea, but still she winced, remembering the gin she'd stupidly had before coming. "No, I'm fine. I won't be here long."

He nodded and took the chair across from her. Then his expression turned serious. "What do you need, Callie?"

For a moment all she could focus on was the sound of her name on his lips. His voice was deep and still sent a warm shiver through her. Three months ago he'd whispered her name in the heat of passion. Had murmured it when she'd kissed the smooth skin of his abdomen. Had shouted it as he'd found his release. More than anything, she wanted to hear him say her name again. Then his question registered, and she straightened her spine.

"Why do you think I need something?"

His forehead creased into a row of frown lines. "I just

assumed…" He let the sentence trail off. "After all this time, I figured if you were contacting me, you must—"

"I don't need anything," she said, holding up her hands, palms out. "I'm here as a courtesy, to let you know something."

His jaw hardened. "You're getting married?"

The way his mind worked was intriguing. She remembered that from their short time together—she'd been constantly fascinated by the things he said.

"No, I'm up for a promotion." Her PR firm had finally given her a chance to make partner—something she'd been working toward for years—and she wasn't going to let the opportunity go.

"Congratulations," he said. "So how does this involve me?"

"They've given me an assignment. If I handle this project well, I'll make partner." At twenty-nine, she'd be the youngest partner in the history of the firm.

He raised one eyebrow. "What's the assignment?"

"The Hawke Brothers' Trust." His company's new charity raised money for homeless children; it had already made a splash with various events, including a bachelor auction, and was now ready to move to the next level. Something Callie was looking forward to being a part of.

"Ah," he said, and rubbed the back of his neck. "I didn't realize Jenna had brought in your company."

Adam's future sister-in-law, Princess Jensine of Larsland, had helped to create the charity and was in charge of day-to-day operations. Callie had suspected Adam wasn't aware that her company had become involved. Which was why she was here, warning him, before she started work on the project.

"There was a good chance we'd run in to each other in a meeting or something, and I wanted to give you a heads-up before that happened."

"I appreciate it. So," he said, offering her half a smile, "how have you been?"

Despite being married, they didn't really know each other well enough to catch up. They had no basic information to catch up on. So she said, "Good, and you?"

"Good," he said, nodding.

It was awkward, so she took a breath and refocused. "I was thinking that maybe we should have our stories straight in case anyone puts two and two together."

He rubbed a hand over his chin. "You mean about us being married?"

"Since I'll be working with members of your family, it's a possibility."

"It won't happen. They don't know I—" He swallowed. "They don't know what happened."

"You didn't tell your family that you got married?" She hadn't expected he would brag about a short-lived Vegas wedding, but equally, she hadn't expected that he'd keep it a secret from his two brothers. In the short time they'd spent together, he'd mentioned he was close to his younger brothers.

He shifted in his seat. "Did you tell your friends and family?"

"I didn't tell everyone, but I told my sister." She moistened her lips. "You seriously didn't tell anyone?"

His face was unreadable. "I don't generally telegraph my mistakes to the world."

Asking her for a divorce had pretty much shown he had thought of their wedding as a mistake, but still, there was something in the way he held himself tall in

the chair—and in his tone as he said it—that had made her feel small and insignificant. She'd thought of their time together as something wild and crazy, something out of character, where they just went too far. She hadn't thought of herself as someone's mistake. It hurt more than she would have expected.

But now that he'd made his feelings crystal clear, the stupid part of her needed to let go.

She took a breath. "While I'm here, we really should talk about a divorce."

"Already underway," he said without hesitation. "I've filled in the paperwork and was just waiting for my brother's wedding to be over before filing it."

"Oh, right. Good." Everyone knew Adam's younger brother was marrying Princess Jensine of Larsland, so Callie could see that he wouldn't want to draw attention when the media could be hunting for stories.

"I didn't want my alcohol-fueled decision to have ramifications for him."

Flinching, she stood and hitched her bag over her shoulder. "I should go. Let me know when you're ready to file the divorce papers."

"Callie." He reached out to her as he stood, and then let his hand drop. It was the first time his voice had held a note of tenderness since she'd entered his office. He'd been the only man who'd ever affected her with merely his voice, and she wobbled. "I'm sorry," he said. "That was probably harsh. I don't want us to part on bad terms."

"It's fine," she said, summoning a polite smile. "But I've taken up enough of your time. I just wanted to give you some forewarning and I've done that, so I'd better get back to promoting the Hawke Brothers' Trust."

He held her gaze for a heartbeat or two, searching her eyes. Then he nodded and stepped back. "Okay. Let me know if you need anything."

Callie smiled and slipped out the door. Halfway down the corridor, her cell rang, and she paused in the reception room to answer it. A colleague's name flashed on the screen: Terence Gibson. He'd recently been up for the same promotion as Callie and his competitiveness had bordered on excessive. Since she'd been offered this project with the chance to win the promotion if she did well, she knew this wasn't going to be a congratulatory call.

"Hi, Terence," she said.

"I can see why the partners gave you this assignment," he said, not bothering to hide the malice in his voice.

She punched the elevator button. "And why is that?"

"Being married to one of the clients will certainly give you an edge."

She froze.

"Oh, you mean they don't know about your marriage to Adam Hawke? Oh, dear. I wonder what upper management will say when they find out. It will hardly make them feel as if they can trust you, and I hear they value open and clear communication in their partners."

The elevator arrived but she ignored it, sagging back against the wall. "How did you…?"

"You really need to work on your poker face, Callie. The expression when they told you it was for the Hawke Brothers' Trust would have told anyone watching closely enough that you had some sort of connection. The question was only about which brother. After a bit of searching I found that you married one of them

three months ago. Although I couldn't find a record of a divorce anywhere. I assume that's where you are now? With your husband?"

Her stomach clenched tight. "What do you want, Terence?"

Despite asking the question she had a pretty good idea of what the answer would be.

"Stand back from this assignment and let them hand it to me."

It was what she'd expected him to say, but still, the gall of the man, the entitled arrogance, was staggering. "You know I won't do that. It would be handing you the promotion, as well."

"Then I'll sell the story to the tabloids," he said, his voice almost gleeful. "I'm sure you can imagine what a PR disaster that will create. They'll love an exposé about the future prince's brother having a drunken wedding in a tacky Las Vegas chapel."

"No." It would overshadow her assignment and ruin her chances of the promotion.

"Then step away now and give me a clear shot at the partnership."

So either she stepped back and let Terence have the partnership, or she stayed and he caused a scandal, meaning he'd probably get the partnership instead of her anyway. Neither of those choices was appealing, but she especially didn't like giving in to blackmail. She needed time to think. To find a third option. She had to stall him.

"Give me a few days to think about it. Even if I tell the partners I can't take the assignment I'll need some time to come up with a believable reason."

"You have one day. Twenty-four hours."

The line went dead.

Callie blew out a breath, turned on her heel and headed back to Adam Hawke's office.

Adam stood when Rose, his receptionist, buzzed to tell him Callie Mitchell wanted to see him again. It had barely been five minutes since she'd left. He told Rose to let her through, and then had a look around the room for something Callie had forgotten. He couldn't find anything. But then, he was hardly focused enough to be sure.

Since she'd first made the appointment yesterday, he'd been unsettled. He'd dreamed about her last night, about their time together. About making love to her. Though that wasn't uncommon—he regularly dreamed about making love to her.

Which just showed how bad she was for his equilibrium. Control over himself and his life was important to him, and Callie made him feel off-center—a feeling he disliked intensely.

Then from the moment she'd appeared through his door this morning, he'd barely had two functioning brain cells to rub together. Hell, he hadn't even greeted her, just made some inane comment about her hair. Though her reply had been memorable...

He prayed this would be a short visit so he wouldn't make a fool of himself by blurting out something worse than what she'd said.

After a knock on his door, there she was again, as if conjured from his dreams, her rich, caramel-brown hair hanging sleek around her shoulders, her olive skin smooth. He knew from experience the taste of that skin,

and his heart skipped a beat as the memory flooded his senses.

"Did you forget something?" he managed to ask.

She shook her head, her silver-blue, almond-shaped eyes serious. Something had changed.

She tipped up her chin and met his gaze squarely. "We have a problem."

He was careful not to touch her and set off more memories as he moved behind her to shut the door and lead her to one of the chairs they'd occupied only minutes before.

Once they were settled, he said, "Okay, tell me."

"A *colleague* of mine," she said, her emphasis on the word *colleague* telling him much, "noticed my surprise when I was given this assignment and started digging. He's found our marriage license and is threatening to tell the tabloids."

Adam swore under his breath. "What does he get out of it?"

"He wants this promotion and he wants me out of the way. He thinks the media coverage of your secret Vegas wedding will overshadow any PR work I do for the trust, and he's probably right. He wants me to refuse the assignment and let him have it."

"Like hell." There wasn't much that Adam hated more than a bully, and he refused to let Callie become the victim of one while he had any power over the situation. "The trust won't work with a man who's blackmailed his way to get the role."

"If I step back and you refuse to work with him, he'll probably still plant the story out of spite. We'd both still lose."

Callie's entire demeanor was professional, but un-

derneath she had to be rattled. Every protective instinct inside him reared up, ready for whatever needed to be done.

"Give me one minute."

He stood, strode over to his desk and pressed the buzzer for his receptionist. "Rose, cancel all my meetings for the rest of the day."

"Certainly. Do you want me to give a reason?"

"Just that something unexpected has come up. Then reschedule them as soon as you can."

"Consider it done."

He grabbed a legal pad and pen and returned to his wife. It wasn't just Callie's job in danger, though that alone would be enough to make him take action. No, he wouldn't let his stupid mistake create trouble for his brother and future sister-in-law. His Vegas wedding had been out of character for him, and since then he'd taken the consequences seriously—he hadn't let himself drink more than a glass or two of alcohol at a time, and rarely let his control slip even an inch. This was just another consequence that needed addressing.

And he could fix this. That was what he'd always done in his family—fix things. The only difference was that this time, Callie was the one with the PR expertise.

"So, how do we handle the PR fallout when the story hits the press?"

A tentative smile crept across her face. "You want me to stand up to him?"

"Well, I certainly don't want you to give in to blackmail." He frowned, searching her features. "What did you expect me to say?"

"I don't know. Thing is, I don't really know you that

well, so it's a pleasant surprise that you're willing to stand behind me."

She might not know him as well as, say, his brothers did, but surely she at least knew this much of his character? "Callie, I know our history is a little unconventional, but don't ever doubt that I'll stand behind you."

"Thank you," she said, and for one brief, shining moment he recognized the passionate woman from Vegas who'd snagged his attention from the moment he'd laid eyes on her in the bar. "That means a lot. And it goes both ways."

"I appreciate it. Now, what's our first move?"

She tapped a bright red fingernail against matching red pursed lips as she thought. "We need to get ahead of the story. Be on top of it and create our own story."

"Sounds good," he said. "How do we do that?"

"We need to come up with our own version of our wedding." She rose to her feet and started pacing, her words coming rapidly. "Create a new truth—it was love at first sight. Make it a sweet story, not the sleazy version that the tabloids will want to print, and get that new truth in the media ASAP to beat the other story. My contacts will help get it out quickly."

Adam made a few notes, and then looked them over. "It doesn't seem like enough—it will be one version versus the other."

"True," she said, holding up an index finger, "but that's only step one."

He smiled. "Good."

"The second part is to give them the current story."

He made another note on the legal pad and asked without looking up, "What sort of current story?"

"Something about us." She stopped pacing.

"About us being together?" he asked warily.

"That would be best." She rested her hands on her hips, her mind obviously going at a million miles per hour. "Perhaps that we're ready to have a real wedding."

He hid the instinctive flinch. If they were to find a workable solution, he needed to be open to all ideas in this first brainstorming phase. "How does that help?"

"Then, the story of our Vegas wedding becomes a very sweet, love-at-first-sight beginning to our current relationship and can't harm my career or your family. I'll let my bosses know before the story appears, and apologize for not disclosing the fact sooner, saying we'd agreed not to tell anyone before the announcement."

"A wedding," he said, this time allowing his skepticism to show.

She shrugged one slim shoulder. "It doesn't have to be forever, just until the story dies down and we can quietly separate and go back to our normal lives."

"How do we explain the intervening months?"

"I'm not sure. Give me a moment."

Again, she tapped her nail against pursed lips and, as he watched, he sat back. She was even more beautiful in real life than she'd been in his dreams last night. They'd been back in the Vegas hotel bed where he'd kissed that same lush mouth and covered her naked body with his. His blood began to heat. He stared at the light fixture in the ceiling as he brought his wayward body back under control.

"Okay," she said, gracefully sliding back into the chair across from him. "What if we say we gave it a go at the start but circumstances tore us apart. However, we never lost touch and recently we've begun to work through our problems and can finally announce

that we're ready to begin a life together as husband and wife."

He released a long breath, mentally checking all angles. "That roller-coaster history will feed in to the explanations when we break up again afterward. What will it take to convince them that we didn't just make this story up as a stunt?"

"Besides the story itself, which we'll give to an entertainment journalist I trust, I'll have friends leak details to key journalists. We'll also need to appear in public together, and do some media interviews. Then we'll have the wedding."

The last item on her list caught him off guard. His mouth dried. "You really want to go through with an entire wedding?"

Callie, on the other hand, seemed entirely unfazed by the prospect. Apparently she had nerves of steel. "We're already married, so it won't change anything legally. Either way, we'll still need to get a divorce at some stage."

Adam swallowed hard. She was right. Besides the cost of a wedding, which would barely make a dent in his bank balance thanks to the success of Hawke's Blooms, marrying her again wouldn't make any important difference—they were already married. But being around her, spending significant amounts of time near that lush mouth, just might change everything...

Two

Four and a half hours later, Adam looked around his brother Liam's living room at his collected family. Liam and his fiancée shared the sofa, a baby in each of their laps. On the opposite sofa were his youngest brother, Dylan, and his fiancée, Faith. Dylan and Faith now split their time between New York and LA; Adam was lucky they happened to be in town for this meeting. His parents were in two armchairs near Liam's elbow, and he and Callie rounded out the group.

Everyone was chatting in twos and threes, catching up on each other's news. But it was time to face the music. Adam's gut clenched tight.

He turned to Callie and quietly said, "Ready?"

"As I'll ever be," she answered, her expression not giving away much.

Bracing himself to lay out his mistake in front of

the people whose opinions counted the most, Adam cleared his throat. His family quieted and turned to him, waiting.

"Thanks for adjusting your schedules so you could come out here on short notice. I needed to introduce you to Callie Mitchell. Callie is taking over the PR for the Hawke Brothers' Trust."

Both his brothers raised eyebrows at him, but Jenna jumped right in. "I'm thrilled to meet you, Callie. You probably already know, but I head up the trust, so we'll be working together."

Callie smiled back. "I'm looking forward to it."

"However," Liam said, his head cocked to the side, "this raises the question of why you're introducing her to all of us and not Jenna."

Dylan held up a hand like a stop signal. "Are you about to try and talk us in to some crazy-ass PR stunt like the bachelor auction?"

Adam snorted. "As I recall, that stunt seemed to work out well for you." He looked pointedly at Dylan's hand holding Faith's—she was the person who had bought the package of three dates with Dylan at the auction.

Dylan grinned, acknowledging the point, and then leaned in to kiss Faith's cheek, which had turned pink.

"So why are we all here, then?" his mother asked.

Adam drew in a breath and cast another quick look at Callie, to ensure she was coping with his family's antics. Besides being a little tense—which was to be expected under the circumstances—she seemed fine.

"Callie and I..." he began, wishing he was anywhere but here. "We knew each other before she took this account."

Dylan made a sympathetic sound. "Callie, sweet-

heart, if you've dated my brother, let me apologize now. He can be a little—"

"Uptight," Liam interrupted.

"Yeah," Dylan said without missing a beat. "Let's go with uptight."

Adam pinched the bridge of his nose. His life was unraveling and they wanted to take the opportunity to rib him?

"She didn't date me," he said when he knew his voice would be even again. "She married me."

After a moment of stunned silence, the room erupted into questions, each being called more loudly than the one before. Even the babies, Jenna's daughter, Meg, and Liam's daughter, Bonnie, joined in on the action, laughing and waving their arms around.

Callie looked over at him, her eyes wide. He didn't know much about his wife, but from her reaction he guessed she didn't come from a boisterous family. This was a baptism of fire into the Hawke clan.

"Sorry," he said, and offered her a tight smile. He loved his family, but they tried his patience at least half the time. He turned back to the horde. "If you'll give me a chance, I'll let you know what happened."

The noise immediately stopped, and Adam could breathe again. "Callie and I met at a conference in Vegas several years ago. We've spent time together at the same conference for three years running and at this last one, we made a spur-of-the-moment decision to get married."

Liam was first to find his voice. "I assume alcohol was involved?"

"Please tell me there was an Elvis impersonator officiating," Dylan said, clearly loving the entire debacle.

Adam kept his voice even. "Alcohol on both sides, and no Elvis impersonator."

His mother leaned forward in her chair. "From the fact that this is the first we're hearing about it, you clearly didn't plan on staying married. So why are you telling us at all? Are you hoping to make a go of it now?"

"Hey!" Dylan said before Adam could reply. "I just realized why you refused to be part of the bachelor auction. You were already married."

Adam winced. The auction had taken place just after he'd arrived home from the fateful weekend in Vegas. He might not have been telling the world about the wedding, but neither would he lie and pretend to be a bachelor. However, he ignored the question and turned back to his mother.

"Callie was given this account by the partners of her firm without them knowing about our connection. Unfortunately, a colleague of hers found out and is hoping to blackmail her into handing the project over to him so that he can get the promotion when it's completed."

"That's awful," Faith said. "I hate petty politics like that. Can't you tell the partners?"

Callie leaned forward. "I could, but the story would probably get out anyway, and I think with Adam's connection to Larsland's royal family through Jenna, combined with his profile here in LA, the tabloids would have fun with the story."

"And," Adam added, "that could be disastrous for the trust. Donations could dry up. Not to mention the impact it could have on the coverage of Liam and Jenna's wedding."

Both Liam and Jenna opened their mouths to speak,

but Callie got in ahead of them. She was a quick study in how to deal with his family, and he appreciated that.

"It's okay," she said. "We have a plan."

Callie looked to Adam, as if for permission to explain. He nodded—it was her idea, so it was only fitting that she explained it.

"We're going to take control of the story and announce our new relationship. We'll speak to some journalist friends of mine and have it run in the media, complete with photos. The story will then be about an unconventional start to a sweet relationship. Hopefully, the interest will die down and we'll be able to go back to normal sooner rather than later."

"New relationship?" his mother asked hopefully.

Adam almost laughed. Of the entire crazy story, *that* was the phrase his mother had focused on.

"Sorry, but the story is fake. Callie and I will wait until any interest has blown over, then quietly get a divorce. The only ones who will know the truth are the people in this room and Callie's family."

His mother looked disappointed, but there was nothing he could do about that. Besides, she'd soon be gaining two new daughters-in-law. She was doing well enough without him having to add to the count.

"I'm worried you're doing this for us," Jenna said with a hand on Liam's thigh. "You don't have to—we'll be fine."

They might be fine, but he'd be damned if he'd let his drunken mistake hurt his brothers or Jenna's family. It was his mess and he'd clean it up.

"Callie and I have discussed the potential ramifications on your family, Jenna, but also on the trust and

Callie's career. We've agreed this is the best course of action."

"What can we do to help?" Liam asked.

"We have the situation in hand," Callie said. "All you need to do is play along and attend the wedding."

Faith sat up straighter, as if she'd had an idea. "I can do a story on the wedding flowers on my TV segment if that will help."

Faith had recently started a job with a nationally syndicated gardening show, doing regular segments on flowers and floristry. The job was based in New York, and now she and Dylan split their time between New York and LA.

Jenna nodded. "Liam has a new flower, a snow-white tulip, almost ready to go. Instead of an event for this one, we could use the wedding as its launch. That will give the media something else to focus on besides digging for the truth."

That could help. Liam's work breeding new strains of flowers had been part of the reason their company had made a mark in the world of flower retailing. Jenna had organized red-carpet launches for the past two new blooms, and Faith's skills as a florist had ensured the most recent, the Blush Iris, had been presented to best effect, garnering them maximum exposure.

"It's gorgeous," Faith said, turning her excited gaze to Jenna. "Since you weren't firm on a name yet, perhaps we could tie it in? Call it the Bridal Tulip."

Jenna and Faith fell into a conversation about the flowers, while his parents took the opportunity to welcome Callie into the family, even if only temporarily. Adam watched, until his brothers approached him, blocking Callie from view.

Liam pulled Adam to his feet and clapped him on the back. "I can't believe you'll be the first of us to get married."

"Will be?" Dylan said. "He already *is* married. We're going to have to watch his drinking from now on."

Despite knowing it was a good-natured joke, Adam bristled at the thought of having to be watched like a child by his younger brothers, of all people. He tried to move away, but his brothers had boxed him in.

"You know," Liam said, pretending to think, "I don't remember the last time I saw him drunk."

Dylan grinned. "Now we know why. It makes him feel matrimonial."

Ignoring them, he shouldered his way past, reached for Callie's hand and then raised his voice to be heard over the din. "Much as I'd love to stay and enjoy Liam and Dylan's brand of support, Callie and I have to leave. We're meeting with her family, as well, tonight."

Within a few minutes, they had extricated themselves and made it to the car. Yet, even as he started the engine, his shoulders wouldn't relax. No one liked to have their screwups made into a joke, but still, it had rankled more than it should have for his family to witness the consequences of the only time in years he'd lost control.

And this farce was only just beginning…

Callie glanced over at her husband's strong profile, and a shiver raced down her spine. She'd spent most of the day with him, but there was something different about being in close quarters together in the dark cabin of the car. More intimate than a large, bright office and much more personal than a room with his entire family.

She felt the pull of him more strongly here, with nothing to claim her attention but his masculine beauty. His scent. Him.

His hands were firmly gripping the steering wheel and he seemed unsettled.

"That went okay?" she ventured.

"Sure, if you like publically admitting to your drunken mistakes and having them turned into wisecracks by your brothers."

At the words *drunken mistakes*, she cringed. Her reaction was stupid since she already knew Adam regretted their marriage, but still, she couldn't help it. It was like a slap in the face.

No point being squeamish now, especially when it was her job that was forcing them to make their situation public. She sat up straighter. "Let's put your brothers behind us and move on."

"Fine with me," he said, rolling his broad shoulders. "Fill me in on your family so I'm prepared before we arrive. Are they likely to mock? Chase me with a shotgun?"

"No, it'll be all safe and calm. My parents are both teachers, happily married and loving parents. They'll want to know the details, but ultimately they'll support whatever I choose to do."

"Siblings?" he asked as he smoothly overtook a car full of teenagers who had their music up loud. She tried not to be mesmerized by the way his hands and arms worked to control the car.

"One sister, Summer. She's also my roommate." And best friend. In fact, Summer was the only person Callie had told about Adam when she'd returned from Vegas. She'd spilled the beans on the spontaneous wedding,

her toe-curlingly handsome new husband and her hope that it might grow into something more one day. A hope that had turned out to be in vain.

"Will she be there tonight?" His voice was deep and rumbling, almost a physical presence in the car.

"She said she'd come for moral support. She already knew about Vegas, and I filled her in on the phone this afternoon, so she's up-to-date on the plan."

She and Summer had always been inseparable. Even since she was ten and Summer was eleven, they'd had a plan to conquer the world. As they'd grown up, the plan had changed a few times, but their ambition hadn't wavered. By the time they'd reached college and found they both had a flair for PR, they'd decided that they'd one day open their own firm, Mitchell and Mitchell. In the meantime, they were working in different firms so they could gather a broader range of skills and contacts. Either one of them making partner would give them the best springboard into their own firm, so it had always been a priority.

Along the way, they were both supposed to find men they loved, but who were also movers and shakers. Men with power and social influence. Men somewhat like the man sitting within touching distance from her now. Her husband.

The remnants of a child's idea of a successful life could still be seen in their life plan, but it was more than that. It was the American dream. Their parents were comfortably middle-class, and happy with their lot, but Callie and Summer had always dreamed of more.

That she had accidentally ended up married to someone who didn't want to stay married only set their life plan back a little. But she and Summer would get through

this and get back on track after Callie was free to divorce Adam Hawke.

As they neared her parents' house, she gave directions until they finally pulled up in the driveway. Summer's car was already here, so they were all systems go.

"What a nice home," Adam said, his tone polite.

Callie looked at the modest, single-story brick house, conscious of how it must seem to him. The gardens were bursting with flowers, but to Adam's expert eye, they would be nothing special—daisies and other plants that were easy to grow. And, though she knew he'd come from humble beginnings, it must have been a long time since he'd been inside a house that wasn't luxurious and stylish. She wondered what he was thinking, but his expression gave nothing away.

"Come on," she finally said. "Let me introduce you to my family."

By the time the mission was complete and they were on their way back to Adam's car with Summer walking beside them, almost an hour had passed.

"That went quite well," Summer said brightly.

Callie returned the smile but couldn't match the wattage. "I think they're disappointed in me."

Adam whipped his head around to face her, his dark brows drawn together. "They should be proud of you. Any parent would be proud to have a daughter like you."

Callie stilled. It was the first compliment Adam had given her since the night of their wedding. And even then, he'd been light on the complimenting front. It sent a happy buzz through her bloodstream, to her fingers and toes, and she was appalled. She couldn't let a simple

compliment from Adam Hawke affect her this much. It would be granting him power over her.

She braced every muscle in her body, bringing her reaction to him under control.

"Thank you," she said through tight lips.

Without looking at her, Adam gave a quick nod, and then thumbed the keyless lock.

Summer watched the exchange with a thoughtful expression before she added, "They're not disappointed. They're just surprised. It will take them a little while to process it all, but they'll be fine. It will take everyone a little time before it feels natural. Including you two."

"We don't have a lot of time," Callie said.

"That's true." Summer folded her arms under her breasts and regarded them both. "I'm just going to come out and say this. You two don't look like a couple in love."

Adam shrugged. "If you're looking for someone who gushes, you've got the wrong man."

Summer shook her head. "It's more about how comfortable you seem around each other. Or, more precisely, how uncomfortable."

"We'll be fine when the curtain goes up," Adam said dismissively.

Callie bit down on her lip. Summer was right. No one would believe the story they were going to try to spin if it wasn't backed up by nonverbal communication between them, and she and Adam weren't in the least at ease in each other's company.

"What do you suggest?" Callie asked.

Summer tapped her index finger against her lips and considered them. "A bit of rehearsal time should do it."

Callie suppressed an involuntary shiver at the

thought of *practicing* touching Adam. Since she'd arrived in his office this morning, they'd barely touched. But memories of touching him freely—of being touched by him—were burned into her brain. No one had ever made her come alive like Adam. She might have been under the influence of alcohol when she said her vows, but she'd been equally influenced by the man himself. By his touch. By his hands. By his mouth.

Even now, in her parents' driveway, she felt her heart pick up pace at the prospect of experiencing his touch again.

Adam, however, seemed unmoved. His decision about their marriage must have been mainly a result of the alcohol. If she wasn't careful, she would make a fool out of herself while they rehearsed. What she needed was a chaperone. Someone to remind her that this was all make-believe.

"Will you help?" she asked her sister.

Summer smiled. "Of course. How about now? We could grab some takeout and go back to the apartment."

"I don't think it's necessary," Adam interjected, everything about him screaming reluctance.

Callie took a step closer, until she was a hand span away, and reached up to cup the side of his face with her palm, ignoring the part of her that demanded she take it further. His jaw was lightly stubbled, and his skin was warm and enticing.

Adam's eyes widened with surprise and his spine went ramrod-straight.

With great effort, Callie took a step back and met his gaze, hoping that nothing in her own betrayed her. "That's what Summer's talking about. We need to be

comfortable enough with each other that our reactions to unexpected touch won't give the game away."

Adam blew out a breath and leaned against his car. "And you're suggesting we practice."

Callie nodded. "Don't worry. It will be aboveboard. Summer will be there as our outsider point of view. If we're going to do this, we need to do it properly."

"Okay. How about you go back with Summer. Give me directions to your place and I'll pick up some food on the way."

As Callie told him how to get to her apartment, her stomach fluttered. She was going to spend the evening practicing touching Adam Hawke.

Or, more precisely, she was going to spend the evening pretending to be unaffected while her husband touched her. And she wasn't even sure that was entirely possible.

Three

Adam shifted the bags of food to one hand and pressed the buzzer for Callie's apartment. When he'd woken this morning, he'd grabbed a quick coffee before heading for the gym. His head had been full of thoughts about the day ahead: a meeting with a potential supplier and some paperwork he needed to catch up on. Not once had he even come close to imagining how the day would truly unfold.

Less than twenty-four hours since Callie had crashed back into his life, his schedule, his family and his life were all in a mess.

He was used to being the one who solved problems, not the one in the middle of the trouble. But one day with Callie Mitchell had turned the tables on him.

And worse, he might be getting ready to participate in a sham of a marriage, but he'd learned one thing

today—his desire for his wife was anything but imaginary. It threatened to overwhelm him anytime she was near. But he had to keep any reaction to her buttoned down. If he was to survive what was coming with his sanity intact, he'd need to keep a very clear line between what was real and what was part of the PR plan.

The door buzzed and opened, and he headed into the foyer and took the elevator to the sixth floor.

Callie was waiting in the doorway to her apartment, giving him a nervous smile, and his shoulders relaxed a little. He was glad he wasn't the only one uncomfortable about the situation.

He held out the bags in offering. "I wasn't sure what you liked, so I got sushi, Chinese and pizza."

Summer popped her head around the corner. "Great. I call dibs on the sushi." She grabbed the bags and headed back into the apartment, leaving him in the doorway with Callie.

She'd changed into jeans and a sky-blue top, and her long, caramel hair was caught up in a sleek ponytail. She looked understated and utterly desirable.

"Look," she said, digging her hands into her pockets, "I just want to say how sorry I am that you're caught up in this."

He frowned, not quite following her thinking. "I signed the marriage license right beside you."

"But no one would ever have known if it wasn't for my job. And my slimy coworker."

"Still not your fault," he said dismissively. "Besides, you never know what journalists would have found once they started digging for dirt when Liam and Jenna's wedding drew closer."

If anyone was to take the lion's share of the blame, it

should be him. Among his brothers, he'd always been the one who could be relied upon to be the most responsible, a trend that had started when they were kids and his parents would leave him in charge of Liam and Dylan. It was one of the reasons they'd voted him CEO of the entire Hawke's Blooms company.

Whenever he'd relaxed his guard too much in the past, bad things had happened. Like when he was thirteen and making out with his first girlfriend behind the sheds after school, and a ten-year-old Dylan had wandered off and been missing for two hours. Adam had been frantic. He'd eventually found Dylan safe, but with cuts and bruises from a fall. Adam had been more careful to watch his brothers after that.

Then there was the time he'd let himself get rolling drunk on a trip to Vegas and wound up married...

He followed Callie into the spacious apartment and across to the kitchen. Summer had pulled out some plates and cutlery and she handed them to him to take to the table.

As he watched the sisters work together, a thought occurred to him. "Have either of you had to do this with clients before?"

Callie's brows drew together. "Pretend to marry them?"

"Ah, no," he said as he put down the food. "I meant coach people to act like they were..."

"In love?" Summer observed, and he gave a curt nod.

Callie pulled out a chair and sat across from where he was standing. "No, this is a first for us."

He should have been disconcerted by their lack of specific experience, yet part of him was glad. If she'd been a professional at being able to fake adoration,

while he was an amateur, the situation would have been too uneven. He hated feeling like he was in someone else's hands.

"Actually," Summer said, "we should be starting now. You two sit beside each other."

His instinct was to keep more distance between Callie and him—to keep out of arm's reach—but the suggestion was reasonable. A couple in love would take every opportunity to be close. He crossed around to the other side and sank into the chair beside Callie's.

This close he could smell her coconut shampoo. It immediately brought back memories of his fingers threaded through her glossy hair. Of it spilling across the pillow while he was above her. His skin heated and suddenly his tie was too tight around his throat. He loosened it and tried his best to appear impervious, which was easier said than done.

He glanced casually at his wife as he spooned fried rice onto his plate. "I assume your plan is that we spend some time near each other so we become accustomed to the other's presence."

"Pretty much," Callie answered. "Though we should do some deliberate things, as well, not just passively sit beside each other."

He stilled. He was only just coping with sitting this close. "Define *deliberate things*."

Callie shrugged as she grabbed a sushi roll from the platter. "Occasional touches. Holding hands. Just so when we do it for the cameras, neither of us flinches. We need to seem used to it."

He relaxed again. That made sense and didn't seem too intimate. As long as he had his reactions to her under control, it wouldn't be a difficult task.

Bracing himself, he reached over and threaded his fingers through hers. "Like this?"

"Just like that," she said, her expression professional. But there was a small catch in her voice. "And we should talk about our jobs, and things that married people would know about each other."

Talking. Far preferable to more touching. Holding hands and talking. He could do that.

He rolled his shoulders back, trying to relieve some of the tension that had taken up residence there. "What do you want to know?"

While they ate their meal, she asked questions about his company and he answered. The entire time, he was pretending to be a man unaffected by the woman he was pretending to be in love with. And it was so far from the truth it was laughable—pretending not to be affected was taking so much of his attention he was lucky he didn't stab himself in the eye with his fork.

"This is going well," Summer said, taking another sushi roll. "Adam, how about you feed her something?"

Erotic images of feeding his new wife strawberries in his Vegas hotel room flooded his mind, and he froze. He'd had so much to drink that day that he shouldn't recall it clearly, but he did. He thumped his chest once with his fist to get his lungs working again.

Suddenly, he realized he hadn't replied, and his face probably had a weird expression. He coughed to try to cover it. Summer and Callie, however, had noticed, and each raised an eyebrow.

"Sorry," he said. "This is just awkward."

While Callie looked down at her plate, Summer regarded him with a quizzical expression. "You've never

held hands with a woman or fed her food? That's all this is."

"If I was involved with a woman," he assured her, "these things would definitely happen, but organically."

Callie drew in a shallow breath and met his gaze, and he was certain she was remembering the same moments he was. When she'd laughed and flirted with him at the conference cocktail party. When he'd rested a hand on hers at the bar. When they'd kissed and his world had tilted. When they'd only just made it back to his room before tearing each other's clothes off. When they'd shared more champagne in the bed and accidentally spilled some on their bodies...

The air felt thick with the memories, and Callie's eyes darkened. Most of the blood in his body headed south, but Adam refused to let himself get carried away. He flicked a glance at her sister, who was watching the interplay from across the table, and sighed. This situation wasn't about what he wanted in this moment. It wasn't about fun or entertainment—they were practicing so the world thought they were in love, and he had a responsibility to play his part. He would do that and do it well.

He locked down every physical reaction to the woman beside him, every stray thought or memory. Then he found a fake smile and gave it all the enthusiasm he had, and fed Callie a spoonful of his rice.

She gave him the same overly bright smile back and opened her mouth to receive the fork.

"That's better," Summer said. "Though, Callie, can you put your fingers around his wrist to hold it steady?"

Callie complied and Adam refused to react to the warmth of her hand encircling his wrist. To the scent

of her skin as she leaned in. To the effect on his body of seeing her lush mouth opening.

"Great," Summer said. "Now look into each other's eyes."

Holding his expression in place, Adam focused on Callie's silver-blue eyes, and thought about the pile of paperwork waiting for him on his desk. Spreadsheets and graphs. Anything to ensure he didn't let himself get caught up in a moment that wasn't real.

Callie looked back at him as she gripped his wrist a little too tightly and ate the food from his fork.

Summer sighed. "That wasn't believable. How about we clear these plates away and try a few poses in the living room?"

Callie winced. It was a small movement, and if he hadn't been this close and focusing on her face, he might have missed it. He turned his wrist so he could grab her hand and gave it a slight squeeze, offering reassurance. As he realized what he was doing, he felt like laughing. He'd never had trouble attracting women in the past— hell, he'd even attracted this very woman in the past— yet here he was, offering reassurance because she was going to have to spend a few minutes touching him.

After the table was cleared, they moved into the living room and Callie's sister spent ten minutes arranging them in various poses. It was awkward and he'd pretty much rather be having a root canal than be arranged like puppets by someone he'd just met. Worse was that he was still fighting the simmering desire for his fellow puppet.

Finally, Summer said, "Hang on. Let me show you something." She grabbed a digital camera and hooked

it to a laptop, then took a few photos of Adam with an arm around Callie's waist. "Have a look at these."

Adam moved to the laptop screen and saw the image. He looked stiff and unnatural, and Callie looked almost pained.

"That's not good enough," he admitted.

Callie bit down on her bottom lip. "We're going to have to try harder." She spun away from the laptop and the evidence of their awkwardness, and took in the room. "What if we put on some music? Maybe we could dance. That would give us something to actually do so we didn't feel self-conscious."

"Good idea," he said. In one sense the closeness of dancing could be dangerous, but if he and Callie took back control of the situation he also might be able to regain control of his body. It was worth a try.

Summer headed for the sound system in the corner, and seconds later, a modern day crooner's voice filled the room. Adam held out a hand to Callie. "Shall we?"

She smiled at the formality of his offer and took his proffered hand. "We shall."

Her palm was smooth and warm; the friction of her skin sliding over his set off a depth charge down deep in his belly.

He guided her to an open space between the living room and the entryway that had polished wood floors and less obtrusive lighting. Then he pulled her into his arms and led them in a simple dance step. With the music filling the air, it felt more natural than the poses they'd been trying.

"You were right," he murmured. "I do feel more comfortable."

"Me, too," she said. "Is it okay with you if I move a little closer?"

He chuckled. "We're supposed to be in love. I think you're allowed to get as close as you want without asking permission."

She stepped in and leaned her head on his shoulder. She felt good there. Felt right. As if his body remembered their intimacy. He took his hand from her waist and wrapped it around her, securing her against him, and she let out a contented sigh.

He imagined leaning down, finding her lips and losing himself in her kiss. Then taking her by the hand down the hall to her bedroom...

Except they had an audience.

And they were pretending.

This wasn't real. He couldn't let himself be lulled into falling for the very story they were spinning for the press. He released Callie and stepped back.

"I, er," he said, and then cleared his throat. "That seemed to go better."

Callie nodded. "I was less self-conscious. What did you think, Summer?"

Summer held up her camera and pointed to the laptop. "Excellent. Once you two started dancing, it was totally believable. Just remember how you did it when photographers ask you to pose."

"Sure," Callie said, her voice a little husky. "We'll pretend we're dancing."

Adam rubbed two fingers across his forehead as he contemplated having to repeat this. "Will do," he said, throwing a glance at the door. He needed some space to clear his head. And to rein in his body. "Look, I should head home. Thanks for your help, Summer." He stuck

out his hand, and Summer shook it. Then he turned to Callie. "Callie, let me know when you have an interview set up and I'll clear my schedule."

"I'll get on it first thing in the morning."

He nodded. After the dance they'd shared, it seemed ridiculous to offer her the same handshake as her sister, but then again, they weren't actually dating. He settled on the same greeting he gave his brothers' fiancées and kissed her cheek.

Then he left the apartment. Quickly. Because the stupid part of his brain had told him to kiss her again. And this time, not on the cheek.

Once he was safely inside the elevator with the doors closed, he thumped his head back on the wall and swore. Next time, he'd have better control over his reactions to Callie Mitchell. Next time, it would simply be like two actors in a scene.

Next time…

He groaned and thumped his head against the wall again as he realized this was only the beginning.

Two days later, Callie found herself with a journalist, walking through the Hawke Brothers' flower markets. She was wearing a pale gold dress and kitten heels, her hair and makeup photo-ready.

Adam was striding a few steps ahead with the photographer, who wore ripped jeans and a faded T-shirt. Adam, in contrast, was in a tuxedo, parting the crowd like Moses at the Red Sea. No one walked the way Adam Hawke did—powerfully, and always with a purpose. The jacket fit his shoulders perfectly, highlighting their breadth and strength. It was mesmerizing.

"You sure lucked out in husbands," Anna Wilson

said as she walked in step beside Callie. Anna was the first journalist she'd called when looking for a place to launch the story. She was already a friend, and she had a reputation for writing good, solid stories on famous people that neither simpered over the subject nor made snarky digs.

"Yep, Lady Luck was kind to me that night." Memories of twisted white sheets and Adam's naked physique rolled through her mind, causing her mouth to suddenly go dry.

"Maybe I should try Vegas," Anna said. "If I'm going to try my luck anywhere, then surely luck's hometown will work as well for me as it did for you."

A stab of unease hit Callie squarely in the belly. Luck hadn't smiled on her in Vegas. It had given her a night in heaven, sure, but the price had been high. Spending this time with Adam now might just drive her insane.

"You're not wearing rings," Anna said suddenly.

"Rings?" Callie repeated.

"You know," Anna teased, "those little bands we traditionally exchange when we get engaged and married."

Callie frowned, surprised at herself for missing this detail. When they'd originally exchanged vows, they'd paid for cheap rings that had come from a tray kept under the counter at the chapel. She and Adam had both taken them off the next morning. Hers was in her makeup case where she'd tucked it after sobering up, and she assumed Adam had thrown his away.

"We're getting new rings for the new ceremony," she said, thinking on her feet. "It's symbolic of us starting fresh."

Anna smiled dreamily. "I love that idea."

Adam stopped in front of a large flower stall with

shelves covered in buckets of bright blooms in every color. He said a few words to the photographer, and then turned to Callie. "How about we take some of the photos here?"

She surveyed the scene. The backdrop would provide color and evoke happiness, and the light was good. "This would be great," she said, moving to take Adam's hand.

He leaned in and placed a lingering kiss on her lips, and her pulse went into overdrive. It wasn't difficult to find the blissed-out expression that she was supposed to be faking—in fact, she knew it was on her face, whether she wanted it there or not.

Anna glanced around and conferred with Ralph, the photographer, and then said, "This is good. How about we start with you replaying that kiss for us?"

Callie glanced up at Adam and he looked for all the world as if he could think of nothing better than kissing her again. He clearly had the acting thing down pat. Of course, he probably did still desire her—chemistry as strong as what they'd shared wouldn't likely disappear overnight, but she was well aware he didn't want to give in to it again. And one thing she'd learned about Adam Hawke in the short time she'd known him was that he had iron willpower.

"It would be my pleasure," he said, and wrapped an arm around her waist, pulling her against him as he lowered his head. This time it was no peck on the lips, it was more. So much more. Tempting, sensual and knowing. It was everything. She slid her hands along his wrists, past his elbows to grip his biceps through his shirt, partly to keep him in place and partly to hold herself up.

He trailed his lips to the corner of her mouth and then across to her ear. Whispering her name, he sent a shiver across her skin and bit gently on her earlobe. She turned her face, searching for and finding his kiss, feeling as if she'd found her home, as well.

They eased apart and Callie held on to his arms for an extra beat, her knees too wobbly to hold herself upright, her mind too dazed to think clearly.

"Adam," she whispered, and in response a lazy smile spread across his face.

"That's great," Ralph said. "Just hang on a sec while I adjust some settings."

Surprised out of the little world she'd been in with Adam, Callie took a step back. She hadn't given one thought to acting during that kiss or its aftermath. She'd forgotten the photographer was there. Forgotten the rest of the world. In that moment, she couldn't look at Adam. Didn't want to know if he was looking down on her with pity for getting carried away, or if he was looking at something else, disinterested in her now that they'd performed for the camera. And if he was as off-kilter as she was? Well, some things were better not to know.

To give herself something to do, she turned to take in the picturesque markets around her, the beautiful displays of flowers of all kinds, all colors, and waited for her breathing to return to normal.

As she turned farther, she felt her dress catch on a bucket of lilies near her feet. Not wanting to hurt the flowers, she picked up her knee-length skirt and took a step back.

"Hang on," Adam said, looking at her hemline. "You have pollen on your skirt."

Callie sighed. Pollen was almost impossible to get

out of fabric, and this was a good dress. She went to rub her thumb over it, but Adam held up a hand. "Wait. Rubbing it will only make it worse."

He kneeled down in front of her and took the skirt from her hands, inspecting the stain. Then he retrieved something from his pocket.

"What's that?" She tilted her head to try and see around him to what he held.

Holding it up for her to see, he gave her a quick smile. "Sticky tape. I always carry a roll when I walk through the markets."

"Just normal, everyday tape?" she asked, skeptical about what he was doing, but prepared to give him the benefit of the doubt.

He nodded. "Best thing for it."

She watched as he ripped off a small strip and carefully laid it across the pollen before peeling it off. There was something strangely like a fairy tale about standing amongst the flowers in a pale gold dress with a handsome man on bended knee before her. The fact that he was doing something as practical as helping with her with a pollen mishap, instead of declaring undying love and offering her his kingdom, only made it all the more perfect. Adam Hawke stole her breath no matter what he was doing.

He stood and held the tape out to her. "All gone."

His voice was low and the sound wouldn't have reached the ears of those around them, which made the moment feel intimate despite the topic.

She laughed softly, unable to help herself—it just all seemed surreal. "I can't believe you just did that."

"You learn a lot of tricks when you grow up around flowers." His green gaze was smoldering, out of pro-

portion to a discussion about flowers and pollen, but then again, whenever he was near, she felt her reactions were out of proportion, too.

She moistened her lips, and his gaze tracked the movement. The idea of losing herself in his kiss again pulled at her, drew her with a powerful intensity, but she wouldn't forget the photographer again. She angled her head to where the others stood, watching them, and Adam gave her an almost imperceptible nod.

He straightened his spine, took her hand and turned to Ralph and Anna. "If we go a bit farther down this way, we can get some shots with the Midnight Lily in the background."

Since the Midnight Lily had been developed by Liam and launched less than twelve months ago, it had become one of Hawke's Blooms' signature flowers. And that fact served to remind Callie that this was business to Adam—this session with the photographer and this entire plan. And that included the kiss they'd just shared.

She'd been in danger of being swept away in a moment that wasn't even real.

She couldn't afford for that to happen again. It would be too easy to fall in love with Adam Hawke, especially if she let herself believe he had feelings for her. That way led to heartache a thousand times worse than what she'd experienced when he wanted to call off their short-lived marriage. They were both just playing the roles they'd agreed to when they'd devised the plan.

Now all she had to do was make sure that she didn't fall for her own lies.

Four

Callie was just out of the shower when she heard her sister call out.

"It's gone live," Summer was saying from two rooms over.

"The interview?" Anticipation quickened her movements as she dried off, put on her silk robe and headed for the living room.

"Yep. I didn't expect they'd run it for a few more days yet."

Callie stood behind her sister and peeked over her shoulder at the laptop screen. All the breath left her body as she saw the page. She and Adam had never had a photo taken of themselves together before—their relationship was hardly significant enough to warrant that—and they'd never shared a bathroom to get ready to go out and caught sight of themselves side by side

in the mirror, so she hadn't seen an image of them as a couple reflected back at her. She'd failed to realize the startling effect it would have on her.

There were a few shots of her with Adam among the flowers, but the biggest photo, the one taking up about half the page, was Adam kneeling at her feet, the hem of her dress in his hand.

"That photo is great," Summer said, pointing to the same one Callie was looking at. "The composition is genius. Was that arrangement the photographer's idea or yours?"

"Ours," Callie said faintly, still trying to take it all in.

"Good work. And your expression is perfect. You look totally smitten. All that practice paid off."

Callie couldn't reply; she just kept staring at the photo. Because her sister was right—the woman in that photo looked completely smitten by the man in front of her. And the scary part was she hadn't been pretending. Neither of them had known their picture was being taken.

Pulling the robe tighter, she slid into a chair, leaving her sister to scroll down and read the story. Callie had bigger things to worry about just now. Like whether she was in over her head...

"Hey, wow," Summer said.

"What?" Callie braced herself, unsure if her system could handle anything more than her new emotions for Adam Hawke being on display for the entire world to see.

"I just checked the magazine's social media pages and they've shared it with the headline, 'Princess Wishes New Brother Well on Vegas Elopement.'"

Callie winced. "That wouldn't have been Anna's headline."

"But it's working. Look how many shares it's had."

Callie watched in astonishment as Summer flicked through the various pages. "I didn't think it would be this popular. We only wanted something to counter possible bad stories."

"You've got way more than that," her sister said, grinning. "You've gone viral, baby."

She blinked. Viral? She'd lived her entire life under the radar—it seemed surreal that people were reading about her, sharing her story on social media. "But why?"

"Never underestimate the pulling power of a princess. Especially when rumors are circulating that the Queen of Larsland herself might be flying over to attend your wedding."

"I hope Jenna isn't regretting being involved."

"I'm sure she understands how the media works. Besides, it's not all about her. That photo of Adam kneeling and you being all adoring is like something straight out of *Cinderella*. What was he doing, anyway?"

"Getting pollen off my skirt." She looked at the photo again, remembering that she *had* felt as if she was in a scene from a fairy tale when it happened.

Summer sighed happily. "Even more chivalrous. That picture is gold."

Callie's stomach clenched. This was moving so fast. "I have to call Adam and warn him." She stood and grabbed her cell but stilled when Summer gasped. That sound hadn't been like any of her other sounds of glee as she scanned the pages, and it made Callie instantly uneasy.

"There's a photo of our front door." Her sister's voice was wary.

A wave of anxiety washed over her, making her skin cold. "They found where I live?"

"Worse than that. That photo was taken this morning."

Her lungs froze. Phone still in her hand, Callie moved to the window and sure enough, there was a small but focused group of paparazzi camped around the entrance to her apartment building.

"They're here," she said, her voice uneven. "It's ironic. We spend a good portion of our working lives trying to get stories to go viral, and the one that has is…"

"You," Summer said as she joined Callie by the window.

"Yeah, me." She wrapped her arms tightly around herself. "I honestly thought this would only make a little splash."

"Good news for the Hawke Brothers' Trust, though, since it got a mention in the article. And good news for the trust is good news for your partnership prospects."

The cell in her hand chimed and she glanced at the screen. Adam. Her heart lurched, and she wasn't sure if it was because she was going to have to fill him in on the developments, or if she was glad to hear from him.

She swiped the screen. "Hi, Adam."

"Callie," he said, his deep voice seeming to smooth its way across her skin. "Have you seen the story?"

"Yes. I was just about to call you about it, actually. There are photographers outside my apartment."

Adam swore. "I'm leaving the office now. Pack a bag."

"Wait. What for?"

"You and Summer are coming to stay with me. My security is better."

Part of her wanted to protest—the secret feminine part that was still shocked about the expression on her face in those photos. But she couldn't afford to let that part take control of her decision. She took a breath and called on her professional side. He had a point—she wasn't looking forward to walking through that mob on her way out.

"That might be best," she said, watching the paparazzi through the window. "But don't come here. I'll leave as if I've been visiting my sister. If everything in our story was true, we'd most likely be living together. I'll pack and send someone back to get the bags later."

Summer started pointing and gesturing, asking if she was going to move in with Adam. Callie nodded, and mouthed, "Wait a sec."

"Good call," Adam said. "What about Summer?"

"She's flying out in a couple of hours and will be away for a few days. Once they realize I'm at your house, they'll abandon this place, so it should be quiet again by the time she gets home."

"Okay. I'll meet you at my house in one hour—is that enough time to pack and drive over?"

"Perfect," she said, trying not to sound reluctant.

"I'll also send someone over to wait with Summer and drive her to the airport. Just in case the vultures don't leave with you."

Callie flicked a glance at her sister. "Thank you, I'd appreciate that."

One drunken night in Vegas was having more ripple effects than she could have predicted—even Summer

was having her life impacted. Now the challenge was to surf those ripples and get good outcomes for everyone. All while avoiding slipping under and drowning.

Perhaps the biggest danger of drowning was going to be moving into her husband's house. Living with Adam Hawke while pretending to be in love with him. Possibly the craziest plan she'd ever made.

Adam waited in front of his beach house as Callie made her way up the driveway. Restless energy filled his body, and it took all his self-control not to fiddle with the coins in his pocket or tap his foot on the ground.

She pulled up in front of him and stepped out of the car, looking around to take in the surroundings. The ocean breeze flirted with her long hair and she put a hand up to hold it off her face.

His heart skipped a beat at the sight of her. Since the very first moment he'd spied her at the conference they'd both attended two years ago, she'd affected him this way. Stolen the breath right out of his lungs and made the world practically tip to the side.

And that reaction was the exact reason he refused to pursue anything with her—the morning after their vows, or now. She made him feel off balance. She crowded his brain. That wasn't a way he wanted to live his life.

When he'd been young, before his family had moved to California, he'd been close to his grandfather. He'd been named for his father's father, and the love he'd had for him had been mutual. The elder Adam Hawke, however, had been crazy about his second wife. *Crazy* being the operative word. She'd been flippant and un-

feeling, and barely tolerated his family—especially a small boy who hung around too much.

His grandfather had done the lion's share of babysitting Adam once Liam and Dylan had come along, and Adam had adored that special time with his grandfather. Then his step-grandmother had decided that five years of her life was enough to spend married to a farmer and living on a working farm, and threatened to leave.

Blinded by love, her husband had sold the farm— his children's inheritance—and used the money to take her on trips and spending sprees. *Anything* to keep her. She'd hung around until the money dried up and then left anyway.

Adam's parents had already packed their belongings into their car and headed for the West Coast to try their luck now that they'd lost the farm that had been their home and provided their jobs.

Broken and alone, abandoned by the woman he'd called the love of his life, Adam's grandfather had taken his own life.

His parents had broken the news and tried to shield the boys from the worst of it, but Adam was older and had demanded to know the details.

That awful day, standing out in their flower fields so that Liam and Dylan wouldn't overhear, listening to what his parents would divulge and filling in the blanks himself, Adam had made a decision. He'd been twelve years old, but he'd known exactly what he was promising himself.

He'd always be the captain of his own ship. He would never fall for manipulating behavior, or let someone influence him into a major decision against his better judgment.

Obviously his grandfather hadn't entered into his second marriage thinking he was handing over control of his life, despite how it had ended up. And that was the reason why Adam had always needed to be extra vigilant. Anytime he'd been dating a woman and started feeling his guard slipping, or that his mind wasn't one-hundred-percent clear and focused, he got out quickly.

Callie was a threat to that.

He didn't need any more evidence than the fact that he'd gotten drunk and married her.

Yes, Callie Mitchell was most definitely a woman with whom he needed to keep up his guard.

As she walked the distance to reach him, he locked that guard in place around him and double-reinforced it. He was impervious.

"This place is gorgeous," she said, her silver-blue eyes sparkling in appreciation as she took in the views.

He allowed a smile. "It's my favorite place." The ocean soothed him; often it was the only thing that could calm his soul. "Come on inside and I'll show you around."

She followed him up the three steps to the wide porch, and then paused at the open front door and said, "Thank you for the invitation."

Wanting to get this done as quickly as possible, he nodded without stopping, continuing through the entranceway and indicating with a wave of his hand that she should do likewise. He took her on a tour of the main parts of the house, allowing her a moment when the view of the Pacific Ocean through the floor-to-ceiling windows in the living room snagged her attention. They finally ended up in her bedroom.

"This is yours," he said, holding the door open. The

walls and trim were all pure white and the floor was polished wood. The king-size bed was draped in a comforter that was all blues and greens, mirroring the brilliant hues of the view through the window. A decorator had furnished the room following Adam's request to keep it simple.

"I love it," she said, looking from the bed to the window and around the room. "I might never leave."

Reflexively, he flinched, and unfortunately she caught the small movement.

"I was joking, Adam. Relax. I don't have plans to insert myself into your life." Then she laughed. "Okay, I suppose that's what this entire plan is designed to do. But I meant in reality. I won't be trying to snag you or anything."

"I didn't think you had ulterior motives," he said truthfully and blew out a breath. "I'm just not used to living with anyone, so this will be an adjustment."

She arched an eyebrow. "You've never lived with anyone?"

"Not as an adult, no. I have a full-time housekeeper, but she doesn't live onsite. For most of the time that she's here, I'm at work so I don't see her all that often."

Callie lowered her voice. "Does she know? The truth about us?"

He was sure his housekeeper was trustworthy—she'd been hired by Katherine, their family's housekeeper who still worked for Liam and Jenna, and Katherine's standards were ridiculously high. But trust didn't come easy to Adam at the best of times.

"I've given her a week off on full pay so we don't have to worry about her discovering our arrangement. She normally cooks for me, but it seemed easier to just

order takeout while you're here and keep everything private."

"That's probably a good idea. But I can cook, and I don't mind making our meals."

That would be cozy. Sharing a meal at night that she'd cooked for them. And cozy home-cooked dinners sounded like the last thing he should be doing while ensuring his guard stayed in place.

He held up a hand. "Your time is valuable. How about we compromise and I'll ring a catering company and get them to deliver some prepared meals. We'll also need to order some groceries for lunches and snacks."

Her eyebrows shot up. "You'll be home for lunch?"

"I've taken a week off," he said, his casual tone belying the fact that he hadn't had a week off in four years. "I told my office that we're basically newlyweds so we're taking some time together. But we'll both be able to work from home."

Callie glanced around the room and frowned. "I wasn't planning on staying here in some kind of lockdown."

"It helps the believability of our story." And if he could feel other reasons tugging at him? They were best left unexplored. "Besides, if we're not coming and going then those photographers at the gate will get bored and leave. After the week, the story will have lost its urgency and we can resume our normal lives."

"Except for the wedding plans," she said.

"Except for the wedding plans," he agreed. "You'll probably want to stay here after the week, right up until the wedding. But the media's attention will move on enough that you won't be restricted here all that time."

"Okay, sure." She fiddled with the hem of her top—the only crack in her facade of composure. "I'll do the

lockdown. My main focus is the Hawke Brothers' Trust account, and if anything that will be easier to work on while staying with a member of the Hawke family anyway. I've brought my laptop, so I can work from this room easily enough."

"I think we can do better than that." He headed for the hallway and opened the door across the hall. "This guest room is also at your disposal. I have some office furniture being sent over from Hawke's Blooms' headquarters. It should be here in the next hour, and we'll rearrange and set it up in here."

She glanced around again and bit down on her bottom lip. "You didn't have to go to that much trouble, honestly."

"It was only a phone call." He shrugged a shoulder. "This is a guest wing, so you won't be disturbed. My home office is off the living room, and my bedroom is at the other end of the house."

Before she could reply, ringing came from her handbag, and she fished out her cell.

"It's my boss," she said, her expression telling Adam that she was bracing herself for the call.

He nodded and stepped toward the door. "You take it and meet me in the living room when you're done."

As he left the room, he closed the door behind him to give her some privacy and headed for the living room. The windows overlooking the ocean called to him, and he drifted over. Being near Callie—having her in his home—and not reacting to her was testing his will. The effort it took to not allow his desire to intoxicate him left room for little else, making it difficult to form coherent thoughts. Watching the rhythmic crashing of the waves calmed him. Restored order to his mind and system.

Her footsteps sounded faintly at first, and then grew louder as she came down the hall and entered the room. But he was reluctant to turn. He'd only just found his equilibrium again and here she was to destroy it.

"Mesmerizing view," she said softly from beside him.

Her floral scent surrounded him. He took a deep breath and let it out slowly before replying. "It is."

She didn't face him, just stood with him, looking out over the expanse of ocean. Eventually, she said, "My boss saw the internet coverage and he's thrilled. He said if it all comes together, the partnership is mine."

"That's great." This situation needed to lead to a whole heap of good outcomes to be worth the tension it was creating inside him, and one of those outcomes was to boost Callie's career.

"Yeah," she said, chuckling, "I implied I knew what I was doing, so he doesn't realize we're just keeping our heads above water."

Finally, he turned to face her, trying to read her expression. "Regrets already?"

She shrugged. "The odds are finely balanced, but we're still on top of things. Still moving forward."

"Why don't I believe you?" She looked calm, professional, but there was something behind her eyes that told him it was another example of the mask she wore for the world.

She glanced up at him, surprise clear in her expression, and then shrugged. "I guess I'm just used to being the one advising clients on how to deal with PR problems, or implementing solutions, not being the one in the center."

He grinned. It seemed that he wasn't the only one who preferred being in control.

"You know they say doctors make the worst patients," he said gently.

She arched an eyebrow. "What are you saying?"

"Just that it would make sense that you're having trouble adjusting to being on the other side of the clipboard."

She rubbed her eyes and gave him a reluctant smile. "I guess that's true. And on the bright side, I'll probably have a much better understanding of my clients when this is over."

"That's always a bonus in business."

She paused and her expression changed, soured. "He also said that Terence, the guy who threatened to tell the tabloids about us in the first place, had offered assistance with the account if I needed it."

Adam wasn't sure whether to swear or laugh at the man's ridiculous optimism. "Terence obviously has some underhanded scheme in mind. What did you say?"

She tipped up her chin. "That everything was under control."

"Good," he said, wishing there was something he could do about the bottom-dweller who'd threatened Callie. The best he could do was make sure that their plan went off flawlessly so she secured the partnership. Her success would be the best revenge.

The security intercom sounded. Adam pressed a button on the wall, gave instructions to the staff from the delivery truck and let them in. Then he turned back to Callie.

"Come on," he said. "Time to set up your new office."

Five

The next morning, Callie met Jenna and Adam in the living room. After she and Adam had arranged her new office the day before, Callie had stayed there, catching up on emails and phone calls and letting people know she'd moved. At dinner, they'd ordered takeout and she'd eaten hers while still working. So, beyond a quick discussion about what to eat, she'd avoided conversation with her husband ever since he'd shown her around the beach house.

Which was for the best—she'd decided that approach would give her the strongest chance of surviving this craziness. She had a feeling that Adam Hawke sometimes saw right through her, and that made her feel... exposed.

Jenna grinned when she saw her and held up a bag. "I brought breakfast. Pastries and muffins."

Callie took the bag and returned the grin. "You're a goddess. Don't suppose you also brought coffee?"

"I can take care of that," Adam said from the other sofa. "Cappuccino?"

Callie finally allowed herself a glance at him. In the short time of their acquaintance she'd already learned that avoiding looking at him helped a lot in coping with his presence. He had the power to overwhelm her senses if she didn't ease into it.

Though, as she raked her gaze over him now, hungry to simply see him, she had to admit that even easing into it wasn't helping this time. Maybe she should try the opposite strategy—look at him as much as she could and build up a tolerance to him.

Develop immunity to his presence.

He raised an eyebrow and she realized she was supposed to be answering a question. What had it been about? *Coffee. That's right, coffee.*

She'd seen a state-of-the-art coffee machine when she was in the kitchen yesterday, so she jumped at the offer. "An Americano would be great, thanks."

"Jenna?" he asked, turning to his brother's fiancée.

"I'd love a cappuccino."

He nodded and left, and Jenna turned concerned eyes to her. "I was hoping we'd have a moment alone." Her lilting Scandinavian accent seemed to grow stronger as she lowered her voice. "I wanted to check if you're all right."

Callie frowned. "Why wouldn't I be?"

"It's just been a bit of a whirlwind. Many people would find it disorienting."

The situation wasn't as disorienting as Adam him-

self, she wanted to say, but she wasn't prepared to discuss something she didn't fully understand herself yet.

"I'm fine," she said instead. "I'm staying in a multi-million-dollar beach house and Adam set up an office in a guest room for me. I'm *more* than fine."

Jenna patted Callie's knee. "I'm glad. But just remember, you married a Hawke, so you're one of us now."

"We're not—" she began.

"It doesn't matter how long this marriage lasts, or that you're exaggerating your relationship at the moment. You're part of the family. If you need help from any of us, say the word."

Callie's throat thickened. Never in her wildest dreams would she have expected such a warm welcome to the family, especially from a princess who must have spent her life surrounded by people wanting to be close to her.

She swallowed to get her voice to work. "Thank you. I appreciate that more than I can say."

Adam reappeared carrying two coffee mugs, and Callie took the momentary diversion to compose herself. She found a blueberry muffin, then lifted her clipboard holding all her printed-out notes on the Hawke Brothers' Trust. She had all the information on her laptop, but found that in meetings, she was able to forge stronger connections with clients if she had pen and paper in hand. It seemed somehow more personal.

"So I've had some ideas about the trust's PR and I think a couple of them really have legs." She'd stayed up late getting all her thoughts together so she could make a strong proposal.

"Excellent," Adam said. "Before you outline them—

Jenna, have you checked the donations for the trust since our story went public?"

"Actually, I've checked often, including just before I left to come here."

"Any fallout?" Adam asked, and Callie held her breath. The last thing she wanted was to have this blow up in the charity's face. Hopefully they'd had an increase.

"They've gone up. In fact, they've *shot* up. Maybe more in the last twenty-four hours than in all the months since we started the trust."

"Really?" Adam said, and leaned back in his chair, obviously pleased.

"I'm so glad," Callie said. "And relieved."

This would be a great lead-in to their new PR strategy. She couldn't wait to get started, not in the least part because it would give her something to focus on besides her husband sitting across from her.

Jenna nodded. "I've been thinking—I'm sure your ideas are excellent, but perhaps we should be focusing on the wedding? Make *it* the PR campaign?"

Callie's gut clenched tight. It was one thing to do some media interviews to spin a story that protected them from potential damage, but quite another to make it the entire focus. To invite more scrutiny and keep herself in the spotlight. But she'd started this—she'd said yes to Adam's proposal in Vegas, and it was her job that foisted her back into his world, her colleague that had created the problem and her plan to fix it with this wedding. If they decided this direction was in the best interests of the trust, she'd see it through.

Her mind rapidly flicked through the pros and cons,

and landed on the biggest issue of making the wedding itself the PR campaign.

"Where do we stand on the ethics of raising money using a fake wedding?"

"I like that you're concerned about that," Jenna said, and then paused, considering. "Any money that's donated to the trust goes to help homeless children—there's nothing fake or dishonest about that. It's transparent and those children are in genuine need. Also, you and Adam are already married, and you really are going to renew your vows, so that's not a lie, either."

Callie leaned back in her seat. They were good points. "But we're pretending to be in love, so the heart of this campaign wouldn't be authentic."

"It seems to me," Adam said, "that rather than a lie, it's more akin to a PR stunt, which happens all the time. Besides, I don't think we're the only couple in the media who are together for reasons other than love."

"You think the ends justify the means?" Callie asked him. "The benefit to the children?"

Adam nodded. "If we wanted to use that strategy, then yes."

"So," Jenna said. "What do you say?"

Callie felt Adam's gaze on her and lifted her own eyes to meet it. His expression was masked but she knew this wasn't his preferred direction, despite him weighing in on the ethics of the situation. She raised an eyebrow, asking a silent question, and she watched his chest rise and fall once before he gave her an almost imperceptible nod that sealed their course of action.

She turned back to Jenna. "It would make sense to

build on what's already working. Keep things moving along."

"If you both think that's the most effective strategy, I'm on board," Adam said. "Though won't it be a vow renewal?"

"Technically," Callie said. "But in the media we'll mainly refer to it as a wedding—it's more romantic." She flipped to a blank page on her clipboard. "The wedding *is* the campaign."

Jenna smiled. "Sounds fun. What do we do next?"

She mentally switched gears from a woman sitting in a room with a princess and a virtual stranger who was actually her husband, to a public-relations professional who needed to come up with a strategy.

She took a sip of her coffee and set the cup back on the side table as she collected her thoughts. "The main thing will be to keep the trust and our wedding firmly tied together in the public's mind."

Adam rested an ankle on his knee. "We'll mention it in interviews?"

"At bare minimum," Callie said, making notes as the ideas came to her. "But we need to plan specific strategies. Maybe we could sell the wedding photos to one publication, with the money going to the trust."

Jenna sat up straighter. "We could do a professional shoot before that, too, and sell the photos for the trust."

"Like engagement photos," Callie said, "except we're already married so we'll need a different term. Why don't we call them wedding announcement photos?"

"I love that," Jenna said. "If it would help, Bonnie and Meg could be in that shoot."

Adam raised an eyebrow. "You wouldn't feel that was exploiting them?"

Jenna shook her head. "I'd have to check with Liam, but people try to take their photo all the time as it is. This would be something we chose, and it's about family and charity. They're two things that are important in how we're raising the girls."

"If you and Liam are sure," Callie said, "two baby princesses will certainly increase the money we raise from the photos."

Jenna dug into the pastry bag and came out with an éclair as she spoke. "Meg can toddle around, so we could make her a flower girl at the wedding and play that up in these photos."

"Great," Callie said. "Adam, how do you feel about the official wedding announcement photo idea?"

He rubbed a hand across his jaw, contemplating. "The part of this strategy that I like is that the photographer will work for us, so we'll control the shoot and choose which photos we pass to the publication. So I'm okay with it."

There was something in the way he said the words that made her think he'd been as unhappy with the surprise picture of him kneeling at her skirt as she was. She gave him a small smile to show she understood, and his gaze softened in response. That simple change in the way he looked at her set off a domino effect in her body, starting with a tingling in her toes and ending with heat in her cheeks.

She turned back to Jenna and refocused on the task at hand. "We'll implement more strategies to link the trust to the wedding—perhaps make a visit to somewhere the trust assists, with a journalist in tow? But the next thing we should consider is the wedding."

"Do you have thoughts on what you want?" Jenna asked.

Callie nodded. "We have to not think of it in terms of *my* wedding, or *Adam's* wedding. We've agreed this is the PR campaign for the trust, so the details have to be ones that suit the charity."

Adam frowned. "I don't follow. How can a wedding suit a charity for homeless children?"

"Well—" Callie tapped her pen on her notes "—we need to make it stylish, but not over-the-top. If it looks like we've spent a ridiculous amount on a lavish wedding that will only imply that we're out of touch and have too much money. Donations would drop."

"Stylish on a budget," Jenna confirmed. "We can do that."

"Also, we make children a visible part of the wedding. Having Meg as a flower girl is a good start, but perhaps the rehearsal dinner could include one hundred children from a charity the trust supports. No photos that night—we don't want those children to feel exploited or have their identities compromised—we just let the media know that it happened."

"So the hundred children have a fairy-tale night," Adam said, approval warm in his voice, "and we keep the wedding and the trust linked in people's minds."

"Exactly." Callie smiled and tried to ignore how much his approval affected her.

"And we have the Bridal Tulip," Jenna said. "Perhaps sales of the flower in the first week after release—which would be the week of the wedding—could go to the trust."

"I love that idea." Callie made a note. "We could link the advertising to the fact that we'll be using it at a vow

renewal and suggest couples who've already married buy a bunch for their spouse to remember their wedding. Adam, is that feasible?"

Adam shrugged. "Sure. From a business perspective, it would mean increased exposure for the flower, which would help future sales. I'd have no problem with that strategy from a sales or charity angle, even without the wedding."

Jenna glanced about the room, and then frowned. "Speaking of flowers, I've just noticed something. I've only been in this house a couple of times before, but I've only realized this time that there are no flowers."

"You live at the flower farm," Adam said pointedly. "Of course your house is full of flowers."

Jenna shook her head. "Yes, but I didn't always live at the farm." She turned to Callie. "I met Liam when I was Dylan's housekeeper—I'd run from my family and my homeland when I found out I was pregnant. I would have never forgiven myself for causing a scandal for my family because I was an unwed mother. I wound up working incognito as Dylan's housekeeper. Dylan lives in a downtown apartment and he has a delivery once a week. When I worked for him, it was the highlight of my week to arrange the fresh flowers."

Callie looked around. Now that Jenna mentioned it, it did seem strange that a man who had made his fortune from flowers didn't have a single one in his house. In fact, besides furniture, the space was practically empty. No personalized…well, anything.

"It would be a waste since I'm at work all day." He waved a dismissive hand.

Intrigued, Callie persisted. "Do you have any on your desk at work?"

"No." He shifted in his seat. "But I do look at photos of flowers several times a day."

Perhaps Adam Hawke needed to slow down and literally smell the roses. He had this great view from the living room, but had admitted he was rarely here. It seemed most of his life was work. But she didn't want to push too hard in front of Jenna.

In front of Jenna? Jenna was his actual family—if anyone was going to press him, she would have more right. Not a virtual stranger who'd been plonked down in the middle of his life.

Uncomfortable with the stark reminder of reality, she changed the subject. "Okay, is there anything else we need to focus on at this stage?"

Jenna glanced from Adam's hands to Callie's. "Do you have rings?"

Callie felt her thumb rub over her naked ring finger of its own volition.

"Not yet," she said to Jenna. "In fact, Anna asked about them at the photo shoot and I said we were getting new ones for our fresh start, but then the whole thing slipped my mind."

"I'll call a jeweler this morning," Adam said. "I'll get them to come to the house with a selection as soon as they can arrange it."

Adam had spoken in a pragmatic tone, yet the idea of looking at rings with him sounded just a little bit magical. Ruthlessly, she pushed the thought away. This was not the time for flights of fancy.

Jenna flicked through her notes and looked up. "What about the bachelor and bachelorette parties?"

Adam cocked his head. "Is that what we'd call them when we're already married?"

Jenna shrugged. "We can call it something else if you prefer. Technically you're not a bachelor, but it's like the vow renewal being called a wedding."

"You know," Callie said, "I think it would be simpler for the sake of the campaign to call them bachelor and bachelorette parties, even if it's not strictly correct. Everyone knows what the term means."

"Suits me." Jenna made a note. "Here's another thought. Since neither of you need a traditional farewell to your single life, how about we do something different with them?"

"How different?" Callie asked.

Jenna smiled. "We could hold them jointly."

"A bachelor-bachelorette double bill?" Adam asked, rubbing his jaw. "Sure, why not?"

Callie's mind kicked into high gear. "That could work. It would be an integral part of the overall strategy, and we'd invite a journalist along to cover the event."

Jenna nodded. "And instead of bachelorette games, we could have some fundraising events during the night."

"That's just the sort of thing that's non-traditional enough to get some traction in the media. I'll start getting some ideas together and send them to you." Callie glanced down and reviewed the notes she'd made. "I think we have enough for now. Adam, if you organize the rings and get things set up for the Bridal Tulip sales to go to the trust in the first week, and, Jenna, if you start setting things up with the charities the trust supports for the children to attend the rehearsal dinner, then I'll get to work on a plan for the rest."

"Done," Adam said.

"Will do," Jenna said. "Faith will be back in town

in a couple of days. Shall we schedule another meeting for then? I know she's keen to do something with the Bridal Tulip on her show, and she'll love the idea of linking it closely to the children. She'll want to be part of the planning."

"That would be great. How about the same time, same place, in two days' time?"

"I'll bring the pastries." Jenna packed her things into her handbag and stood. "Now I'll head home to Bonnie and Meg. As soon as I make it through that throng at your gate."

Callie winced. "That's one aspect of your life I don't envy. They'll fade away for me, but you'll always have the paparazzi following you."

Jenna shrugged one shoulder. "I'm used to it. I grew up with public scrutiny, so I barely notice anymore."

"How do you deal with it?" A princess was probably the perfect person to ask for advice.

Jenna flashed a resigned smile. "You learn to let go of the worry. The media will always want what they can't have."

Callie thought about that for a moment. "So basically, our strategy is going to give them what they want and it will benefit the trust."

"See," Jenna said, walking to the door. "You're smart about dealing with them already. Now you forget about them."

They said their goodbyes and Jenna went out to her car, leaving Adam and Callie standing in the foyer together.

"Forget about them," Adam said wryly.

Callie turned on her heel to face into the house again.

"While we're here in lockdown, we don't have to think about them."

"True, but we might go stir-crazy."

She gave him an assessing look. She hadn't thought about the impact this was having on him besides the inconvenience of having her move in. But it made sense that a type A personality who was used to overseeing a vast company would find this lockdown rather confining.

She wanted to offer to help, but didn't know him well enough to know how.

"Do you want to watch a movie or something?" she offered.

His expression gentled. "Thanks for the offer, but no. I have a lot of work to get done today, including a video call in about ten minutes."

"Right. Of course," she said, feeling stupid for making the offer. "I have a lot to do, too. I'd better, uh, go and do it."

He reached out and grasped her hand. "I really do appreciate the offer. It was sweet."

"Oh, that's me," she said on a dry laugh. "Sweet as pie."

Something that looked like a genuine smile flitted across his face. "I've been thinking about your offer to cook. I should have been the one offering. I can do tacos—refried beans, guacamole, shredded lettuce, tomatoes, cheese, salsa."

He was the one who seemed a little uncomfortable this time, and she smiled indulgently. "Sounds nice."

"All the ingredients are in the fridge, so if you'd like, I can make them for dinner tonight. Say, eight o'clock?"

She froze as she realized that would mean sitting

alone with him, sharing a meal in an intimate setting, all while pretending not to be affected by him—a task that was fast becoming harder than pretending to be in love with him for the cameras.

Then she remembered the new strategy she'd decided on this morning. Spend more time with him, look at him more. Develop immunity.

Dinner would be her Adam Hawke vaccination.

She drew in a breath and nodded. "I can't remember the last time I had a good taco. I'm in."

"Eight o'clock, then."

"Eight o'clock," she said and watched him walk away.

One thing that interested her was that he'd taken a throwaway comment and thought about it. Moreover, he was making an effort to do something.

There was more to Adam Hawke than she'd even suspected.

Adam answered the security buzzer and let the jeweler through the gates out front. Luckily the man had been able to schedule a visit for the same afternoon. Well, either it was luck or enthusiasm over being the provider of rings for a wedding that was getting media coverage. Either way, Adam appreciated that it would be dealt with so quickly. He was no fan of loose ends.

He'd let Callie know the jeweler was on his way and she was waiting in the foyer for him.

"I guess it's showtime again," she said with a half-hearted attempt at a smile.

He dug his hands in his pockets and sought a calm that he didn't currently feel. "We're back to a couple in love."

There was a small change to her stance, a slight stiff-

ening in her spine, but then she relaxed her shoulders and gave him a more believable smile. Still not a real one—he had memories of those burned into his brain from their time in Vegas.

"At least we've had a little practice this time," she said brightly.

"Listen, when he's here, just choose whatever ring you want." He said it casually, just wanting them to be on the same page, but as the words left his mouth he realized how unromantic that had sounded. Sure, they were playing roles and she didn't need romance when no one was looking, but still, didn't all women dream about moments like this? He gave himself a mental slap. He should be sensitive.

"Sorry, that sounded very…"

"Unromantic? Practical?" she queried. He nodded and she chuckled. "Adam, don't worry about my delicate sensibilities. For better or for worse, we're in this together. And if we can't be honest with each other, then who else have we got?"

"Okay, good."

The doorbell chimed and Adam opened it to the jeweler, Daniel Roberts, who was accompanied by a well-built man in a suit carrying a heavy-looking reinforced briefcase.

Adam stuck out his hand to the first man. "Thanks for coming on short notice, Mr. Roberts."

"Good afternoon, Mr. Hawke. Mrs. Hawke. You're very welcome. Thank *you* for choosing us."

Adam slid an arm around Callie's waist as he stepped back to allow the men entry. Interesting how natural it felt to hold her against him. They'd been pretending to be a couple for less than a week, yet already it was

beginning to feel like second nature. Like she fit him perfectly.

They all walked into the living room, which now had more people in it in the past twenty-four hours than Adam could remember ever being there before. Once they were settled, the jeweler brought out tray after tray of exquisite rings.

Callie played her part well by oohing and aahing and looking tickled pink as she modeled various rings for Adam, and he, in turn, smiled indulgently.

He also spent the time acting like a man besotted, which generally involved sitting on the armrest of the sofa she'd chosen and touching her.

Even though she'd given him permission to touch her in these situations, he still wanted to respect her boundaries, so he settled on stroking the skin from her shoulder down to her elbow—a fairly innocuous area. It was silky soft beneath his fingers and every stroke made his gut swoop. The scent of her coconut shampoo surrounded him, cocooning him from the rest of the world. Perhaps spending time together in this charade would be more pleasant than he'd anticipated.

Thankfully, Callie took the lead in choosing the rings, finding a plain gold band for him and offering it up to him for an opinion. He didn't care, as long as he could stay like this, touching her skin, surrounded by her scent, pretending to be in love with her. In some ways, this was a perfect way to spend a day. He could spend some time enjoying being near her, with the safeguard of them both knowing the limitations of their arrangement. Callie wouldn't read too much into it, and he wouldn't get carried away. Control would be maintained.

She offered a pretty solitaire diamond for approval and he murmured, "It's perfect," before dropping a kiss on her temple.

A delicate pink flush stole up her throat to bloom on her cheeks. He knew it was probably embarrassment, but in the role of besotted new husband, he chose to interpret it as Callie liking his touch. A thought more appealing than it should have been.

When they'd made love in Vegas, she'd responded to him with no reservation—something that had moved him deeply. Now that they knew each other a little more, would she still be unguarded with him if they made love? Or would that have been lost because of their complicated relationship?

Of course, the point was moot—she was the last person he should be thinking of sleeping with. If they did, how would he be able to walk away from her a second time? It had been hard enough when they had no ties between them besides a piece of paper. Now? Things were so much trickier.

And one thing was certain—walking away once this was over was imperative. He didn't want their fake relationship to become real. At least on that they were in agreement.

He glanced down at Callie as she tried on wedding rings and a thought hit him with the force of a Mack truck—*were* they in agreement?

Callie had wanted to dissolve their marriage, and seemed uncomfortable with their current arrangement…but what if she was secretly hoping this could turn into something more?

"Very fine choices," the jeweler was saying. "I can see you have exquisite taste."

The man began putting the trays back into the special briefcase, and Adam stood, still reeling over the questions in his mind.

"Thank you, you're very kind," Callie said.

"Yes, thank you," Adam echoed. He moved to the side to give Callie room to stand, but this time he didn't stay close to his wife or touch her. He needed to be certain of what she was thinking before he did that again. Why had they never explicitly discussed it?

He walked ahead and opened the front door for the visitors.

The jeweler stuck out his hand. "I'll give you a call the moment the rings are resized and ready to be picked up."

"I appreciate it," Adam said, shaking his hand.

The two men left and Adam was once again alone with Callie. It was the perfect opportunity to have an honest conversation about where Callie saw their relationship heading, yet part of him wanted to put it off. If she was hoping it would evolve into something permanent he'd have to lay his position on the line, which would hurt her. Callie was the last person he'd ever want to hurt.

Then again, if she really did feel that way, the longer he let it go before addressing the issue, the more she'd be hurt. He had to do it now.

She turned. "I'll just head—"

"Can we talk about something first?"

"Sure," she said, turning back and folding her arms under her breasts.

Now that he'd started, he wasn't quite sure how to word it. The topic called for finding a balance between clarity and sensitivity.

He drew in a long breath. "Ah, I just wanted to touch base with you about our situation."

"What do you mean?" she asked, her head cocked to the side.

"We made this plan that day in my office, and since then it seems to have taken on a life of its own."

She chuckled. "It has rather become a bit of a monster, hasn't it?"

"Do you want to call it off?" he asked, watching her reaction carefully.

Without hesitation, she shook her head. "I want the partnership. And from Jenna's figures, it's helping the trust." She unfolded her arms and tucked one hand into her back jeans pocket. "Do you want to call it off?"

"No, I made a commitment and I'll see it through." He shifted his weight, wishing he'd found somewhere more comfortable for this conversation. "I also need to check that you're not hoping for…more."

She frowned. "More?"

"From me," he said simply. Clearly. No misunderstandings. "From the marriage."

She arched one eyebrow. "You think I'll succumb to your charms and beg you to make the marriage real?"

Adam flinched. Said like that, it did sound over-the-top. "Sorry, I didn't mean to offend you. But I have to make sure that we want the same things. That I wasn't leading you on."

"No one could accuse you of leading me on, Adam," she said drily. "As soon as we're not in front of people, you drop the act pretty quickly."

He felt as if he was missing half the conversation. Was she saying that was a problem? She'd just mocked

him for suggesting she might want more, so surely she *wanted* him to drop the act as soon as he could?

But before he could find the right question to work out what he was missing, Callie had turned away.

"I'll see you at dinner," she said over her shoulder and walked down the hall.

"Sure," he said to her retreating back, and wondered if he'd ever completely understand her.

Six

Callie pushed her empty plate away and sighed in satisfaction. "You undersold your cooking abilities."

Adam shrugged a broad shoulder. "My repertoire is small. Basically the tacos you just had and scrambled eggs. I have dreams of one day branching out into pizza."

Callie laughed—both at the words and from surprise at his easy self-deprecating humor. Adam Hawke liked to stay buttoned up, but she suspected if he ever let his guard down he could be a whole heap of fun.

No, scratch that. She didn't suspect it— she knew it. Their time in Vegas had been amazing. On the way to the chapel, they'd laughed and run through a fountain, and on the way back, Adam had insisted on carrying her over the threshold of the hotel, much to the amusement of the security team and everyone else in the foyer.

"Penny for your thoughts," he said.

She glanced up. "You really don't want to know."

"I offered money, and I'm always serious when it comes to money," he said, a grin dancing at the corners of his mouth.

Still she hesitated. Should she lie and avoid talking about a time she knew he regretted, or do as he asked? She was never quite sure with Adam. Always second-guessing herself.

He fished a hand into his pocket and threw a quarter onto the table. It rolled and did a few lazy spins in front of her plate before falling flat.

She picked up the coin and flipped it over in her fingers, not meeting his gaze as she spoke. "I was thinking about the people we were in Vegas. Would those people even recognize the man and woman sitting at this table?"

His fingers started tapping on the side of his wineglass, until he looked at them, as if surprised to find them moving without his permission. They abruptly stopped. "You mean me, don't you? You're basically the same, if a little more subdued without the alcohol."

She dared a glance at his eyes. They were the dark green of a deep, stormy ocean, and they made her heart catch in her chest.

"I guess I did, yeah." She took a sip of her wine and then studied him over the rim. "I saw a side of you that you rarely let out to play, didn't I?"

His fingers began to tap again, before they once more abruptly stopped. "Do you want to get out of here? I'm going stir-crazy."

It was the same phrase he'd used earlier when talking about the possible problems of their living arrange-

ment, but now he was admitting to feeling trapped. It seemed quite a strong admission coming from a man who usually kept his innermost feelings and reactions locked down tight, and part of her was glad he'd shared even this small snippet with her. But that didn't mean she was going to leap at his suggestion.

"I know that now that we've changed the plan to the wedding becoming our PR strategy we don't need to be in lockdown anymore. In fact, we'll probably want to be seen together a couple of times before the ceremony— maybe dinner out or something. But I don't think I'm up to being that public just yet."

"There's only one guy out in front now," he said with a dismissive shrug, "and if we go out the back door down to the beach, he won't know."

It seemed too easy after the drama of the past couple of days. "What about other people?"

"It's usually pretty deserted at night, but I have some sweats you can borrow to make sure no one recognizes us."

The idea of escaping the four walls around them without causing a spectacle was too good to pass up.

"Let's go," she said.

As she cleared their plates, Adam left and returned a few minutes later in nondescript gray sweatpants and a matching hoodie. He passed a black set to her.

"You'll have to roll the legs up, but not too much— you're so tall that I think I only have a couple of inches on you. The top will swim on your frame, though, sorry."

She took the clothes and held them against her chest. Even though they were clean, they smelled of him and she had to fight the impulse to breathe in the scent. "Ev-

erything I brought is brightly colored, so I'll be much less visible in these." Even if she would be completely surrounded by his scent.

A few minutes later she'd changed and they were heading down the outdoor stairs that separated his yard from the beach. A gentle breeze blew, and the moonlight sparkled on the inky water. They made it through the soft sand to where the edges of the waves played around their bare feet.

"I always forget how much I love the beach," she said, trying to take it all in at once. "I live in LA, but hardly ever take time to enjoy its treasures."

Maybe Adam wasn't the only one who needed to stop and smell the roses. When things returned to normal, she was going to make some changes, starting with regular visits to the beach.

"I know what you mean. I bought the house for its location, but…" His voice trailed off.

"But you're at work most of the time," she said.

He let out a short laugh. "Something like that. Do you want to walk?"

"Sure."

For a couple of minutes, they walked in silence until she broke it by saying, "Look, I'm sorry for what I said back at the house. How you live your life is none of my business."

"If it's anyone's business," he said with humor in his gaze, "it would be my wife's."

She sighed and splashed at the water with her toes. "I guess that's the problem. We've crossed lines back and forth so many times that we're going to wind up making mistakes about where they are now."

Silence descended around them once more, but it

was far from comfortable. There was tension in it beyond what had been between them the past couple of days, and it was all coming from Adam. There was clearly something on his mind, so she waited, hoping he'd start talking.

"I saw you looking at the family photos along the wall in the dining room while I was fixing dinner," he finally said.

She stole a quick glance at him, unsure if he was annoyed, but he seemed not to have a problem with it. So she nodded. "You have a very photogenic family."

He seemed to ignore the compliment. "Did you see the older man who was in lots of the photos where we were children?"

She had noticed him. Tall, with striking looks and silver hair. "You look a lot like him."

"My grandfather, Adam Hawke." He said the words without inflection. Without emotion. "I was named after him, and people often told me that I was like him."

"Looked like him?" she asked, sensing there was more to this.

"Looks and personality. I was always fairly serious and responsible, which probably isn't too unusual for an oldest sibling, but it was more than that."

"Your grandfather was serious and responsible, too?" she asked gently, unsure how far to push.

"All his life." He folded his arms over his chest as he walked. "Right up until his second marriage." His expression turned bitter.

"I take it you didn't like his new wife."

"She didn't like me, or any children. But my grandfather couldn't see that. We'd always been close—when my parents had two more babies, he was the one who

babysat me. He taught me to ride a bike." Adam looked up at the starry sky before letting out a humorless laugh. "He used to tell me all the time that my father would inherit the farm from him, and one day it would all come to me."

She'd known this wasn't going to be a happy story from the start, but a feeling of foreboding was growing in her belly.

"What happened to the farm, Adam?" she asked.

"His wife said she was leaving because she hated being stuck on the farm. So he sold it and spent all the money on her." His voice became flat, hard. "It didn't matter enough that we were all living on that farm, or that my dad was working it. My grandfather sold it anyway."

Her heart squeezed tight. Having met his parents and brothers, she hated thinking of them in that situation. "So that was your family's home and income gone in one swoop?"

"Pretty much. My parents had saved a little so they used that to move to California and start fresh."

"And your grandfather?" she asked warily. The fact that there had been no recent photo of him was telling.

Adam drew in a deep breath and shuddered as he released it. "After the money ran out his wife left anyway. And so he shot himself."

Callie found Adam's hand and intertwined their fingers, wanting to offer as much comfort as he'd allow. After a moment's hesitation, he squeezed her fingers back.

"How old were you when he died?"

"Twelve."

"What an awful thing for a child to go through. Es-

pecially when you'd been so close to him." If only she could do something to take away the pain, but realistically, she knew that nothing could, except maybe time.

"I learned something that day," he said, sounding resolute. Determined. "You might feel like you're in control of your life. You might think you're on top of the challenges, the way that my grandfather did before he married. But that control can snap at any time, and you lose *everything*."

A lightbulb went off, and Callie finally had an insight into why Adam was so determined to stay in control all the time, and it only made her want to know more. Though one thing didn't add up.

"Why are you telling me this? You think I'm after your money like your grandfather's wife?" She didn't really believe he thought that way about her, but needed to hear him deny it.

Adam shook his head abruptly. "The story wasn't about her. It was about him. About what happens when someone like him—like me—throws caution to the wind."

And suddenly it all made sense. "You keep yourself locked down not because you're less wild than your brothers, but because you're afraid you're the wildest of the three."

"Everybody always told me I was like him," he repeated as if that explained everything.

"That doesn't mean you are," she pointed out.

"Some people go to Vegas and have a drunken one-night stand. I took it a step further and got married."

Everything kept coming back to that snap decision three months ago. "You weren't the only one," she said ruefully.

He continued without missing a beat. "My family wanted to turn a roadside stall of homegrown flowers into their very own store. I created a national company that's still expanding."

"That's a great outcome." The first time she met him, she'd been almost as impressed by his success as by the man himself. Almost.

"It is." He shrugged, as if dismissing the achievement. "But I have a tendency not to do things by halves. If I'm not careful, I get carried away. The only times that works well for me is if I take a considered, logical approach."

"Our wedding wasn't logical or considered," she conceded, and he laughed.

"No, it wasn't." He blew out a long breath. "I learned something with my very first girlfriend."

"Is this going to be a dirty story?" she teased, hoping to lighten the mood a little.

"I was thirteen. How dirty can it get?" he said with humor in his voice. Until he started talking again. "I was supposed to be watching my brothers after school until my parents picked us up, but I was crazy about a girl and I convinced her to sneak behind the shed and make out. Long story short, Dylan went missing on my watch and when we found him he was covered in cuts and bruises."

"Having met Dylan, I have a feeling he spent much of his childhood getting himself into mischief." And probably his adulthood, too.

"Which was even more of a reason to keep a close eye on him," Adam said, clearly disgusted with himself. "But I was carried away and let my guard down."

She tried to imagine a thirteen-year-old Adam, al-

ready serious, but flush with first love. "You were only a kid yourself."

"Maybe, but it was exactly the same thing that happened with my grandfather. Obsessed with a girl and forgot my responsibility to my family."

Her eyes stung, but she blinked any sympathy away before he noticed. He wouldn't welcome it.

How hard had he been on himself back then? She'd bet more than the quarter he'd given her that he'd been harder on himself than anything his parents had dished out.

"I'm guessing you broke up with that girl."

"The next day. I had to."

The jigsaw pieces fell into place. "And anytime you felt yourself getting close to a woman since then, you break things off?"

He didn't need to answer—the way he rolled his shoulders back and glanced over to the horizon told her. They might not be emotionally close, but they were married. His internal alarm must be deafening.

"You're warning me off, aren't you, Adam?"

"No, I'm filling you in. We have a false sense of intimacy around us because of our situation and I don't want you to come to hope that I could give you more than I'm capable of giving."

"I'm not asking for more."

"I know that."

"And I—" She stopped walking and dropped his hand as his earlier words replayed in her head.

The story wasn't about her. It was about him. About what happens when someone like him—like me—throws caution to the wind.

It hardly seemed possible that someone with as much

self-control as Adam Hawke could be worried about his reaction to a woman. To her.

"I get to you, don't I?" she said, hearing the wonder in her own voice.

He didn't bother denying it. "I think our twenty-four-hour marriage already proved that you're a potential trigger for me." He stopped walking again and glanced around. "I think this is far enough. We should start back."

Everything inside her seemed to be unsettled. Agitated. Thrilled. He'd wanted her when they hooked up in Vegas at the three conferences, but he'd played it so cool afterward each time that she'd assumed his attraction to her was nothing particularly strong. Nothing especially urgent. Nothing near how much she had wanted him. Still wanted him.

Wordlessly, she followed his lead. Since the day in his office, when she'd told him about her coworker's threat and they'd embarked on this plan, she'd been feeling at a disadvantage. She'd understood that she had a stronger attraction for him than he had for her.

She'd been wrong.

He was just better at hiding it. More practiced at denying himself.

The newfound power was exhilarating, setting her pulse fluttering.

"You still want me," she said, though she didn't need the confirmation.

"Of course I do." He stopped and faced her. Framed by the star-studded sky, his skin luminescent in the moonlight, he seemed different from both her Vegas groom and her housemate who kept his emotions tightly

leashed. His eyes held a potent mix of surprise and open desire.

"You didn't know?" he whispered.

She swallowed. "You're very good at playing your cards close to your chest."

"That was for my own benefit." He winced, clearly uncomfortable with the confession. "More denial than secrecy."

"I thought I was in this hell alone." Despite his own admission, as soon as the words left her mouth, she wished them back. He may still feel desire for her, but he clearly didn't want to let things develop between them.

She looked over his shoulder at the surf pounding behind him, trying to find her equilibrium. In Vegas, even after they'd sobered up, she'd been infatuated with him. In all honesty, she had been since the first conference where they'd met and she'd spent the night in his bed. By the third conference, when he'd suggested saying vows, she'd been halfway in love with him. His quick backtracking the next morning had taken those fledgling feelings and stomped all over them. Not quite broken her heart, since she hadn't handed that to him, but close.

Her gaze found his again, and she felt the connection like an electric jolt.

If she let herself develop feelings for him now—and that would be such a simple thing to do, given the way he was looking at her, his expression open and troubled—it wouldn't be as easy to shrug off the hurt when he turned away again. In fact, she had a suspicion it would be harder than anything she'd ever had to overcome before. And yet, she couldn't look away.

Couldn't make herself start walking again. Couldn't stop wanting…

"You're not alone," he said, his fingers brushing her hair back behind her ears.

As he touched her cheek, her breath caught and his gaze dropped to her mouth. The sound of the ocean receded and all she could see was him. Adam. His lips were slightly parted, his chest was rising and falling in rhythm with hers.

If she had felt this way about any other man, any other time, she would have leaned in and kissed him, but this was Adam who had just trusted her with his deepest fears about losing control. She had to wait for him to decide. That was if she survived the time it took for his decision. Every moment of hesitation felt like a lifetime.

Her tongue darted out to moisten her lips, and he watched the motion. Her skin grew warmer, and still she waited.

Finally, with a groan, he reached out and wrapped his arms around her, pulling her to him. His mouth landed on hers, all heat and need and heaven, and it felt as if they'd never been apart. As if this was where she always wanted to be.

She leaned into him, feeling the strength of his frame as he drew her closer. His tongue stroked along hers, causing a sinfully glorious sensation. The touches they'd shared during their charade were like a candle flame compared to this bonfire. Lost to the magic of his kiss, she reached her hands to thread through his hair.

"Adam," she murmured. In response, he eased back.

For long seconds all she could hear was their loud breaths before the rest of the world began to intrude.

His expression was stunned, which pretty much summed up how she felt. Their chemistry was as explosive as ever.

"Maybe we should keep walking," he said, and she nodded. For some reason a public beach felt more intimate right now than a house with only the two of them.

They headed for home, walking close, but not touching.

"I'm thinking it might have been better if we hadn't had this conversation tonight," she said once her breathing was even.

"The conversation or the kiss?" His tone was lower, rougher than before.

"Both, but I meant the conversation. We're pretending to be head over heels for each other when the cameras are on. Keeping the line between fantasy and reality would be an issue for anyone in a similar situation, but we've just blurred the line a little."

"You think keeping it firmly in place was easy these past few days?" As they walked, he stroked a hand down her back, sending shivers across her skin. "Shutting down my response to you when other people left the room? Hauling myself back when the camera was packed away?"

"There's no alternative—we got ourselves into this situation." Except there was another option, one she'd been refusing to consider. But perhaps now was the time...? "Okay, what if there was? An alternative."

Dark eyebrows swooped down in a frown. "Stage a breakup?"

"No, the plan is still working for the trust and my career. But we're stuck together, alone, letting the world think our marriage is real." Her heart skipped a beat

as she contemplated saying this aloud. "Why not take advantage of the perks of the situation instead of fighting them?"

"Isn't that dangerous considering what we just discussed? This can't go anywhere." His words weren't enthusiastic, but he didn't move away from her side as they walked; his expression didn't close off.

It was a good point to have in the back of their minds, but it didn't have to stop them. "We've already slept together. More than once. And this time we're going in with our eyes open."

They reached the stairs that led to his house, and he turned to her.

"Are you saying you want to have a fling with me, Callie?" His voice was low and as dark as night.

A fling? It sounded so deliciously decadent. Her heart fluttered, and she had a moment's doubt—could she be involved with Adam Hawke again, share his bed, and not start to hope for more? She looked away, then back to her husband. Of course she could. If he could keep his heart guarded, then she could, as well.

"If we're not expecting it to develop into more, what could it hurt?"

He took a step closer. "Are you sure?"

"If you're willing to try it, then I'm in." She crossed her fingers behind her back for luck, hoping she knew what she was doing.

His gaze dropped to her lips and lingered a moment before returning to her eyes. "Then I have a proposal."

"You've been there and done that. I have the marriage certificate to prove it."

The corners of his mouth twitched. "A proposal of a different kind."

"I'm listening." In fact, he had every last scrap of her attention.

"We go inside now and give ourselves tonight." He traced a warm palm down her arm. "One night to share a bed, and we reassess in the morning."

Her body had gone into meltdown at the mention of sharing a bed, but she forced herself to think through what he was offering. "What do you think will be different tomorrow?"

"We make sure we're both happy with the arrangement. Neither one of us feels…emotionally compromised."

"Emotionally compromised? You say the sweetest things." She drew in a breath. "And if neither of us does?"

A slow smile spread across his face. "Then we consider turning this into a fling for the duration of our sham marriage."

Every nerve ending in her body lit up and buzzed. She had trouble finding her voice, until finally she whispered, "Deal."

Seven

Adam led Callie by the hand through the house to his bedroom, resisting the urge to haul her against him the entire way. If he did that, they wouldn't make it to his room, and it was of burning importance to make love to her in his bed.

The other times they'd slept together, the situation hadn't quite felt real. It wasn't just that they'd been drinking, it was also because they'd been at a conference in Vegas, away from their everyday lives. For three years running, they'd carved a slice of time together that didn't have to mesh with their reality.

Tonight things would be different.

Tonight, it was real.

As they reached the threshold to his room, he paused and glanced at Callie. Perhaps because it would be more real than anything that had come before, he needed to

make extra sure she was fully on board with the step they were about to take. Nothing would be the same after this.

Her gaze steady on his, she leaned against him and cupped the sides of his face in her palms. Then she stood on tiptoes and kissed him. Everything inside him burst to life, as if he was hyperaware of each cell in his body. And each cell wanted one thing—to be closer to Callie.

With her mouth moving over his, he gripped her hips, digging his fingers into the flesh there, anchoring him to the world. To have her pressed along the length of him, kissing him, was almost too much sensation at once, but he wanted more.

He tore his mouth away and tugged her toward his bed. Still fully clothed, he half laid, half fell onto the mattress, bringing her with him, and then resumed the kiss. Her mouth was hot and sensuous, and part of him felt as if this was the same kiss from three months ago, that it had been merely interrupted.

He pulled his sweatshirt over his head and then also stripped off the sweatshirt he'd given her. The feel of her skin against his chest was heavenly and a groan of satisfaction rumbled deep inside him.

"I've missed touching you," he said, his voice barely a rasp.

She found his hands and brought them to her breasts, holding them over the cups of her bra for a long moment. "Then by all means, touch me some more."

The note of teasing while her eyes were practically glazed with need was pure Callie. He rolled onto his back, taking her with him so that she was above him, straddling his hips, her torso bare except for the white

lace bra, and he took her up on the invitation to touch her some more.

His fingertips stroked down her sides, across her slightly rounded abdomen, back up to her collarbone. Her skin was smooth and silken and he might never get enough. Then he found her breasts once more and brushed across their peaks with his thumbs. Callie's thighs tightened around his hips and her breath picked up speed. He repeated the motion, this time paying more attention to her reactions. A slow smile spread across his face—she liked it when he did this.

He should already know her likes and dislikes, but the alcohol had distorted his memories. Reaching behind her, he unhooked her bra and tossed it to the side of the bed. He was going to need more freedom to discover everything he wanted to know.

He lifted himself to a seated position on the covers with Callie still straddling his lap, his hands on a journey of investigation. And everything he learned was like a secret as old as time, a secret he was privileged to be granted.

She tried to wriggle back and make room for her own hands.

"Oh, no," he said, staying her hands. "I've been dreaming of this moment. I need a chance to explore."

She smiled and rested her hands on her thighs, allowing him this.

"Thank you," he said, punctuating it with a kiss on her collarbone, then another. When he reached her shoulder, he scraped his teeth across the skin, tasting as he went. She was faintly salty, with a trace of soap… and something extra—something that was hers alone.

He laid her down on the cover and pulled the track

pants from her legs, taking her underwear with them. The sight of her naked was one thing he had retained complete memory of from their twenty-four-hour marriage and the times they'd come together before that, and yet…she still amazed him.

"Callie."

Her gaze softened. "Nobody's ever looked at me the way you do."

He prowled over her on all fours, leaning in to whisper, "Then they were blind," before taking her earlobe into his mouth, glorying in her gasp.

He kissed a path down her body, until he reached the juncture of her thighs. She deserved to be worshipped, and he set about doing just that. Every whimper that escaped her lips urged him on, every time she writhed under his mouth made him want to push her further. When she reached her peak and shouted his name to the ceiling, a surge of satisfaction filled his chest.

He pulled himself up the bed, holding her as she floated back to earth, feeling more content than he could remember. Finally, her eyes fluttered open and he wanted to do it all again, to make her call his name, so he raised himself on one elbow and trailed a hand over her stomach.

She gently pushed him back against the pillows.

"It's my turn to explore," she said, her eyes sparking. His pulse spiked. He reached up and gripped the headboard and then nodded. "That's fair."

Her fingers lightly caressed his chest, sending goose bumps racing across his skin, and, as she moved down lower, his abdomen clenched tight at her touch. Then her tongue began to follow the same path, her teeth nip-

ping every few heartbeats. He was on fire. The things she did to him with mere touches… It was craziness.

She moved farther south, and her mouth found him hard and ready. Her tongue licked up one side then down the other, and he gripped the headboard so forcefully he was surprised it didn't break. Her hand joined her mouth, and he groaned out her name, trying to restrain his body from thrashing against the sheets, knowing he couldn't stay completely still, but not wanting to break the contact with her mouth.

She moved higher, to his stomach again, then higher still, until her pelvis was over his groin, pressing down with luscious pressure. She kissed him, and he released his grip of the headboard to wrap his arms around her, finally touching her again.

Holding Callie in his arms was everything. The friction of skin on skin as they moved was bliss, almost more than he could stand. Not breaking their kiss, he rolled them over until they were side by side, and hooked a knee over her legs, wanting to touch her everywhere at once. His heart thundered in his chest, his mind swam. This was more than making love, but what did that make it?

Her hands began a journey down his sides, over his thighs and back to grip his length. He rested his hands on hers to hold them still. He needed to find protection before things went too far and he lost capacity for thought altogether—a place he was already dangerously close to. The only problem was, where would he find any? He didn't normally like people in his personal space, so even when he was seeing a woman, he rarely brought her here. He squeezed his eyes shut as

he forced his brain to reengage. Bathroom. There was a box in his private bathroom.

"Hold that thought," he said and came close to breaking the land-speed record on the way to retrieve a condom.

When he made it back to Callie's side, she put her hand out. "May I?"

He handed it over without hesitation. He'd be crazy to say no anytime she wanted to lay a hand on him. As she opened the foil packet, and then held him in one palm and started rolling the condom down his length, he let out a low groan. The torment of her touch, of it never being enough, was going to kill him.

He eased down to lie along the length of her, pulling her close, needing to feel as much of her body against his skin as he could. As he kissed her, she threaded her arms around him, lightly trailing her fingernails down his back and digging into his buttocks in a delicious nip of sensation.

The kiss became more passionate, his body's demands more insistent, and when Callie began to writhe against him, clearly needing more, he rolled her beneath him and settled himself in the cradle of her thighs. Her hands still gripped his rear end, encouraging him, so he reached down and positioned himself, and then found her silver-blue gaze. How could he have forgotten how exquisite it was to have this woman in his bed? Never again—he'd remember every second of tonight for the rest of his life.

With deliberate slowness, he stroked into her and then held still, savoring the sensation of Callie holding him inside her. But too soon, the insistent beat in his body demanded he move, so he lifted his hips before plunging back again.

She lifted her legs and wrapped them around his waist, changing the angle, and he clenched his jaw as he fought for self-control. He wouldn't let this be over too soon. They'd only agreed on one night, and, though he would definitely vote for many more, he was acutely aware this might be the last time he made love to her. He wanted to make the most of it.

Once his—admittedly tenuous—grip on control was back in place, he began to move again, and she moved with him, finding their rhythm, moving together in a ragged harmony. His body urged him to rush headlong to the goal, his mind wanted him to slow down and take in each detail. The result was somewhere in the middle.

His eyelids grew heavy, but he fought to keep them open, gaze fixed on her face. In that moment, she was the most beautiful woman in the world, her skin glowing, her eyes hungry. For him. It made him burn for her even more.

Each stroke seemed to spark every nerve ending in his body, made his pulse race faster.

She was close, he could see it in the tension in her muscles, in the way her breath was coming in short pants. He reached between them, to the place they were joined, and stroked, and she froze, clenching around him and calling his name, until he couldn't hold on any longer and followed her over the edge. Everything inside him, around him, dissolved into bright light and all there was in the universe was Callie. *Callie.*

Callie.

Callie woke curled around Adam. He lay on his back, one arm above his head on the pillow, the other holding her firmly against him. His breathing was even in

sleep, and she carefully inched up on an elbow to look at him in the early-morning light streaming through the window.

His dark hair with its hints of deep mahogany was striking against the white pillow. Her gaze traveled languidly from there, past defined cheekbones to a jaw covered in day-old stubble. He was a picture of masculine beauty, and something moved in her chest as she watched him.

"Regrets already?" he asked without opening his eyes. His voice was gravelly with sleep, and it seemed to reverberate through to her soul.

She eased back down and snuggled into his warmth. "Just looking at what I've got myself into."

His chest rumbled under her ear with a lazy chuckle. "And do I pass muster first thing in the morning?"

"You'll do," she said, her voice teasing.

His eyes blinked open and focused on her. "You'll more than do. Early morning in my bed suits you."

The comment triggered a contented warmth, which spread through her body. In fact, this could easily become her favorite place to wake up, but she didn't want to scare him, so she didn't reply. Instead, she stretched against his luxurious sheets and glanced around the room.

She hadn't paid much attention to the master suite when they'd come in last night, but it deserved a good look. It was huge, done in the same white-on-white color scheme as the rest of the house, with indigo-blue blinds and comforter. A deep navy blue sofa sat beside a bank of white doors to closets that must hold all his clothes and personal items.

"You like plain decorating," she said.

"I like simplicity."

She turned back to face him. "Is this another facet of what you were talking about last night?"

"About only being able to cook tacos and eggs?" The corners of his mouth twitched.

He was being deliberately obtuse, and it delighted her to see him so relaxed. She lightly punched him on the arm and said, "Strangely enough, I wasn't thinking of cooking. I meant about you keeping your wild side under control. You deliberately keep things simple and plain. Not a lot of color, no flowers in the house, nothing to rouse the passions."

"There's you," he said and reached for her.

She went into his arms because it was still a novelty to have him unreservedly want her there, and because he was Adam. It was possible she would never deny him anything.

"In all seriousness," he said once he'd tucked her against him again, her face comfortably nestled under his chin, "we said we'd talk about this—about us—this morning. How are you feeling about moving our relationship in this direction?"

"You mean us starting a fling?" It had been his word, and she wanted it on the table, no confusion.

He nodded. "What are you thinking today about us having a fling while you're staying here? I've probably got another quarter around here somewhere if these thoughts cost as much as last time."

"These thoughts are free." She rubbed a hand over his chest as she spoke. "Having to keep my guard up around you, quite frankly, was exhausting. If we continue, besides the obvious advantage of more nights like last night, I'll have a place I can be relaxed."

"I want you to be able to relax while you're staying in this house," he said, his voice gentle. "That would mean a lot to me."

The unexpected moment of tenderness moved her, and she reached up to place a kiss on his lips that was full of appreciation, though it quickly escalated into something much more. More beguiling. More intimate. More spine-tingling. Just more.

Long moments later, she broke away and lay back against the pillows to catch her breath. His darkened gaze followed her, his chest rising and falling in a similar heavy rhythm to hers.

"What about you?" She laid a hand along the side of his face, the day-old stubble exquisitely abrasive against the flesh of her palm. "How are you feeling about us?"

"Now that I have you back in my bed, I'm reluctant to let you leave again, so I'm all for this plan. In fact," he said, trailing fingers down her side, "I think we should explore the finer points of the plan this morning."

"I'm open to exploring that option," she said, and kissed him again. Whether or not she survived this fling with her heart intact, she had a feeling she was in for the time of her life.

It had been two days since she and Adam had agreed to have a fling, and they'd spent a good portion of that time in his bed. Even when they'd been doing something else, her mind had been filled with memories of making love with him, or plans to maneuver him back to his bedroom.

Today, though, they were having their official wedding announcement photos taken. They'd booked their own photographer to come out to Liam and Jenna's

flower farm, and Callie had asked her friend Anna, the journalist, to come along, as well. They'd already brokered a sale of the photos to another magazine with the money raised going to charity, but Anna was covering the rehearsal dinner next week and wanted to attend the shoot as part of the lead-in to the piece she'd write.

There had been a stipulation—which she'd expected—that at least one photo would include the princess, Meg, and the princess-to-be, baby Bonnie. Callie and Jenna had decided to also include Liam, Dylan, Faith and Adam's parents in the photos.

Callie's own family had been invited, as well, but had declined. Her parents and Summer were private people, and Callie had understood their decision and supported it.

So all eight adults and two babies of the Hawke clan found themselves standing among rows of flowers in their Sunday best, laughing and ribbing each other. The photographer called out various instructions, many of which were ignored as the boisterous conversation flowed.

Callie's professional side was watching the scene even as she posed. Some photographers would have insisted that the subjects fall into line, but this one was savvy enough to want to capture the energy and love in the group. And there was a lot of love.

Suddenly, everything in Callie's chest pulled tight and she felt very alone. The occasion might have been about her wedding, but she was the only one in the group of ten people who didn't belong. The others all loved each other; even Faith, the newest addition, had clearly been welcome with open arms, and was now integral—Liam joked with her, Bonnie went smiling into

her arms and Dylan looked at her as if his world began and ended in her eyes.

Callie knew she had no right to feel bad about it—she had her own family at home, including a sister who was her best friend. But something deep inside yearned to be part of Adam's family, too. To have that casual ease of familiarity with other people who loved him.

Her body went rigid. *Other* people who loved him? No, she did *not* love Adam. She'd promised herself she wouldn't let that happen, and she couldn't afford to break that promise. Stuffing any remnants of the thought into a far recess of her brain, she forced herself to smile.

"You okay?" Adam whispered near her ear.

"Couldn't be better," she said brightly.

He moved closer, his lips resting on her ear, voice low. "You probably haven't had enough sleep lately. Completely my fault. As soon as this is over, you'll go straight to my bed."

A surprised laugh burst out before she could stop it. The last thing she'd expected him to joke about when they were surrounded by his family was making love. His eyes danced as he leaned and brushed a chaste kiss over her mouth.

As they pulled away, she was aware that the group was quiet. She glanced around and found them all watching her, their expressions ranging from Adam's mother's glee, to misty-eyed happy sighs from Jenna, to a knowing grin from Dylan.

A blush crept up her throat to her cheeks and, despite knowing it would only encourage them, she hid her face in Adam's jacket while she composed herself. The whole family cheered.

"Okay," the photographer called out. "I think I have enough. How about we move over to the roses? Just the bride-and-groom-to-be for these."

The group dispersed and, as they made their way, her friend Anna caught up to her.

"Thanks for inviting me out," she said, glancing at Adam, who was deep in conversation with the photographer a few steps away.

Callie smiled. "Thank you for coming out. The more coverage the photo shoot gets, the better for the trust."

"You know," Anna said, "when you first told me about this, I wondered if it was an elaborate PR stunt."

Callie's heart skipped a beat. "You did?"

"Well, you have to admit it was a big coincidence that you landed the trust's account and suddenly you're marrying the CEO of Hawke's Blooms."

"We were already married," Callie pointed out carefully.

"Which would be enough to disprove it if we were talking about regular people, but you and Summer are very good at your jobs—this isn't too complicated for you to pull off. Somehow. With smoke and mirrors. And maybe a time machine."

Callie's lungs constricted until she could barely draw in enough breath. Had Anna guessed the truth? Was she warning Callie that she was about to expose her? Or maybe she was only fishing.

"What do you think now?" She worked to keep her voice even.

"The day I did that interview with you, you and Adam were awkward together at times, but I could see that was probably because you were nervous about the

story, and it was your first time being photographed together. But today…" Her voice trailed off.

"Today," Callie prompted.

Anna smiled. "I think that no one who saw you and Adam Hawke together could doubt you're in love."

Relief at fooling a journalist warred with unease about her friend's supposed insight. They were playing roles, sure, but Anna had picked up their awkwardness at the first interview, so she was perceptive. And Anna thought they were in love.

Was Callie coming to feel too much for Adam Hawke? Or was she becoming a better actress?

Adam fell into step beside her and slid an arm around her waist. Without thinking, she leaned in to him, wanting his strength and support as she grappled with the questions her friend had raised.

"See," Anna said, her voice a little smug. "You can't fake that."

Adam looked down at her. "Can't fake what?" His voice was casual but she knew the wariness behind it.

Callie found a short laugh, as if the idea was crazy. "Anna wondered when we first announced our relationship if it was a PR stunt."

She knew from experience that he was good at locking down his emotions so it was no surprise when he merely raised an eyebrow. "It's a fairly complicated and personal plan to be a stunt."

Anna shrugged. "But not beyond Callie's abilities. However I was just telling Callie that no one who sees you two together—how sweet and attentive you are to each other when no one else is looking—could doubt how much you love each other."

Adam pulled her tighter against his side. "I have no

reason to hide what she means to me. My life changed the moment I met her."

Callie suppressed a grin. She had to hand it to him—he'd given the journalist what she wanted, and what they needed her to believe, but he hadn't lied.

Anna had her notebook and pen already in hand. "Can I quote you on that?"

"Absolutely," he said.

"Any reply?" she asked Callie.

Callie thought for a moment. It seemed right to say something just as truthful. "There's no one like Adam Hawke. He makes every day brighter and inspires me."

"How does he inspire you?" Anna asked, her hand scribbling as they walked.

"He's brave. He sees what he wants and goes after it, no concerns about the risk of failure. It's one of the reasons Hawke's Blooms is such a huge success." She found his ocean-green gaze and smiled. "To have all that enthusiasm and energy and determination beside me every day couldn't fail to inspire me."

They'd reached the roses, and Anna backed away, still making notes as the photographer positioned Callie and Adam in front of a shrub bursting with white blooms.

Once everyone else was out of earshot, Adam ran a finger under her chin, drawing her gaze up.

"Did you mean that?" he murmured.

"About you being inspiring?"

He nodded. "I can't always tell when you're saying things for effect, or exaggerating so people believe the story."

"I meant every word." She cupped the side of his face in her palm, wanting him to understand that among

their exaggerations, she was completely serious about this. "You might think it's a failing that you get *carried away* by things, but I think it's one of your strengths. Who else would have committed to this crazy plan and then seen it through?"

He leaned in and kissed her forehead, then met her gaze again. "As it turned out, going along with this scheme has been one of my better ideas."

Careful not to ruin her makeup for the photos, or to leave a trace of lipstick on him, she reached up and placed a delicate kiss on his lips.

"Ready?" he whispered.

Taking a deep breath, she nodded and turned to the photographer. "We're ready. How do you want us to pose?"

"No need," the photographer said cheerily. "I got everything I need."

She looked from him to a grinning Anna and back again. "When?"

"While you were talking." He shrugged, as if that was obvious. "They're sweet photos. They should come out well."

"Right then," Adam said, straightening. "What next?"

The photographer picked up his equipment. "We'll just take a few close-ups of the rings, maybe in the house so I have more control of the light, and we'll be done."

Anna and the photographer headed back to the house, and Adam laced his fingers through Callie's, a rueful smile dancing around his mouth. "It seems this is getting easier with practice."

"Seems so," she said, but her earlier unease about their relationship returned. Was it easier to pretend to be in love because it was becoming closer to the truth?

Pushing the thought aside for now, she changed the subject. "Do you mind if we stay a bit longer after these last photos? Since Jenna and Faith are both here, we were thinking it would be a good time to do some more planning for the wedding, as well as the rehearsal dinner and the bachelor-bachelorette party."

"Sure," he said. "There are a few business things I'd like to discuss with Liam and Dylan anyway, so it's good timing."

She leaned in to whisper in his ear. "And after that I'll take you up on that offer to go straight to your bed."

"I'll make my meetings quick," he said, deadpan, and she laughed.

But as they drew closer to the house, she sobered. She was about to plan her wedding to this man, but once that happened, it would be the beginning of the end. As soon as their vows were spoken, they would start planning their separation.

And every day spent in Adam Hawke's company, in his bed, made the prospect of that separation more devastating.

Eight

By the time they left Liam's house, Callie was restless with wanting Adam. After the photographer and Anna had left, they were just with Adam's family, who all believed she and Adam were putting on an act for the camera. And, of course, they had been.

But then, to keep things simple, they'd pretended for his family not to be involved at all, which was also a lie.

The truth was in some messy place in between, and couldn't really be explained to anyone, so they'd spent the afternoon acting more like business associates than two people who were desperate for a chance to be alone together.

Once in the car, they were silent, but the air vibrated with the tension of all the subterfuge.

At the first red light, Adam glanced over. The heat in his green eyes was unmistakable, making her skin

flush. She swallowed. The light changed, and he accelerated, but no words had been exchanged.

At the next light, again he glanced over, and this time she reached and out laid a hand on his thigh. A tremor ran through his body.

"San Juan Capistrano back to LA is not a quick trip," he said through a tight jaw. "We're not going to make it if your hand continues on that path."

"Are you suggesting we stop somewhere along the way?" The idea of Mr. Cool and Controlled being so overtaken by his passions fascinated her.

He grimaced. "I'd rather make it back to my place."

Grinning, she retracted her hand. "Will that help?"

"It's a start." He blew out a breath. "But we should talk. Tell me about something that's not dangerous."

Something not dangerous? The only topics she could dredge up were all dangerous. She tucked her hair behind her ears and tried again. "What do you want to know?"

"How about when you were growing up? I know the basic details, but tell me what it was like."

She settled back into her seat and thought over her childhood. Then she began to talk. She told him about the school swimming meet where she'd come third in the two-hundred-meter freestyle event, and the year she and Summer had dressed up as dalmatians at Halloween. About the time she'd gotten so addicted to solitaire that she fell behind on her schoolwork, and when her family had traveled to New Mexico for summer break.

Adam asked questions and laughed in the right places, and some of the tension in the car relaxed. It was nice spending time with just him, where they weren't

pretending to either be in love or not involved at all. Just being.

However, when they pulled in to his garage and stepped out of the car, the mood changed. Or rather, it adjusted. For the most part, they'd been ignoring the simmering heat between them on the drive home, but now that they'd arrived…

He took her hand as they walked through the front door and an electric tingle raced from her fingers up her arm to her spine. She'd been waiting for this moment all day.

As he opened the door, they both stopped. There was a trail of rose petals on the floor, leading from the entryway to the hall to his room.

"When did you do this?" she asked. He'd been with her since they left this morning, so it wouldn't have been easy.

"It wasn't me," he said grimly. He glanced around, and found a note propped up on a side table. As he scanned it, he said, "Dylan. He called my housekeeper on her vacation and got her to set it up. It's a surprise from all the staff at Hawke's Blooms. Apparently they all wanted to do something for us, and they said it with flowers."

She scooped up some of the delicate petals and rubbed them between her fingers. "It's very sweet of them."

He cut her a glance. "It is sweet of them, but we've just spent half a day with my brother and he failed to mention it. That part is less sweet."

She held the petals to her nose. "They smell divine. Let's see where they lead."

"I think we can guess," he said wryly.

No one had ever done anything like this for her before, and whether they were suffering under a misapprehension or not when they organized it, it was still lovely, and she intended to allow herself to appreciate the indulgence.

"Let's follow the trail anyway," she said and set off down the hall. Sure enough, the petals led straight to Adam's bedroom, and his comforter was liberally strewn with them, mainly in reds, pinks and whites. There were huge bunches of roses in the same colors in vases around the room and the air was heavy with their rich scent.

Adam came to stand behind her, and she could feel the heat emanating from his body. She leaned back into him.

"It's beautiful," she whispered.

He stroked a hand down her hair. "No, you're beautiful." He kissed the top of her head. "I need a shower. Liam had us standing out in the sun for most of the meeting, going through the rows of his upcoming flowers."

Despite knowing his shower would be quick, and he wouldn't be far away in the attached bathroom, impatience pulled at her. "I'll be here. Waiting."

"Or..." he said, turning her in his arms.

"Or?" she asked, blinking up at him.

"Or you could join me." He tugged on her hand, drawing her into the bathroom with a smile that promised much.

"That could work, too." She allowed herself to be led, and when they reached the shower, allowed herself to be undressed. Adam quickly shucked down his own

clothes and turned on the water, testing the temperature with a hand. Then he pulled her beneath the spray.

The warm water was sensual as it poured over her body, but the feel of his slickened skin sliding against hers as he adjusted the water and reached for the soap was better.

"I can't imagine why I've been showering alone since I moved in."

He squirted liquid soap into his hands and began to lather. "You're always welcome in my shower." With hands on her shoulders, he turned her and rubbed the lathered soap over her back. "In fact, I encourage it."

Strong hands stroked over her shoulders and down her back, curving over her buttocks before starting at the top again. She let out a contented sigh. "Will those be full service like this one?"

Her earlobe was sucked into the warmth of his mouth, and a shudder raced down her spine. Then his lips were at the shell of her ear. "You haven't seen full service yet."

He turned her again so that she was facing him and squirted more soap into his hands. Then, slowly, ever so slowly, he washed every square inch of her, paying special attention to her breasts.

"I've heard these can need more washing than elbows and legs," he murmured as he soaped up the peaks of her breasts.

Her blood pumped insistently through her veins. "Your attention to detail does you credit."

"I'm glad you think so," he said, sliding his hands lower, "because I've heard a rumor that there's another part that often needs even more washing."

An ache between her legs throbbed, begging for his touch. "I think it's your duty to investigate."

He stepped behind her and pulled her against him with an arm beneath her breasts, while the other hand continued its descent. "Oh, I plan to."

When his fingers hit their target, her knees wobbled, but he held her firm. The slow, slick movements were designed to drive her out of her mind, and they were working. She moaned his name, and felt him hardening against her buttocks, but his hand didn't falter.

The warm water gently beating down on her skin, Adam at her back, his soaped hand circling and rocking her: it was too much all at once and her release came upon her in a roar of sensation, overtaking her completely then ebbing away, leaving her limp in his arms.

He held her for long moments, kissing her face, before letting her stand on her own once she was ready. The quick, practical movements of his own cleansing routine were in sharp contrast to the lush strokes he'd used on her, but she still admired the process.

The water stopped and he patted her down with a thick towel.

"I could get used to this way of showering," she said on a happy sigh.

He waggled his eyebrows. "That's my nefarious plan. Then you'll be naked in my shower each morning."

Once he was dry, as well, he interlaced their fingers for the few steps back into the bedroom. The curtains were drawn, hiding the magnificent ocean view, but it gave them privacy, which she preferred in that moment. Adam flicked a switch and downlights came on around the edges of the room, creating a magical atmo-

sphere. The rose petals that covered the bed practically sparkled in the light.

She dropped Adam's hand and crawled onto the bed, luxuriating in the rich, creamy texture of the petals against her shower-sensitized skin. Eyes closed, she stretched just to feel their caress.

The mattress dipped, and Adam's arms came around her. "If that's your reaction, I'll make sure this bed is covered in rose petals every night."

"You know, I've always thought it sounded romantic, but it *feels* divine, too." With every movement, the flowers' scent was released until it surrounded them. "Try it."

Adam lay flat on his back, moving his arms above his head as if making a snow angel. "You know what? You're right."

She gathered a handful of petals and sprinkled them over him. "You've never done this before? You're the head of one of the biggest flower companies in the country and you've never lain on a carpet of rose petals?"

One corner of his mouth quirked up. "My brothers were always more hands-on with the flowers. Liam with growing them, and Dylan selling them."

"Even when you were young? Before you ran the company?"

He nodded, his gaze on her hand as she let another handful of petals fall over his chest. "My mother and Dylan were the mainstays of the roadside stall, where we started selling the flowers—I don't know if you noticed, but Dylan can sell anything to anyone. And Liam started helping Dad from a very young age. He was more interested in science and getting the technical details right in growing the best plants."

"And you?" she asked softly, feeling as if she was prying, but dying to know what went on in his mind.

"Me?" He shrugged and pulled her closer. "I had a vision. Right from the start I could see that we had all the ingredients to make it work. Dad could grow anything and Liam could produce new and unusual flowers. Mom had a keen eye for what the customer wanted and Dylan could charm anyone into parting with their money. They just needed someone to dream big for them and turn it into a business plan."

She could imagine Adam when he was young, already driven and focused. "You certainly came through on that."

"They all came through on their parts, too," he said, his voice filled with respect and affection.

She wondered if he had any idea of what he'd really contributed. There were lots of groups and families who had "all the ingredients to make it work," but that didn't mean much without someone with business savvy. Someone who could conceptualize an idea then turn it into reality. From the sound of it, Adam had done that partly through sheer force of will.

One question tugged at her—he'd made it his mission to look after his entire family but who was looking after him?

"You're an amazing man, Adam Hawke," she said, and then reached up to kiss his jawline.

"Oh, you think so, do you?" In the space of seconds, his tone had changed from serious and reflective to something altogether more wicked. It sent her pulse racing.

He rolled them over, pinning her beneath him, his gaze mischievous. "How amazing?"

"Quite," she teased back.

One corner of his mouth quirked. "That's it?"

She pretended to think about it, which was difficult, given that her breathing had become uneven. "Yes, I think that's about it. Quite."

"What if I do this?" He scooted down and took the tip of her breast into his mouth, tugging gently and swiping with his tongue. The action seemed to tug at the very core of her being, setting every nerve ending alight.

"That's good," she said, though her voice was higher than normal.

"Good, huh?" He reached over to the box he now kept in his bedside drawer and withdrew a packet. In seconds, he was sheathed and poised above her. "It seems that I've gone backward from quite amazing to good."

All she could see was him above her as he rested his weight on one forearm. Then she felt his hand come between them, his thumb moving expertly, making her forget any trace of conversation.

"Still only good?" he asked as first one finger then a second slid inside her, his thumb still the center of her world.

"Um," she said. Her skin was hot, so hot. *What was he talking about?* "Yes?"

"You were telling me whether I was merely good, or quite amazing, or maybe something more." He sounded maddeningly patient, but she could feel the evidence of his arousal pressing against her thigh and knew that his nonchalance had to be costing him.

"More. You're more than amazing." She couldn't think of any words that meant more than amazing in

the moment, so she hoped the intent would be enough to satisfy him.

His hand disappeared but before she could miss it, he'd parted her thighs wider and was resting his weight on his knees between them. "I think you're pretty amazing, too," he said, his ragged voice finally showing how affected he was. Then he slid inside her.

She arched up to meet him, feeling the perfection of him filling her, stretching her, but still needing more, needing movement.

"Adam." It was more of a moan, a plea, than anything, and he seemed to understand, because he began to move, to find the rhythm that suited them both, and she rose to meet each thrust, an ebb and flow that they'd practiced enough now to create naturally.

Their movements released more fragrance from the rose petals beneath her, and the sound of Adam's rough breathing near her ear made her heart beat faster. Pressure was building inside her, around her, propelling her higher, the momentum driving her further.

He moved his pelvis somehow, and the friction was suddenly different, better, harder, and everything coiled tight then exploded in waves of glorious sensation from her toes to the top of her head and beyond, as if she was too big for her body.

As she came down, the motion continued, with Adam keeping the rhythm going before his entire body stiffened and he shouted his release into the curve of her neck. As he slumped, she wrapped her arms around him, wanting more than anything to be the one who held him. The one who would always catch him. The one who would be there for him.

And for this sweet moment, she was.

* * *

"Another glass?" Adam asked two hours later, holding up the bottle of red.

"Just a little one." Callie held her glass out as he poured the wine, and then settled back into the deck chair on his balcony and breathed in the view. The sun would be setting soon over the Pacific Ocean and the colors were vibrant.

"I'm going to miss this house once this is all over," she said on a sigh. "You have to promise me you'll take advantage of it more, even when you're back to working long hours."

Adam was silent for a moment, so she glanced over. He was deep in thought, his gaze on the far horizon over the water.

"I don't have a quarter on me," she said, "but I'll offer the last piece of brie for your thoughts."

The corners of his mouth quirked and he took a sip of his wine before reaching for her hand.

"I was thinking about what you just said. About after this is all over." The weight of his gaze landed on her. "What if it doesn't have to end?"

Callie's heart picked up speed, racing double-time. "I'm not sure what you're asking."

He let out a long breath. "I'm not sure, either. All I know is I'm not ready for this to end."

She remembered him saying that whenever he grew too emotionally close to a woman, he backed away. If he was willing to continue things, that meant he didn't have feelings for her.

The realization hurt more than she would have expected. She didn't know quite what she felt for him, but whatever it was, it clearly wasn't reciprocated.

She carefully placed her glass on the small table between their deck chairs and crossed the few steps to the railing. She'd known this was a plan with a time limit, and Adam had been completely up-front about not being able to offer more than they'd agreed to, but clearly some naive part of her had been holding on to a shred of hope...

She felt him come to stand beside her. "Callie?"

"I don't know," she admitted with a small shrug.

He was silent for a beat, and when he spoke, his voice was low and tender. "What, specifically, don't you know?"

"Anything." She let out a humorless laugh. "Everything." Finding his gaze, she bit down on her bottom lip. "Except that I'm not ready for this to end yet, either."

His eyes softened, and then heated. "Well, let's not let it."

Her hands trembled. That sounded so easy, and yet...

"If we continue, there's a good chance one of us—" namely her "—would become emotionally compromised."

"If you're worried about hurting me, Callie, don't be. You know I've become good at guarding my heart over the years. And if you're worried about you falling in love with me, there are things we can do about that."

Curiosity piqued, she grinned. "So how do you plan to stop me falling in love with you?"

"We'll start with a visit to my brothers," he said with a poker face. "They'll be eager to fill you in on all my failings. No fledgling love could withstand the way they'll gleefully delve into my faults. And it will all be true."

She crossed her arms under her breasts, smothering a laugh. "And if it's not enough?"

"I'll be sure to stomp around the house and be cranky for an hour each night." He rubbed a hand over his lightly stubbled jaw. "Maybe buy some unattractive underwear."

She let her chuckle loose, but as it faded, she turned to face the ocean. If he thought those few things would stop her falling the rest of the way in love with him, he was sadly deluded about the effect he had on her.

"In all seriousness," he said, pulling her closer, "surely we'd have fallen in love by now if it was going to happen? We've been pretending for the world, and spending all our time together, not to mention burning up the sheets on my bed. If we've held out this long, I think we can make it a bit longer safely."

The skin on the back of her neck prickled, and she rubbed a hand under her hair, trying to ease the sensation. "So you think we should continue our fling indefinitely?"

"We'll already be married. All I'm saying is that we could hold off on the divorce as long as the arrangement is still working for us. As soon as one of us wants to call it quits, the divorce is put in motion, no questions asked."

It sounded so clinical. The opposite of how their marriage had begun, all passion and excitement and spontaneity. Now their divorce would be denied the same energy, of ending in a bang of emotion. Instead, their marriage would slowly peter out until nothing was left, and one of them wanted to move on.

"Let me think about it," she said with an attempt at a smile. "My mind is so full of next weekend's rehearsal

dinner, and the bachelor-bachelorette party, there isn't much room to think clearly."

It was an excuse and she saw in his eyes that he recognized it as such, but he didn't call her on it, and for that she was grateful.

"Take all the time you need," he said and fetched their wineglasses. "Now tell me the latest on the rehearsal dinner and our combined bachelor-bachelorette party."

Back on safer ground, she took a sip of her wine and filled him in on all the arrangements she, Jenna and Faith had made in the past couple of days. But even as she spoke, a small part of her mind kept drifting to his suggestion. To the idea of extending her time with him. In his bed. Married to him.

And she wondered—when the time came and he called it quits, would she be able to walk away from Adam Hawke?

Nine

Adam tugged at the collar of his tuxedo and cast another glance around the assembled guests on the four-hundred-foot super yacht. He was looking for Callie, which was pointless, because he'd positioned himself next to the entrance so he wouldn't miss her and she definitely hadn't boarded yet.

Many of the guests for the joint bachelor and bacherlorette party had already arrived, and were milling about drinking the champagne the waitstaff was distributing. Several people had stopped to congratulate him. He'd been polite, but had ensured he could still see new guests over their shoulder.

A hand clapped him on the back, and Dylan's voice came from beside him. "Adam, my favorite brother."

"Hey," Liam said, coming from behind.

"Best to let him think that," Dylan said in a stage whisper to Liam. "It's his night, after all."

Adam snagged another glass of champagne from a passing waiter's tray and tried to ignore his younger brothers. They always found the most inconvenient times to get in his face.

"I haven't seen Callie yet," Liam said, frowning as he looked into the crowd.

"She's not here." Adam adjusted his position so he could see past Liam in case Callie was arriving as they spoke. "She didn't have anything formal enough at my house, so she went to her place a few hours ago to get ready."

"She and Summer are holding back to make a grand entrance?" Dylan asked.

Adam snorted out a laugh. "Nope." That was so not Callie's style.

"Okay, listen. Since this is essentially your bachelor party, I have a few ideas. How about—"

"No," Adam said, swinging his gaze to Dylan. "Nothing. Not one thing, I'm warning you."

The youngest Hawke brother held up his hands. "Okay, okay. I wasn't serious."

Liam chuckled. "I told you he wouldn't be in the mood for jokes."

Adam heard the comments as if from a distance, because he'd just spotted Callie. The world stopped spinning and all he could see was her. She was in a figure-hugging bloodred gown, with lips and nails painted to match. Her caramel-brown hair, glossy under the lights, was swept back from her face and trailed down past her shoulders. Her beauty shone so brightly it held him captive. The need to touch her, to have simple skin-on-skin contact, was overwhelming.

As she drew closer, she caught sight of him and their

gazes locked. He noticed the slight falter in her step, and his chest swelled.

When she reached them, he held out a hand for her, and she came into his arms as if she truly belonged there. For a moment, as he felt her against him, he let himself imagine it was true—that he'd found someone he could love, the way Liam loved Jenna, and Dylan loved Faith.

But it was dangerous to think that way. He was different from his brothers. He didn't have the same luxury of falling in love.

No matter how breathtaking Callie was in that dress, or how she made his heart sing.

She eased back, and he murmured hello and kissed her cheek, careful not to ruin her makeup. Then she was claimed by Dylan and Liam, who had already greeted Summer, and were now congratulating Callie on the success of the rehearsal dinner two nights earlier.

The dinner had been a resounding success. The adults had all dressed as characters such as fairy godmothers and princes, and the looks on the children's faces when they saw them and the room decorations had melted the hearts of everyone there. Jenna was already considering making a dinner for children aided by the trust an annual event.

Callie modestly protested. "Your fiancées and Summer did most of the work."

Liam shook his head. "That's not the way Jenna tells it. And the next day when Anna Wilson's article about it hit the web, the trust had another boost to its donations, which looks like it will have a long tail."

While Liam spoke to Callie, Adam pulled Summer into a brotherly hug.

"Good to see you again," he said, meaning it. He was coming to see Summer as a sister, much like Jenna and Faith.

It was a funny thing—he'd spent most of his life in a family that was dominated by men, with his father, two brothers and himself, and only his mother holding the flag for women. Now he had a wife, three sisters-in-law and two nieces. The gender balance had definitely tipped in the other direction. He liked it.

"You, too," Summer said. Then she laid a hand on his forearm and pulled him back a step, where they couldn't be overheard. "I've finished writing the vows for the wedding. I have a copy in my purse, or would you rather I email them to you so you can check them over?"

Vows. One more detail that he was glad he didn't need to take care of himself for this wedding. "No, I trust you. With your PR experience, you'll be much better at this kind of thing than I would. Whatever you've done is fine."

Callie finished with his brothers and came to stand beside him again, lacing her fingers through his. Summer discreetly slipped away, following his brothers back to mingle with the crowd—something he and Callie should do, as well, but he wanted a little time alone with her first.

"I missed you," he said, close to her ear.

She shot him a teasing look. "Did you think that before or after you saw this dress?"

He chuckled. "Before. After I saw it my thoughts went in another direction entirely."

The teasing light faded from her silver-blue eyes and her expression became serious. "I missed you, too."

Everything inside him seemed to settle into place.

That was a good omen for their continuing the fling after their wedding. Surely, if she missed him, she wouldn't be keen on running off straight away. But he wouldn't ask. He'd told her she could have as much time to think about it as she needed and he'd meant it.

"Regardless of what you said to my brothers, I know you did most of the work organizing the rehearsal dinner and this party tonight. And it's very good work. Both events have come off flawlessly."

She smiled and seemed to stand taller. "Thank you. Your standards are high, so I appreciate that feedback."

"In fact, I've been thinking that your work is so good, that perhaps you should be working for Hawke's Blooms." In truth, the thought had only just occurred to him, but it made complete sense. She was good at her job and their company could use someone with her skill set.

She dropped her voice. "How do you think that would go once we divorce?"

It was good she was looking at the issue from all sides—it was one of the things he liked about her—but he couldn't imagine ever having a strained relationship with Callie. They got on too well.

"That won't be a problem for us," he said, shrugging a shoulder. "Unlike most divorces, ours will be a well-planned and friendly parting."

"You don't think it will be—" her teeth worried at her bottom lip as she searched for the word she wanted "—awkward to see each other at work once we're no longer involved? No longer sleeping together?"

He rubbed a thumb over the inside of her hand, trying to soothe away her concerns. "If we're no longer involved, it means that what we've had will have run

its course. When I look into the future, I see us still being friends."

She blinked. She obviously had a different vision of their future, but that didn't mean his was wrong.

"The offer is on the table," he whispered just as an older couple approached them. Callie introduced them and she and Adam spent the next hour mingling with their guests, sometimes together and sometimes individually.

"Adam," Callie said a little later, laying a hand on his arm.

He turned to find her standing behind him. She was radiant.

"There you are," he said and kissed her cheek. "Ten minutes is entirely too long to be away from me."

She gave him a quick smile, and then stepped away to reveal two men standing with her. "Adam, I want you to meet two of the partners at my firm, John Evans and Ted Parker."

Adam shook the men's hands, resting one arm securely around Callie's shoulders.

John, the taller of the men, planted his hands on his hips. "Good to meet you, Mr. Hawke." Then he turned back to Callie. "I have some news you might be interested in about Terence Gibson."

Adam felt Callie tense beside him. It was the name of the coworker who'd tried to blackmail her into giving him the trust's account.

"Oh?" she asked politely.

John nodded. "He seemed unnaturally interested in your work on the Hawke Brothers Trust account, so I pressed him for a reason, and he told us what a bad choice you'd be for partner."

Callie's face paled, but Adam saw red. After all her work, would they really believe that guy's trash talking? He cleared his throat. "The opinion of one coworker hardly seems to be enough to base an important decision on."

John's expression gave nothing away. "I'm afraid he had quite a detailed list of the disadvantages to us of promoting you. Coincidentally, he also had reasons we couldn't promote Michael, Angela or Diane."

Callie's eyes widened. She obviously hadn't realized how broad an agenda her coworker had. "They're great workers, especially Diane—"

Her boss held up a hand. "We agree. And after we started asking the right questions, we realized Terence had been undermining his coworkers for some time, which is not the way we like our team to operate. So we fired him."

"You fired him," Callie repeated.

John's mouth pulled into a tight smile, but it was far from warm. "Just thought you might like to know. Anyway, I'm going to find one of those waiters and grab another glass of that very fine champagne you're serving. Congratulations again to you both."

And suddenly the partners were both gone.

"Are you okay?" Adam whispered near her ear.

Callie only had time for a quick nod when Summer made a beeline for them through the crowd. Her cheeks were a little flushed, possibly from the champagne, but her eyes said she was focused.

"How do you think it's going?" Adam asked her when she reached them.

"Definitely a success," she said with barely contained delight. "Hey, since we're creating new traditions all

over the place by having the bachelor and bachelorette parties combined, how about another new tradition?"

"Should I be worried?" Adam asked.

Summer grinned. "Just a dance between the happy couple. Do you two have a special song?"

"No—" Callie said, just as Adam blurted out, "'The Lady in Red.'"

Summer glanced down at Callie's bloodred dress and grinned. "Good choice. I'll tell the DJ."

After she left, Callie smiled at him. "That was quick thinking."

"Actually, it's a coincidence that your dress tonight is red," he said, still considering how much to say. Almost by unspoken agreement, they'd never talked about the night they'd met. The time they'd spent together over the three conferences hadn't involved much talking at all, and ever since she'd hurtled back into his life they'd barely mentioned their time in Vegas. But for some reason tonight felt like another first and had him thinking back to that time.

He lowered his voice. "Do you remember the first night we met?"

"At the conference a couple of years ago?" she asked, tilting her head to the side.

He nodded. "We were sitting at the bar the first night."

She'd been a few places down the bar and he'd been watching her, mesmerized. She'd turned away a couple of guys who'd tried to hit on her, so he'd wondered if she just wanted to be left alone. Then their gazes had snagged as she took a glance around, and he'd felt a connection, and knew he had to try his luck, even if she might shoot him down.

"You asked me if you could buy me a drink," she said, her voice nostalgic and hypnotic.

"Not very original of me, I know." In fact, he'd been tongue-tied for the first time in his life. Possibly his first clue that maintaining self-control around this woman was going to be difficult.

"It worked." She moistened her lips. "I'd been trying to think of a line to introduce myself to you."

"Really?" He'd had no idea, and it changed the way he thought about that night. Made it even more special, because it meant she'd felt it right from the start, just as he had.

"If you hadn't come over—" she arched an eyebrow and looked as majestic as she had that night "—you probably had about four minutes before I found a line and came to your bar stool."

"Now part of me wishes I'd waited, just to hear your line." He grinned and was rewarded with a laugh. Her eyes, already impossibly large with the dark makeup, shone from within, and he wondered if he'd ever be able to look away.

"It would probably have been worse than yours," she said, shaking her head.

He waited for their amusement to subside, before he said, "And do you remember what song was playing in the bar?"

She frowned. "No." Then her eyes widened. "'The Lady in Red'? Seriously?"

He nodded, inordinately pleased with himself. "You weren't wearing red that night, but it was definitely playing."

"And you remembered," she said, a touch of awe in her voice.

Keeping her gaze, he placed a kiss on the back of her hand. "That moment is indelibly etched in my memory."

There was an announcement that dancing was about to start, and then the strains of "The Lady in Red" came through the sound system.

Adam put out his hand. "Would you like to dance?"

Callie took Adam's hand and walked with him out to the dance floor, but it felt as if they were doing more. Taking a step into their future.

The old-fashioned ballad was designed for swaying so many other couples joined them on the dance floor. And it was also a thinly disguised chance to be in each other's arms and sneak a kiss or two.

"Are you enjoying yourself?" he murmured near her ear. "You wouldn't have rather had a stripper, or a toilet-paper wedding-dress game?"

"A bachelorette party like that would have been awkward with a journalist along." She nodded in the direction of where Anna was collecting quotes from their friends and family to go with the article she'd write about tonight. "And what about you? An opportunity for drinking and strippers has passed you by."

He caressed her back slowly. "I'm sure I'll cope with the disappointment."

His hand was warm through the fabric of her dress. She could stay like this for hours, just being close to him.

"I made a decision tonight," she said, her voice dreamy even to her own ears.

"Just tell me it's not about sleeping somewhere other than my bed tonight. I have plans for the removal of this dress."

She smoothed her hands over his shoulders as they danced, loving the shape of him, and especially the freedom to touch him whenever she pleased.

"It's about the future removal of dresses."

He leaned back and looked at her with a hopeful gaze. "The fling?"

"It's working for us, so it seems silly to stop at an arbitrary date like the wedding. I agree that we should continue while it still works for us."

He lifted her off her feet and spun around. People made way for them and gave them indulgent looks, which was the advantage of displays of affection at your own prewedding party.

"I can't tell you how happy I am about this," he said as he settled her down again.

The song ended. The next one was modern with a faster beat, and she didn't feel like dancing to it in the heels she'd worn, so she suggested they get a drink. As they went their separate ways in the crowd and fell into conversation with their guests, she found that they were looking for each other across the room, and when she would find him, his gaze would heat and she could feel the answering burn across her skin.

Continuing to sleep with him even after they no longer needed to pretend felt right. In fact, maybe it could turn into something more. Everything inside her lifted, glowed at the thought.

Obviously Adam would be resistant to the idea at first, but that was merely his fear. It shouldn't take long for him to realize they enjoyed each other's company, respected each other, had a passion unlike any she'd had before. They had shared intimate stories with each

other about their backgrounds. When they'd first married, they'd practically been strangers, but this time...

This time it seemed to be a recipe for a happy marriage.

The idea was so bright and shiny that for a moment she forgot to breathe. Adam shot her a quizzical look from the other side of the room and she realized she probably had a goofy grin on her face. The older woman she was talking to patted her hand and mumbled something about brides and newlyweds then left, but Callie was still stuck on the sparkling possibility that she might have a real future with Adam.

She smoothed down her dress and found her composure, but inside she was still buzzing.

Could it work...?

Ten

Feeling as content as she could remember, Callie sat in the backseat of the limousine, Adam's arm around her shoulders, as they arrived back at his place from the marina.

The night had gone off without a hitch, and she felt closer to Adam than ever. Everything was wholly perfect.

"You awake?" he said softly when the limo pulled up.

She arched her neck back to look at him. "I am. Just thinking over the night."

"My favorite part was our dance," he murmured.

It was one of her favorite parts, too, but there was something that had underpinned the night, something she couldn't quite put her finger on, that made the entire experience magical.

The driver opened her door and Adam released her with a quick kiss to her forehead before she stepped out.

They went through the routine of walking through the house and getting ready for bed, with minimal conversation but sleepy smiles, and within ten minutes, they were under the covers together.

"We didn't get to talk much about your decision tonight," Adam said, smoothing the hair back from her face. "But I have to tell you how happy I am about it."

Callie snaked an arm over his waist and snuggled in. "I am, too. It feels right."

A few minutes earlier, she'd been feeling exhausted, but now that she was alone with him, talking, touching, suddenly she wasn't as tired anymore.

She started to trace a pattern over his torso. "Would you like me to show you how right it feels?"

His fingers traced a mirror image on her back of the pattern her hand was making. "Oh, I think I could be talked into that."

She stretched to reach his mouth and kissed him. His breath was minty, his lips ready for her and hungry. Heat filled her body, and she moved farther over him, the abrasion of the light dusting of hair on his chest a delicious friction.

"Callie," he groaned and pulled her tighter. "What you do to me..."

His skin was hot to touch, and she couldn't get enough. She slid her palms over every square inch she could reach. The need to be close was the driving force, one she couldn't resist. Didn't want to resist. The man she loved was...

Wait...

Everything stopped, even the breath in her lungs.

The man she loved?

Was that her mind playing a trick with words, or was

it true? Stomach churning, she flicked through memories, feelings, any information she could dredge up until the pieces of the jigsaw started to fit into place—she'd been so incandescently happy tonight on the yacht as they talked about a future together. She felt herself light up from inside whenever she saw him. And it was his touch, and his touch alone, that she craved like a drug.

She flinched. Oh, yeah. She was in love with him.

What a stupid, stupid thing to let happen. This plan had never been about love—it was a straightforward arrangement to convince everyone else they were in love.

Had she fallen into her own trap? Believed the lies she and Adam had been spinning for other people? Perhaps pretending to be in love with Adam Hawke had seeped into her subconscious somehow and become tangled with her real feelings until now they were inseparable.

Whatever the cause, there was no doubt that it had happened. And now, instead of happy, it just made her feel emotionally vulnerable.

"Something's changed," he said. "Are you okay?"

She didn't want to explain, not yet. Not until she'd had time to think it through properly. So instead, she hid her face against his chest and placed a kiss against the warm skin beneath her lips. "I'm fine."

His abdominal muscles clenched as he lifted himself into a half-sitting position, trying to see her face. "Would you rather we stopped?"

She needed him now more than ever—needed the mindless moments and the release before she had to face the situation she'd created. She rolled onto her back and pulled him with her, until he was above her. "No, I

don't want to stop. I want you to stay close, as close as we can be. I want you touching me."

His eyes softened, and he leaned down to claim her mouth in a scorching kiss before whispering against her lips, "Then stay with me."

There was no mistaking what he meant—she must have zoned out for a few seconds after her realization, and her actions would have seemed more like an automaton's. But staying emotionally engaged with him while making love now, while she was raw from the discovery, was like ripping out her still-beating heart and handing it to him. The only way to survive was to try to hold a little of herself back. At least until she had things clear in her head.

She kissed him again, taking his mind off his request, and moved beneath him in the way she knew would drive him wild. A shudder ripped through his body, and he kissed a path down the side of her throat, nipping at the sensitive skin, making her writhe. And then his hand was between them, working its magic until her hips bucked with wanting him.

And yet, a small part of her, detached and clinical, seemed to be watching them from above. Keeping her heart safe.

"Give me a second," he said, and reached for the bedside table. He sheathed himself quickly and then was back by her side, making her feel beautiful and desired.

He lifted her knees and wrapped them around his hips, and she nudged him with her heels, impatient. Wanting. Always wanting with Adam.

As he entered her, she discovered that holding part of herself back hadn't been enough. The intensity was too much. She squeezed her eyes shut, unwilling to risk

him seeing everything she was feeling, but he wouldn't let her keep him out.

"Open your eyes, Callie," he said, and when she didn't, he kissed each eyelid in turn. "Please don't hide from me. Let me see you."

The comment about hiding from him hit home, but it was the "please" that did it. Her eyelids fluttered open and she was confronted with Adam's deep green gaze. It was unwavering, inviting her to fall away with him, and she did.

He moved within her and the pressure built, taking her higher, higher than she'd ever been, the intimacy of being joined with the man she loved overwhelming. His hands moved over her even as he stroked into her, and he whispered her name in her ear, roughly, as if he was as lost as she. Higher, she flew higher, until she hit the peak, crying out that she loved him, and then crested the wave, feeling him follow her, before slumping, spent, to her side.

For several minutes she floated on a blissful cloud, not moving, not thinking. But slowly, the nagging memory of what she'd said crept into her mind.

She'd called out that she loved him.

Had he heard her? She tried to remember if he'd reacted, but those moments were hazy at best. Was it possible that he'd flinched when she'd said it, or was that her imagination?

The worst part was, despite saying it without thinking it was true.

As she lay in his arms, she made herself face reality. She was in love with Adam. Head-over-heels, lost-her-mind-crazy in love.

And there were consequences of falling in love with Adam Hawke...

She couldn't have a fling with the man she loved. Couldn't stay married and share his bed until he grew tired of her. She'd end up with a heart torn to pieces.

And she couldn't walk away—she'd made commitments to the trust, and to her bosses. And even after they were over, would she be able to walk away from him? Leave Adam when he still wanted her? She couldn't imagine having that level of internal strength.

And that fact meant she needed another way forward. A new plan.

Adam curled into her, letting out a contented sigh, and she squeezed her eyes shut. She'd give herself this one night to enjoy him and then work out that new plan tomorrow.

Callie woke slowly the next morning, and before she was even fully aware, the memory of the night before came crashing back. She was in love with Adam. She'd told him—screamed it to him, actually.

Her stomach swam. She opened one eye, then the other, and found his side of the bed empty. She gave thanks for small mercies. She needed a few minutes on her own. More than a few, but she'd manage with what she could get.

She dragged herself into the shower and threw on some clothes, the whole time thinking through possible solutions. Several ideas occurred to her, but no one plan that would work for everyone. Keeping her feelings a secret was no longer an option thanks to her chattiness.

Unless...

What if Adam had changed his feelings, too, and was just as worried about bringing it up with her?

If he'd had a change of heart, or was at least open to exploring that possibility, then they could try a relationship for real. Sure, there would be a lot of pressure since they were already married, but nothing they couldn't overcome with a little dedication.

She owed it to herself, to their relationship, to at least try.

She smiled. It was funny that only last night on the yacht she'd been having similar thoughts—that perhaps they could try to make things work. But then she'd realized she loved him, and that she couldn't have a fling with a man she loved, waiting for him to become bored. And here she was now, full circle, wondering if there was a chance he would return her feelings, hoping…

Searching through the house, she found him on the balcony with a coffee in one hand, scrolling through online newspapers on his laptop.

"Good morning, beautiful," he said when he saw her.

"Morning," she said, not knowing how to start the conversation now that she was here.

"There's more coffee in the pot, if you want some."

Coffee would definitely help, and going to get it would give her a little more time to organize her thoughts. She headed into the kitchen.

When she ventured back to the balcony, steaming mug of coffee in hand, Adam closed his laptop and put it on a side table.

"How did you sleep?" he asked, and then watched her over the rim of his mug as he took a sip.

She tucked her feet up under her on the deck chair. "Pretty heavily, I think."

She was surprised she'd slept at all, given that her mind was worrying over what her heart had been busy doing, but the exhaustion must have caught up with her.

"Me, too," he said, and she knew from the look in his eye that he was crediting their presleep lovemaking.

The lovemaking that had brought her face-to-face with reality. She took a breath. It was time. If she didn't address this now, it would only drag out.

"Adam, there's something I want to talk to you about." She took a sip of coffee for courage and he waited. "About us."

"If you're embarrassed about what you said, don't be." He shrugged, as if it was nothing more than telling him the coffeepot was empty. "People get carried away in the heat of passion."

She blinked. That answered the first question about how he'd taken it last night. If she wanted the coward's way out, all she had to do was nod, agree and change the subject. Everything could go back to how it was before she'd blurted out the truth during her release.

Despite part of her wanting that easy route, she knew it wouldn't solve anything. She couldn't live with their current plan of continuing their fling after the wedding, until Adam wanted to move on. It would be Adam moving on, not her. She was in love and here for the long haul. And waiting around for the ax to fall? Purgatory.

The only way forward that gave her a chance to keep her sanity intact was to tell him the truth and give him the chance to rise to the occasion.

"So this might seem crazy," she said, noting the waver in her voice but being unable to doing anything about it, "but what if I wasn't just 'carried away'? What if love has crept into the equation for us?"

He was suddenly alert. Every muscle in his body seemed to tense, his gaze sharpened. "You know that was never part of the deal."

Carefully, she put her mug down on the little table between the chairs and found his gaze. "Well, it seems there's some bad news coming for you. Because I love you."

He looked dumbstruck. "No, you don't."

Annoyance wriggled in her belly. "You don't get to tell me how I feel."

"You're right. I'm sorry, I was just caught off guard." He rubbed a hand over his eyes. "Okay, thinking on my feet—maybe this will work well for our marriage."

His solution hit her with the force of a brick in the center of the chest. He thought she would stay in a one-sided marriage? It took her long moments to even find her voice again.

"Adam," she said slowly and carefully, "I don't want a sham of a marriage for the rest of my life. I don't even need a big wedding, second or otherwise. All I need is a man I love, who loves me back."

His face went white. "I've been up-front with you. You know that can never be me."

And there it was. The death knell to her hopes and dreams of a future with him. She was vaguely surprised she was able to sit straight in her chair, unemotional. If she'd been considering options earlier, she might have thought she'd dissolve into tears, but part of her felt detached—the part that was keeping her safe. Whatever it was, it was helping her dignity in this moment, so she was grateful. There would be time for grieving later.

Adam still looked at her, pale-faced and dismayed, and she realized she needed to release him. He hadn't

done anything wrong. In fact, he'd stuck to what they'd agree on.

"It's okay, I know." She even tried to smile for him, but couldn't quite pull it off. "I know. I guess I just hoped..."

He pushed out of his chair and crouched down in front of hers, finding her hands and squeezing them. "I'm so sorry, Callie. I really am. But I can only offer you the plan we agreed on. I wish it was different."

The moment he took her hands, any illusion of detachment or control over her emotions evaporated. The full force of her life falling apart hit her and she started trembling, deep inside. She gulped in air, trying to keep herself balanced. Adam frowned even more than he had been and stroked her forehead; but pity was not what she wanted from him, so she shakily removed his hand. He didn't release her other hand, however, or move from crouching in front of her chair.

She swallowed, moistened her lips, took a breath and said a prayer that her voice would be steady. "Then we need to start talking about a new plan."

His eyes widened. "Don't abandon this one. Your partnership—"

She held up a hand in denial. "If I don't get the partnership, then so be it."

He sat back on his haunches, his face closing off. "Then what do you want?"

She almost laughed. Almost. What she wanted was not even close to being an option. But then she had nothing to lose, so why not give it to him straight?

She lifted her chin and met his eyes, despite hers burning with unshed tears. "Honestly? I want you. I want you to be by my side. But fully here, not with the

mask you wear for the rest of the world. That mask you've put back in place in the last thirty seconds. You, open and willing to enter into a true partnership with me."

His shoulders slumped, as if in defeat. "I can't offer you that. All I can offer is myself as I am."

She'd known that would be his answer before she'd laid it all out for him, yet it still felt as if she was being torn in two. The tears she'd been holding in check started to escape, but she didn't let them have free rein. She still had to pack her things and drive away. She'd need clarity for both those tasks.

Swiping at her face, she stood. "I have to go."

"Don't leave over this," he said, his voice edging on alarm as he came to stand beside her. "We can work past this. I don't want to lose you."

She paused, blinked hard and looked out over the Pacific Ocean. It was impossible to look at Adam while she was refusing him. "It's too late for that."

And it was. She could never be in a relationship with a man she loved but who couldn't give her his love back. The only remaining question was whether she could go through with the wedding for the sake of the charity…

He cleared his throat. "What about the wedding? We've made it the heart of the trust's PR campaign."

It was no surprise their thoughts had been along the same lines—this wedding had been dominating their lives since the day she'd arrived in his office. After all that work—hers, Adam's, Jenna's, Faith's—*could* she walk away?

The weight, the complexity of what she was contemplating pushed down on her.

She glanced up at him, and he held her gaze. It hurt

deep inside, down to her soul, to even look at him. And then she realized that even if she wanted to, she'd never be able to pull off pretending to be happy on her wedding day. The guests, the media, everyone would see through her.

She'd damage their work more by staying than leaving.

She swallowed hard and found her voice. "I'll write up a statement from both of us, saying we deeply regret that we're separating and asking for understanding."

It wouldn't be the first time the public heard about a split just before a wedding, and she sent up a little prayer that the trust's stream of donations would survive any scandal.

He took a shuddering breath, then another. "Are you going back to your place?"

She chanced a look at him and found anguish almost strong enough to rival her own in his features. Her first instinct was to soothe him, take away his pain, but she had to stay strong or she'd give in and stay in a one-sided marriage with him forever.

She wrapped her arms around herself, trying to hold herself together through sheer force of will. "I'm not sure yet. I just need to disappear for a few days. I'll be back and I'll be back to work with Jenna on a new campaign for the trust, but not yet."

It would be torture still being a part of his world after their personal life had detonated, but she wouldn't walk away from a commitment—she'd been handed the trust's account and she'd see it through. Given Jenna was the head of the trust, she might be able to avoid Adam until his presence no longer tormented her. If that day ever came.

He opened his mouth to say something, and from his expression, she knew it was another attempt to get her to stay, so she jumped in before he could say it. "Please, Adam. Please just let me disappear until I have my head together."

It seemed as if there was a war being fought inside him in the moments that followed until finally, his jaw tight and his eyes unnaturally bright, he gave a sharp nod and stood back.

Her heart breaking, Callie set off to pack her things and leave before she could change her mind.

Eleven

Callie threw the suitcase she'd taken to Adam's place onto her own bed, unzipped it and blindly stared at the contents. Tears made everything in front of her blur, but she needed to check that she had everything she needed before she left again, so she swiped the tears away. Having no idea where she was headed didn't help the packing situation in the least. All she knew was she needed to be far, far away for a few days.

The apartment's front door opened and closed, and then her sister appeared in her bedroom doorway.

"Hey," Summer said, "I didn't know you were coming over today. Picking up more clothes?"

Callie didn't reply or look up. Couldn't. It was all she could do to keep it together at the moment so she could keep packing.

Summer came around the other side of the bed and plopped down. "Hey, are you okay?" Then she must

have seen the tears because she jumped up and pulled her into a hug. "Oh, sweetheart, what's happened?"

The sympathy was too much to take, and Callie burst into sobs against her sister's shoulder. She'd been holding back, not letting herself cry since she'd spoken to Adam, knowing that once she started she might not stop. The priority had been getting her things together and driving home.

"It's okay," Summer said, stroking her hair. "Whatever it is, I promise we'll fix it together, just like we've always done."

"You can't." Callie's voice was high and she was hiccupping, but she and Summer had been interpreting each other's crying voices since they were kids.

"Is it Adam?"

Callie nodded wordlessly.

Summer swore. "I'll kill him. Where is he now?"

Miraculously, one of her sobs turned into a stuttering laugh, and she pulled away to wipe her eyes with her sleeve. "It's not his fault."

"Tell me what happened and I'll be the judge of whether it's his fault or not." Summer's voice held a little humor, but there was an edge to it, as well.

Callie sank down onto the side of the bed, and her sister sat beside her with an arm around her shoulders, waiting.

She took a couple of steadying breaths, hoping her voice would work properly. "Nothing more than me wanting to have my cake and eat it, too."

Summer sighed. "You fell in love with him, and wanted the fake marriage to be real."

"Yeah," she said, dropping her head into her hands. Somehow it felt worse to have it said aloud, not to men-

tion being so obvious that her sister had guessed it on her first try.

"Knowing you," Summer said in a soft voice, "and watching you from the beginning, I have to say I've been expecting this. You started off acting, but it changed. And then you weren't acting anymore."

Callie risked looking up, worried about finding judgment or pity in her sister's expression, but all she found was loving acceptance, and that gave her the confidence to open up a little more. "For a while I was kidding myself that the acting was getting easier with practice, but you're right. It wasn't acting."

"I knew for sure the night on the yacht." Summer lay back on the bed and pulled Callie with her so they could look at the ceiling as they talked. "I had my fingers and toes crossed that it worked out between you two. He was making you so happy."

"He did," she said with a nostalgic smile. "He really did, for a while."

"Did you tell him?" Summer turned on her side and propped her head on her hand.

Callie swallowed hard and tried not to let the tears take over again, but as she remembered the scene—and the outcome—she almost lost the battle.

Finally, she was able to nod, and whispered, "About an hour ago."

"And…?"

"And—" she looked back up at the ceiling, wanting to say the words as if she was merely reading a menu "—while he's happy for us to sleep together during our fake marriage, he can't offer me any more than that."

"I'll kill him," Summer said again, shaking her head.

"So, you told me what happened and now I get to tell you whether it's his fault or not. It is."

"You can't blame him. I'm the one who wants more than we agreed to. I guess I just got greedy." She bit down on her trembling lip and looked away.

There was silence for a few beats before Summer said, "You want to know what surprises me the most about all of this?"

"That I was stupid enough to fall for my own spin?" She rubbed her hands over her face, trying to refresh herself.

"Nope," Summer said, her tone brooking no disagreement. "That he said no to you wanting more when he's in love with you."

"See, this is the problem, though." Callie sat up, scooting up to lean against the headboard. "He's not in love with me."

Summer shot her a meaningful look. "Oh, he's in love with you. Believe me, it was as plain in his eyes as your love was in yours. He's just refusing to admit it for some reason."

Callie had a sneaking suspicion that her sister might be right, which was why she'd given Adam the chance to confirm or deny it. He'd done neither, and that had told her more than anything.

She shrugged to cover any evidence of the trembling that was coming from deep inside. "Even if you were right, isn't it all the same, though? He doesn't love me enough to overcome his fears and create a future with me. Either way, there's nothing there for me."

Summer looked as if she wanted to say more but held her tongue, and when she steered the topic to a side issue, Callie was appreciative.

"What about the wedding and the PR plan for the trust?" Summer asked.

The wedding. That had been a wrenching decision. Many people had put work into that plan, and she was tossing all of that away. She felt sick about doing that to them, but it would tear her in two to go through with the charade now, and seeming happy on the day was way beyond her acting skills. People would see through her in minutes and realize the entire plan had been a fake from the beginning.

"I'm calling the wedding off," she admitted, her voice shaky. "I just can't do it. The trust has already had a solid increase in donations, and I'll work harder than ever on a new campaign. I'll make sure the charities don't suffer because I've made a mess of things."

Summer glanced at the half-packed suitcase. "Where are you going?"

"I don't know. Somewhere away from here for a few days." She'd thought she'd figure that out as she went along. All her carefully laid plans were ruined, so perhaps it was time to try a different way.

Summer's face suddenly lit up. "My boss has that place at Long Beach we use for clients, and I know it's vacant this week because I was making the arrangements today for the next person. I'm sure I can swing the use of it if you want."

A house that was already set up and a short drive sounded perfect. "If you're sure, that would be great."

Summer reached out and grabbed her hand. "Do you want me to come with you?"

She'd been wondering the same thing. Company to distract her was wildly appealing, but in some ways, she didn't *want* to be distracted. Deep inside, some-

thing was telling her she needed the time to release and to heal.

"You know what?" She spoke gently, so it didn't sound like a rejection of her sister's sweet offer. "I think I need some alone time. Besides, I need to start making cancellations for—"

"Don't give that a second thought," Summer said over the top of her. "I'll call Jenna and Faith, and between the three of us we'll sort that all out. You just have some time for you."

"You're the best. I'll write a statement that you can release and email it to you." Overcome with gratitude, she hugged her sister tightly. When she released her and sat back, her thoughts returned to Adam. "One thing— just in case Adam calls, don't tell him where I am, no matter what he says. I know he can be persuasive."

"Oh, believe me, your location is not what I want to tell him—"

She took her sister's hands in her own. "Please don't. If you're right and he does love me, then this will be hard enough on him already."

"Okay, I promise," Summer said grudgingly. "But only to give you peace of mind on this, not because I think it's the right thing."

Callie smiled through the remnants of her tears. She knew full well she'd lucked out in the sister department. As soon as she felt human again, she was going to repay her for all the support over the years. However, how she would do that was a question for another day. Today was for allowing herself to grieve for what she'd lost.

A small voice at the back of her mind piped up, pointing out that she couldn't lose what she'd never had. And that was true. She sighed, scooped a top off the bed and

added it to the things already in the suitcase. It sure felt as if she'd lost a lot. Though, if she was ruthlessly honest, she'd also gained.

"You know what?" she said, turning to Summer. "Something has come out of this. I've changed. I'm a different person than I was before I met him."

Summer paused in trying on a long-sleeved top she'd fished out of the suitcase. "In what way?"

"I've changed my mind about what's important in life." She thought back over who she'd been and who she was now, trying to pinpoint the difference. "I think I've been clinging to superficial things. Being with Adam, planning this society wedding, the media coverage— all of it has put things in perspective."

Summer arched an eyebrow. "You mean *we've* been clinging to superficial things?"

"Maybe," she said with an indulgent smile. "Once I come back I think we need to have another look at our life plan. It could do with some refining. Maybe we should start our own business sooner rather than later, and focus more on what we actually want, not what we thought in college we'd want by now."

"Sure." Summer took off the top and returned it to the suitcase. "I'd be up for that. In the meantime, you keep packing, and I'll make some phone calls about the place at Long Beach."

Callie watched her sister leave the room and then turned back to her suitcase. Long Beach didn't seem far enough away to give her psychological distance from Adam, but then, she wouldn't have that even if she traveled to Australia.

As her eyes filled with the never-ending supply of

tears, she grabbed a tissue and pressed it against her face. Would she ever get over Adam Hawke?

On the night Adam was supposed to be marrying Callie, one week after he'd last seen her, he was instead sitting at his desk at work, searching Callie's social media profiles for a clue as to where she'd gone. A noise caught his attention, and he looked up to find his brothers standing in the doorway. He swore under his breath. This was the last thing he needed. He was strung so tightly he was practically vibrating, and his brothers had a habit of pushing his buttons.

He stretched his arms over his head and rubbed his eyes. Since it was a Sunday night and he was the only one in the office, he was surprised he hadn't heard them walking along the corridor, but then he'd been pretty engrossed in his search. Unfortunately, Callie still hadn't posted anything on any of her social media pages.

At first after she'd left he'd comforted himself with the age-old method of denial. That had lasted less than twenty-four hours before reality had sunk in.

He loved her.

And if he was honest, he'd probably known for a while. Known it when she'd asked for a future with him, but couldn't admit it because it scared him more than anything in his life. His love for Callie made him feel vulnerable, stripped all his defenses away. How could he keep the world a safe place for his family, for himself, for the woman he loved, when he felt so out of control? He'd learned early that bad things happened when he let down his guard. People had gotten hurt. It wasn't something he could risk, so when he'd felt it slip-

ping with Callie, he locked his heart down even more tightly than ever before.

He'd been stupid. So determined not to let down his guard, not to fall into the same trap as his grandfather and make himself vulnerable to a woman, or to *anyone* besides his parents and brothers. But it had happened nonetheless. He'd give her the sun, the moon and every star in the sky if she asked.

The thing about Callie, though, was that she wasn't wired to be able to ask him for something that would hurt him. He knew with as much confidence as he knew anything that Callie would give that sun, moon and stars right back to him if he asked it of her.

His grandfather's feelings had never been the problem. It was the person he'd chosen to give his heart to. And by choosing Callie, Adam hadn't even come close to making the same mistake as his grandfather.

Of course, now that he'd realized this, it was too late. Callie was gone, leaving a huge gaping hole in his life. He'd tried everything he could think of and, true to her word, she'd disappeared.

Liam cleared his throat. "Are we interrupting?"

Resigned, he glanced over at his brothers. "What can I do for you two?"

Liam stepped forward into the room. "We're here to offer you some advice."

Adam sighed and tapped his pen on his desk. This was new. And unwelcome. "If you're worried about the trust—"

Frowning, Liam shook his head. "We've already told you that we have faith that when Callie says she'll create a new campaign, she'll pull it off. She's good. The trust will be fine."

Adam called on his last shred of patience. "Then advice about what?"

"Callie," Dylan said. "Between us, we have some expertise in the matter of being left by the women we love."

"Lord help me," Adam mumbled and pinched the bridge of his nose. "You need to leave. Now."

Instead of leaving, his brothers both took a seat across from him. Adam pressed the security button under his desk. He had no time for this—he had to find Callie. Then he went back to his web search.

"You can ignore us," Liam said, "but you need to hear this."

Adam scowled at his screen. "No, I really don't. And you should go."

The sound of running footsteps came from the corridor, getting louder, until his six-foot-four head of security appeared in the doorway, ready for action. Jonah liked to rotate through all the positions in his team to keep his hand in and stay abreast of the situations, so tonight must have been his turn as a night guard.

Liam looked from the guard back to him. "Seriously? You called security on us?"

"I'm busy. I asked you to leave and you declined." He turned to his guard. "Jonah, will you please see my brothers out?"

"Certainly, Mr. Hawke." The guard took a step into the room, and Liam and Dylan both held up their hands in surrender.

Adam had met Jonah back when they'd opened their first store and Jonah had been a homeless teen sleeping on the front door stoop. After Adam offered him a job and supported his career, Jonah's loyalty to him was beyond question.

"Adam," Liam growled, and Adam felt like smiling for the first time in days. Maybe his brothers' arrival had been good for him after all—seeing them thrown out of the building should help his mood considerably.

"Hang on," Dylan said. "Jonah, you work for Hawke's Blooms, and the three of us are joint owners. That means all three of us are your boss. Any two of us can overrule a decision made by the third." He turned to Liam. "Motion to overrule the cranky one behind the desk?"

"Seconded," Liam said. "Motion is passed. You can stand down, Jonah."

Jonah swung around to Adam, his raised eyebrow asking how he should proceed. Adam swore again. It wasn't fair to put an employee between them in a family fight.

"You can return to your desk, Jonah." He offered an apologetic smile. "Sorry to involve you."

The guard looked unconvinced. "Are you sure, Mr. Hawke? I can stay in the corner here and keep an eye on things if you'd like."

Adam sighed, resigned to his fate. "No, I'll be fine."

With one last look at Liam and Dylan, Jonah left.

"You know," Dylan said, frowning, "after that stunt, I don't think we should offer our help."

"Good. That's settled." Adam turned back to his computer. "I'll see you later."

Liam's chair creaked as he sat forward. "No, he's annoying, but he helped both of us when we were in the same situation. We owe him."

"No, you don't," Adam said in exasperation. "You can go."

Ignoring him, Dylan crossed an ankle over his knee. "Do you know what time it is?"

"Late," he said dismissively.

"It's two o'clock in the morning."

Adam shrugged. Even if he'd been at home, he wouldn't be able to sleep. His bed reminded him of Callie, and when he lay in it, he could almost feel her body pressed to his, hear her soft breathing, smell her floral shampoo on his pillow. He gave himself ten minutes a day to lie there, holding her pillow, missing her, but to get any sleep he used the sofa.

"You're in bad shape." Dylan tried to appear sad, but couldn't quite hide an undercurrent of amusement at his brother's misfortune. "As I was saying before we were interrupted by someone *calling security on us*, Liam and I have some expertise in being left. Though I should point out that the woman I love only went across state lines, whereas his woman left the country."

"Hey," Liam said. "She comes from another country. She was going home."

Dylan waved a hand in the air. "Whatever. What we need to do now is make Adam realize he's making a big mistake so that he goes after her."

Adam glanced at the ceiling and prayed for patience. "You two always were slow. I've been looking for her for a week. She's not at her place and she's not answering her cell. She's disappeared without a trace."

Liam sat back, all comfort and ease. "You couldn't have been looking too hard. Jenna and Faith had lunch with her yesterday."

Adam went still and then rounded on them. "Where is she?"

Dylan shook his head. "They won't tell us. Faith said something about the three of them needing to talk

about how stupid the Hawke men can be. Which is crazy, because I—"

Adam held up a hand. "Get Faith on the phone. Or Jenna."

Dylan shrugged. "Neither one of them will break. Those two are better than the CIA with secrets. You might have better luck with Callie's sister."

Adam shook his head as he blew out a breath. "Summer said she didn't know where Callie went."

Summer had been his first phone call as soon as he'd realized what a humungous mistake he'd made. She'd taken a message and promised to pass it on as soon as she heard from Callie, but had said she couldn't make any promises about when that would be since Callie was incommunicado. Adam hadn't been willing to wait, so he'd kept looking.

A self-satisfied smile danced around Liam's mouth. "She was at lunch with the others yesterday."

Adam swore again. "So they've closed ranks."

Part of him was pleased that Callie had people who supported her enough to create a shield around her, but dammit, how was he supposed to find her if none of them would talk?

"You look like you could use some advice after all." Dylan was far too smug for Adam's tenuous grasp on control. His brother was clearly unaware just how tightly Adam was currently gripping the armrests of his chair.

"The only thing I need," Adam said through a tight jaw, "is information about Callie's whereabouts. You've both admitted you have no idea where she is, and are unable or unwilling to talk your fiancées into sharing the information."

"What have you tried?" Liam asked.

"Everything. I've left about a billion messages on her cell, checked in with her sister, her parents, the friends I've met and her work, trawled through her social media pages, called random hotels at places where she likes to take vacations."

Liam frowned, suddenly serious. "Have you considered she doesn't want to be found?"

"Says the man who followed a woman to another country after she ran away from him."

"True," Liam said, his eyes full of sympathy, "but Jenna's family helped me speak to her. And she helped Dylan find Faith. If Jenna and Faith won't help this time, and Callie's family won't help when they know where she is, perhaps it means you should let her go."

Let her go? Simply give up? The emptiness inside him screamed in rebellion. Besides, she might not want to be found now, but that was because he'd said crazy things to her, before he'd realized what she meant to him. That she meant everything to him.

At the very least he owed her the truth. He just hoped with every fiber of his being that she let him give her a whole heap more than that.

He straightened his spine and stared down his brother. "There's something I need to say to her. If I say it, and she still wants to be left alone, I'll do it." His heart would break in two, but he'd honor her wishes.

Dylan rubbed his stubbled jaw, apparently considering Adam's words, and then nodded. "Well, if she won't listen to you, perhaps it's time you do something she can't ignore."

Hysterical laughter bubbled in Adam's chest before dying in his throat. "Like what?" Did they realize he'd

tried everything he could think of already? Why else would he be in his office at two in the morning, chasing flimsy leads?

Dylan turned to Liam. "Seriously, I can't believe we voted to make him the boss of the company." Then he faced Adam again. "I don't know. You're the ideas man, and you're the one who knows Callie. But it had better be something she won't expect, so she knows you're serious, or it's not worth doing at all."

Adam started to frown, but then an idea struck him, one so simple yet so perfect that his heart leaped to life again. He could do this. He'd explain everything and show her he was serious. He reached for the phone and started leafing through papers, looking for Callie's friend Anna's number.

"You do remember it's after two in the morning, right?" Liam said.

Swearing, Adam dropped the phone and speared his fingers through his hair. Now that he had a plan, every second it was delayed was agony, but his brother was right. He'd have to wait a few more hours.

He stood and reached for his suit jacket. "Time you two went home," he said and herded them out his office door. "Actually, why are you here at this time of night, anyway, and not at home with those fiancées you worked so hard to win over?"

His brothers shared a look before Liam said, "Jonah."

"The security guard who was going to throw you out was the one who called you?" Adam huffed out a laugh. "He's always taken his job of looking out for the staff seriously. I'll have to give him a bonus."

"Right after you find Callie, right?" Dylan said from beside him.

"Oh, yeah." Adam closed his office door behind him, feeling a sliver of optimism starting to glow in his chest. "Nothing's happening before I do that."

Twelve

When her cell rang, Callie was reading a book in a deck chair on the veranda overlooking the beach. She checked the caller ID, an action that had become second nature in the past week.

Since the announcement of her split from Adam had gone public, her phone, email and social media had gone crazy. The only calls she'd been taking were from her parents, Summer, Jenna and Faith. She'd had a few from random friends, but unable to face the world just yet—or the world's questions—she'd decided to return the calls when her impromptu vacation was over.

Although there was one person she'd made herself call on the first day—John Evans, her boss. She'd explained the hiccup with the Hawke Brothers Trust account, and promised that she was working on a new campaign. He hadn't been impressed, but was prepared

to give her a chance. She had a meeting scheduled with him next week to look over her new ideas, which meant she needed to start having those ideas soon...

This time the call was Anna Wilson, and Callie debated whether to answer or not. Anna was a friend, but she was also a journalist, and she was probably hoping for a scoop on the breakup. Admittedly, Anna hadn't been part of the flurry of online stories and gossip pieces that had broken out since she'd left Adam. Many of those articles had claimed a secret source who had all sorts of completely untrue morsels of information, and who was likely Terence Gibson. Anna had stayed silent so far, but perhaps she now wanted to wade into the water.

Callie sighed. Her vacation was coming to an end and she was going to have to start facing the real world soon, and Anna was probably a good place to start, so she thumbed the answer button.

"Hi, Anna," she said as brightly as she could manage. "How are you?"

"Hey, Callie. I'm good, thanks." There was a short pause on the line. "I was just wondering... Have you seen my column today?"

Yesterday, when she'd seen the headline, "Anon Source Claims Hawke Wedding a Scam," she'd sworn off the web. There was nothing she could do about Terence having a field day at her expense, but she didn't have to put herself through reading it. "Sorry," she said, tucking her legs up underneath her. "I haven't had a chance."

"You should have a look."

"I'm actually in the middle of something. I'll grab a

few minutes later this afternoon." Or perhaps tomorrow. Or even the next day.

"Now, Callie. It's Adam."

A chill raced down her spine. "What do you mean, it's Adam? Is something wrong?"

"He has a message for you and it's running in my column today."

Callie leaned back in her chair, the sudden rigidity in her muscles dissipating. There was no way Adam would have done something so public about something that was private. He must have given an interview about the trust, or about the company, and mentioned her name when questioned. His words might even have been written for him by Jenna, to keep it on the track they'd decided to take.

Callie ran her free hand through her hair. "Okay, thanks. I'll check it out."

"Really, Callie. You need to see this." Anna's voice was insistent, which was strange. "Promise me."

Her stomach clenched. It was clear that there was more to this. "I promise. I'll look at it now."

They ended the call, and Callie retrieved her laptop from her suitcase where she'd put it yesterday after the sham headline. In the time it took her to boot up her computer, her cell practically exploded with messages. She checked a few and they were all saying the same thing. Adam had left her a video online. Adrenaline spiked through her system. He couldn't have actually addressed something to her, could he...?

When the laptop displayed its welcome screen, she opened her browser and found Anna's column. Before she'd braced herself, Adam's face appeared on her screen, as dear and beautiful as she'd remembered. A

harsh pressure pushed against her chest, making it hard to draw breath.

And yet, it was Adam like she'd never seen him before. She'd seen him disheveled from lovemaking. She'd seen him after he'd had too much to drink in Vegas. She'd seen him windswept on the beach. But this? This Adam had eyes that were wild and untamed. He seemed to be exerting no control over himself to keep his guard up. He wasn't trying to keep part of himself hidden.

And he was doing it in front of the world.

His words finally registered—she'd been too busy looking at him, desperate for his face, that she'd paid no attention to what he was saying. Clicking on the play button, she dragged it back to the beginning and listened.

"Callie, I've tried every method to find you that I can think of, and a few more. I was stupid, I know that, and I'm begging you to overlook that fact. Hoping and praying that I haven't destroyed your feelings for me. If that's happened, I understand, and all I can say is I'm sorry. For everything."

Hot tears built until the image on the screen blurred and she blinked them away, unwilling to miss a second of Adam's message. She still couldn't believe this was public, that he was saying these things, knowing that anyone could see.

"If there's a chance you could ever feel the same for me again, then all I want to say is, I love you." He paused and swallowed. "I love you so much I've been going crazy without you. Not knowing where you are."

A stab of guilt pierced her chest at causing him pain. When she'd left, she'd only been thinking of her own

emotional survival, and had no expectation that her leaving would cause him this much sadness.

"I'm sorry, Adam," she whispered at the screen, but his recorded message continued on regardless.

"I guess you could say I'm emotionally compromised after all," he said and offered a sad smile.

She let out a surprised laugh through her tears.

"One last thing, Callie. If you do still feel the same, if it's possible that you still want me, I'll be waiting at the place it all started. This week—same day and time, at the place I first proposed."

The video ended, but she was lost in the memory of walking past a small Vegas chapel and his saying, "Hey, I have a crazy idea. Let's get married." And fueled by alcohol and infatuation, she'd pretty much squealed a *yes* then jumped up and hugged him,

It had been a Tuesday, about eleven o'clock at night. She double-checked her computer's calendar—it was Monday. He wanted to meet her tomorrow night at 11:00 p.m. in Vegas.

Everything inside her wanted to go, to meet him and feel his arms around her again. She'd been lying awake every night since she'd left him, dreaming of a chance to be held by him again. But something even stronger was gnawing at her belly, holding her back.

There was no question he was being genuine on that tape. He'd exposed himself in a way she'd never thought he was capable of. But what if he regretted it now?

He'd made declarations to her before, made vows, and then changed his mind the next morning. Would he even be waiting in that chapel, or was the tape something he'd made in the middle of the night and already

regretted? Was he working with his lawyers right this minute to get the video taken down?

And even if he made it to the chapel tomorrow night, would he change his mind in a day, a week, a month or a year?

The sad truth was, she wasn't sure if she could trust him with her heart. Was a potential future with Adam Hawke worth the risk?

Callie huddled closer to her sister under the bright yellow umbrella as they trudged down the wet Las Vegas street. Her thoughts were all crammed together in her head so hard, all jumbled, and none of them clear enough to even consider properly.

"Stop it," Summer said.

Callie flinched and then frowned at her sister. "What?"

"I can hear you second-guessing yourself from here."

"Actually, I haven't first-guessed yet, so there's nothing to second-guess." She'd been too busy replaying Adam's message in her mind to do much more than walk in a straight line.

"Oh, come on," Summer said, rolling her eyes. "You're here. That's a decision."

Callie placed a hand over her chest, as if she could brace her heart, and then admitted the awful truth. "It might not even be an issue. I don't think he'll come."

"Of course he'll be here." Her sister waved her concerns away with a flick of her wrist. "No one who saw that video—which is everyone in the country—could doubt that he's head over heels about you. Plus, you're a trending topic on social media and the consensus is

definitely that you'll both turn up. The people have spoken and they're demanding a happy ending."

"That's lovely of the people," Callie said, trying not to cringe at being the topic of so many conversations, "but I don't think the weight of public opinion is going to affect Adam's decisions."

"Well, *I'm* sure he'll come." Summer gave her a smug smile. "I hate to say this, but you knew I would at some point… I told you he loves you."

A seething mass of confusion churned in her gut. How easy it would be to simply believe what he'd said. It would be a dream come true. But life was rarely that simple.

She glanced over at her sister and tried to explain. "Adam changes his mind quickly. Last time, it was less than twenty-four hours after promising me the world that he asked for a divorce."

"You two barely knew each other back then," she pointed out.

"Which is why I was blindsided." In some ways, the pain of that time was still fresh. It was sitting on the sidelines, warning her, trying to keep her safe from being hurt in the same way again. "Now I know him and I understand how much he hates being…emotionally compromised."

"But you're here, you're going to meet him, so what's the plan?"

Callie stopped and looked out over the light but steady rain that hit the pavement and the palm trees, and was bouncing off the umbrellas of people around them.

"I'm waiting to hear what he says and I need to see him in person for that, not a video message. I'll know by his eyes." She had to see how deeply he was affected.

In the meantime, the agony of having no idea if this was real or not was killing her.

As they rounded a corner, Adam came into view. He stood alone, a large, black umbrella shielding him from the rain. A few feet behind him, his brothers and their fiancées stood huddled together in an alcove in front of the chapel.

At the sight of him, her body froze, as if it had gone into internal meltdown. She couldn't take another step, couldn't even feel—her emotions had become numb, as well.

He wore dark trousers and a coffee-hued shirt, his hair clearly damp, his shoulders tight. Tension flowed off him in waves as he scanned the area around them. She'd never seen a man more magnificent.

As soon as he saw them, his shoulders relaxed a fraction and he strode over. Summer squeezed her hand and nodded her greeting to Adam. Adam returned it and edged his umbrella over Callie. As soon as she was covered, Summer scurried off to stand in the alcove with Adam's family.

Adam's gaze was dark and intense. "I wasn't sure you'd come."

"I wasn't sure you'd be here, either." She was still cushioned by the emotional numbness, or she would never have been able to get those words out as evenly.

"Didn't you see the video?" he asked, his voice rough. "I told you I'd be here."

"You forget, I've been through this with you before and you changed your mind once you had time to think it through." She'd tried to say the words gently—this was about having the truth on the table, not about accusations, but still she saw him flinch.

"That was different, and so long ago. Everything has changed."

She glanced at the chapel with its flashing neon lights, and then over at their siblings and partners, all gathered and pretending not to be watching them, and her emotional numbness dissolved. The emotions of the past few weeks came crashing in on her in a tidal wave, and it was all she could do to stay upright.

She rubbed a hand over her eyes and then looked at him. "Adam, what are we doing here?"

"You tell me. I'm here to marry the woman I love. What about you?" His eyes were unwavering, challenging.

She shrugged one shoulder, determined to keep her distance until she was ready. "I'm still thinking about that one."

"If it helps your decision, I've done a lot of thinking, and I've let go of the comparisons to my grandfather. I'm more like my brothers than I ever was like him, and Liam and Dylan are stronger men, better men, with Jenna and Faith in their lives. I want that. I'm ready for that. With you."

That did help, but there was more, and she hardly dared ask…

There was no moving forward until she heard his answer, so she straightened her spine and asked outright. "What about your self-control? Letting your guard down?"

"Not an issue. When we were together, I was letting my guard down without even realizing it." His Adam's apple bobbed up and down. "I thought control was the most important thing in my life, but it's not. You are."

He reached into his pocket and drew out a velvet box.

She recognized the logo of the jeweler who'd customized the rings they'd chosen.

Her bottom lip trembled, so she bit down on it to keep it still. "You really want to get married here, and not at a fancy place with all your friends?"

"You were right. The fancy version we were planning was about everybody else—the trust, the media, your job. That suited our purposes at the time, but what I want now is something stripped back. Something that's just you and me and the promises we want to make to each other. Although," he said with the trace of a smile, "I can't promise my words will be as pretty as the ones Summer wrote for me."

A huge lump lodged itself in her throat, and she had to swallow twice before she could get her voice to work. "I'd rather plain, stumbling words that were heartfelt and yours alone than all the pretty words in the world."

Adam's eyes misted over, and she knew in that moment, beyond any doubt, that he felt this as deeply as she did, and he was making a commitment to her for life, not until he changed his mind. The sight was beautiful and it filled her with joy.

He leaned in and kissed her. It was like stepping off a ledge, flying in free fall, without having to worry about the landing, because this man would always be there for her, she knew that now. Just as she'd always be there for him.

At a certain point, she'd wondered who was there for him, and had desperately wanted to be that person. And now she was. It was almost too much to contemplate all at once.

Dylan's voice rang out. "Are we having a wedding or what?"

Adam raised an eyebrow in question, his gaze steady on her. "Callie? It's your call. You know what I want."

Her heart felt as if it was hitting her rib cage on every beat. "If you're proposing again—"

"I am."

"—then yes. A thousand times yes."

Adam dropped the umbrella, gathered her up in his arms and kissed her again. A cheer went up from the combined family group and she smiled against his mouth, but didn't break the kiss. The light rain was soaking her dress and dripping down his face, but she didn't care. Nothing mattered but being in his arms again.

When they finally broke apart, he lowered her to her feet. "Come and marry me, Callie."

Heart overflowing, she picked up the discarded umbrella and took his proffered hand. While they walked with him into the chapel, she was unable to look away from the man at her side. At the door, they were met with hugs and well-wishes.

Liam said, "Should I tell the celebrant we're ready?"

"Yes," Adam and Callie said together, smiling at each other as they left Liam to organize the details.

Faith carefully reached into a large handbag she had in the crook of her elbow and came out with a small bouquet of the Bridal Tulip, interspersed with tiny blue flowers.

She slid off a clear plastic cone that had been protecting the flowers and handed the bouquet to Callie. "I had it ready, just in case."

"It's perfect. Thank you," Callie said, touched.

Faith again reached into her bag and came out with a single snowy white tulip and pinned it to Adam's lapel.

Then she stood back and grinned. "You might be having a simple wedding, but we couldn't have a Hawke brother getting married without *any* flowers."

"Or something borrowed," Jenna said from beside her. She had a glittering tiara in her hands. "This also counts as something old, since it's been in my family for several generations."

Callie took the tiara, her heart in her mouth. If this had been in Jenna's *royal* family for generations, then it was quite possibly priceless. "These diamonds are real?" she asked, hardly daring to consider the possibility.

"Shhh," Jenna said with a sparkle in her eye. "I'm not really supposed to bring it out without a bodyguard. But I don't think Adam is going to take his eyes off you tonight, so it should be safe."

Adam took the tiara from her fingers. "It's beautiful, thank you, Jenna." He slid it onto Callie's head and smiled. "A princess for a night, but queen of my heart forever. I love you so much, Callie Mitchell. I love you with everything inside me."

The tears she'd been holding back finally started to slide down her cheeks. Since her face was already damp from the rain, she didn't need to wipe them away. Everything just blended together.

As Jenna stood back, Callie could see Faith was pinning single tulip buttonholes to Liam and Dylan's jackets and then she handed Summer a bouquet consisting of a single tulip and tiny blue flowers.

Dylan stepped forward. "Faith said you have something blue in the flowers and that Jenna brought something borrowed and old. So you just need something new." He pulled out a long silver necklace with a locket.

"I had this made for your original wedding—wait, no, that would have been your second wedding. Man, you guys need to stop getting married!"

Callie laughed and kissed Dylan's cheek. "Thanks."

"Open it," he said, and she did. It was a tiny picture from the official wedding announcement photos, which was strange, because he'd thought their wedding was a sham when he would have had this made.

Before she could ask, he said, "I wanted you to know that even after your official wedding ended, you'd always be a part of this family. No matter what was going on with Adam and you, the rest of us would always be there for you. Of course, now you're making it all official and real, so this doesn't have the same meaning—"

His words cut out when she threw her arms around his neck. "Thank you, this means a lot."

The celebrant appeared and called them in, so the group moved into the chapel, but Callie hesitated, tucking her damp hair behind her ear.

"What is it?" Adam asked.

"What about our parents? Neither set is here." This wasn't the wedding with the complete guest list that they'd been planning, but she was sure all four parents would hate to miss the event.

"My parents are babysitting Meg and Bonnie so Liam and Jenna could come, but Dylan has them on a video call, so they can watch." He nodded to where they could see Dylan through the arched door, talking into a phone cradled in his palm.

Surprised, she swung her gaze back to her groom. "You told your parents about tonight before you knew whether I'd come or not?" He was always so guarded

and unwilling to share information that would make him emotionally vulnerable that this didn't make sense.

"I have nothing to hide. I want you, and I'm happy for the world to know it." He kissed her forehead, then the tip of her nose and each cheek. "Also Liam said he asked Summer for your parents' contact details a few minutes ago, and they're calling your parents now." On the other side of the short aisle, Summer was talking to someone on a tablet screen, then she handed it to Jenna and moved to the front of the pews, beside a waiting Liam and the celebrant.

Callie shook her head in amazement. "Considering this wasn't planned, everything seems to be falling into place."

Adam grinned at her. "I have no idea what we were doing, spending all that time planning the other wedding. This one took hardly any effort at all."

"Just a video message," she said and then placed a hand over his heart. She could feel its steady thump through his shirt and jacket. "Adam, I understand how difficult it would have been for you to make that message. It means a lot."

"It resulted in you coming here tonight, so it was nothing." He leaned in and kissed her lightly on the lips in the sweetest of kisses.

Prerecorded organ music started playing, and Adam eased back and held out his arm. "Ready?"

"Wait!" Summer called to the room and then whispered something to the celebrant, who flicked a switch on a panel to his side and the music stopped. Summer pulled an MP3 player from her pocket and connected it to the panel with a cord the celebrant handed her, then

thumbed a button on the player. The room was flooded with the introductory notes of "The Lady in Red."

Adam chuckled. "I think that's become our song."

"It's perfect," Callie said, and walked down the aisle on the arm of the man she was going to spend the rest of her life with.

Ten minutes later, they were married. Again. Each of their five guests threw streamers and popped party poppers. Then they all headed back to a suite Liam had booked for a low-key reception, filled with champagne, room-service food and as much love as one room could hold.

After only an hour or so, Callie met Adam's gaze from across the room. Within seconds, he was at her side. "Ready to get out of here?"

Callie smiled. "Absolutely."

Adam cleared his throat and raised his voice. "Thank you for everything you all did tonight. It's time for us to go."

"You have to throw the bouquet first," Jenna called from the sofa.

They all looked around the room. Everyone was paired off except Summer, who said, "I'm fine. Don't throw it just for me."

Faith gently turned Callie by the shoulders. "It won't be just for you, Summer. Jenna and I aren't married yet, and we don't know which wedding will come first. We'll all play."

Callie picked up her bouquet, turned her back to the women and threw it over her head. When she turned around, Summer was holding the tulips with a look of resigned humor.

Then Adam slid his arms around Callie from behind,

and she forgot all about everyone else. All she wanted was to be alone with her new husband.

Sliding her hand into his and interlacing their fingers, she tugged a smiling Adam toward the door. Toward the rest of their lives.

* * * * *

If you loved this story
pick up these other HAWKE BROTHERS
books from Rachel Bailey

THE NANNY PROPOSITION
BIDDING ON HER BOSS

Available now from Harlequin Desire!

If you're on Twitter, tell us what you think of
Harlequin Desire! #harlequindesire

COMING NEXT MONTH FROM

HARLEQUIN® Desire

Available November 3, 2015

#2407 BREAKING BAILEY'S RULES
The Westmorelands • by Brenda Jackson
When Bailey Westmoreland follows loner Walker Quinn to his Alaskan ranch to apologize for doing him wrong, she can't help but stay to nurse the exasperating man's wounds...and lose her own heart in the process!

#2408 A CHRISTMAS BABY SURPRISE
Billionaires and Babies • by Catherine Mann
When Alaina Rutger wakes from a coma with no memory of her husband or their newly adopted son, she must face the mistakes in her past to reconnect with her surprise family...all in time for Christmas.

#2409 COURTING THE COWBOY BOSS
Texas Cattleman's Club: Lies and Lullabies
by Janice Maynard
Case Baxter learned the hard way with his first marriage that becoming involved with an employee never works out. So what's a cowboy to do when he falls hard for his gorgeous new maid?

#2410 ONE WEEK WITH THE BEST MAN
Brides and Belles • by Andrea Laurence
When wallflower Gretchen McAlister is chosen as the fake wedding date of sexy movie star Julian Cooper, they don't have to fake their chemistry for the camera. But is the best man ready to become Gretchen's groom?

#2411 PREGNANT WITH THE RANCHER'S BABY
The Good, the Bad and the Texan • by Kathie DeNosky
Rancher Nate Rafferty's on-again, off-again lover is pregnant with his baby! Now that she's back, how can she refuse to marry him? She says yes to one month living on his ranch. Now that he has her where he wants her, he won't take no for an answer!

#2412 A CEO IN HER STOCKING
The Accidental Heirs • by Elizabeth Bevarly
Struggling single mom Clara Easton is stunned when her three-year-old inherits a massive fortune from the man who never acknowledged his son...and who also has a gorgeous, wickedly sexy twin brother dead set on wooing her.

SPECIAL EXCERPT FROM

⬥HARLEQUIN® *Desire*

When Bailey Westmoreland follows loner Walker Quinn to his Alaskan ranch to apologize for doing him wrong, she can't help but stay to nurse the exasperating man's wounds, putting both their hearts at risk...

Read on for a sneak peek at
BREAKING BAILEY'S RULES,
the latest in New York Times *bestselling author*
Brenda Jackson's
WESTMORELAND *series.*

Bailey wondered what there was about Walker that was different from any other man. All it took was the feel of his hand on her shoulder... His touch affected her in a way no man's touch had ever affected her before. How did he have the ability to breach her inner being and remind her that she was a woman?

Personal relationships weren't her forte. Most of the guys in these parts were too afraid of her brothers and cousins to even think of crossing the line, so she'd only had one lover in her lifetime. And for her it had been one and done, and executed more out of curiosity than anything else. She certainly hadn't been driven by any type of sexual desire like she felt for Walker.

There was this spike of heat that always rolled in her stomach whenever she was around him, not to mention a warmth that would settle in the area between her legs.

Even now, just being in the same vehicle with him was making her breasts tingle. Was she imagining things or had his face inched a little closer to hers?

Suggesting they go for a late-night ride might not have been a good idea, after all. "I'm not perfect," she finally said softly.

"No one is perfect," he responded huskily.

Bailey drew in a sharp breath when he reached up and rubbed a finger across her cheek. She fought back the slow moan that threatened to slip past her lips. His hand on her shoulder had caused internal havoc, and now his fingers on her face were stirring something to life inside her that she'd never felt before.

She needed to bring an end to this madness. The last thing she wanted was for him to get the wrong idea about the reason she'd brought him here. "I didn't bring you out here for this, Walker," she said. "I don't want you getting the wrong idea."

"Okay, what's the right idea?" he asked, leaning in even closer. "Why did you bring me out here?"

Nervously, she licked her lips. He was still rubbing a finger across her cheek. "To apologize."

He lowered his head and took possession of her mouth.

Don't miss
BREAKING BAILEY'S RULES
by New York Times *bestselling author*
Brenda Jackson, available November 2015 wherever
Harlequin® Desire books and ebooks are sold.

www.Harlequin.com